HIGH PLAINS
P R E S S

Esther Hobart Morris

The Unembellished Story of the Nation's First Female Judge

To Brian
Best always
Kathryn, S.C.

Esther Hobart Morris

The Unembellished Story of the Nation's First Female Judge

Kathryn Swim Cummings

with a foreword by Will Bagley

HIGH PLAINS PRESS

Front Cover illustration by Mark Schuler
© Wind River Studios Holdings, Inc, 2019
For information or prints contact: Wind River Studios at
artworkoriginals.com

Library of Congress Cataloging-in-Publication Data
Names: Cummings, Kathryn Swim, author.
Title: Esther Hobart Morris : the unembellished story of the Nation's first
  female judge / Kathryn Swim Cummings.
Description: Glendo, WY : High Plains Press, 2018. | Includes biblio-
graphical references and index.
Identifiers: LCCN 2018031302 (print) | LCCN 2018031456 (ebook) |
  ISBN 9781937147204 (ebook) | ISBN 9781937147198 (pbk. : alk.
  paper)
Subjects: LCSH: Morris, Esther Hobart, 1814-1902. | Women judges--
  United States--Biography. | Justices of the peace--Wyoming--Biogra-
phy. |Judges--United States--Biography. | Women--Suffrage--United
States.
Classification: LCC KF373.M575 (ebook) | LCC KF373.M575 C86
  2018 (print) | DDC 324.6/23092 [B] --dc23
LC record available at https://lccn.loc.gov/2018031302

FIRST PRINTING
10 9 8 7 6 5 4 3 2 1
Manufactured in the United States of America

HIGH PLAINS PRESS
403 CASSA ROAD, GLENDO, WY 82213
WWW.HIGHPLAINSPRESS.COM
ORDERS & CATALOGS: 1-800-552-7819

This book is dedicated to
William Robert Dubois III,
distinguished representative of the Morris, Slack, and Dubois families.

"My idea of the woman question in Wyoming
is that while we enjoy the privilege of the elective franchise,
we have not been sufficiently educated up to it."
ESTHER MORRIS

Esther Morris, in a letter to Isabella Beecher Hooker, sister of Harriet Beecher Stowe, in the January 31, 1871, Chicago Tribune. *Hooker reportedly read the letter at the Suffrage Convention in Washington, D.C.*

CONTENTS

Part Three:
"I Do Not Withdraw from the Woman's Cause"

The part titles and chapter titles are from Esther Hobart Morris's letters except for those of Part One and Chapters One, Two, Six, Eighteen, and Twenty which are from the pamphlet "In Memoriam" written by E.A. Slack; Chapter Seven which is from Ken Burns's "The West"; Chapter Thirteen which is from a letter by Robert Morris, and Chapter Twenty-one which is from T.A. Larson's *History of Wyoming*.

FOREWORD

I N 1869 WYOMING Territory became the first government in the world to grant women the right to vote. As justice of the peace in the mining boomtown of South Pass City in 1870, Esther Morris became the first woman to hold office in the United States. She has never had a good biography and deserves one.

Kathryn Swim Cummings's *Esther Hobart Morris: The Unembellished Story of the Nation's First Female Judge* fills the bill, and more. The book reveals Ms. Cummings's decades of hard work and devotion to her subject. She also shares a character trait with her hero: Ms. Cummings is persistent and knows how to stick with a task until it is accomplished. I like to say that writing is the hardest job on Planet Earth. I warned Kathryn, but she simply refused to listen to good advice and give up. The book you hold in your hands is the result of her dedication.

Esther Hobart Morris was not a frontierswoman. Like the typical men and women who actually make history happen, she was much more ordinary than extraordinary. With her longtime interest in abolition and women's emancipation, she and her family had moved from New York to Illinois and sent a son to serve in the Civil War. She only moved west to Wyoming Territory with her husband and three sons after the war at age fifty-six. Within a year she had applied for and was accepted as justice of the peace for Sweetwater County, making her the first woman in the United States to hold judicial office.

Though this achievement led some to call her the "mother of woman suffrage in Wyoming," many have downplayed her actions and muddied the waters of her legacy. Cummings's biography situates Morris's personal life amid the events of America's epic mid-nineteenth century national history: the Women's Rights Movement, the Civil War, and westward expansion, as well as the growth and politics of Wyoming Territory. She draws upon excerpts from family correspondence and great photographs of Esther and her family, as well as interviews and census documents, to trace the enterprises of the Morris family as they joined the national migration and left their marks on Wyoming and the West.

Cummings's research and hard work are obvious and admirable. She has gotten good measure from the family letters long available at the Wyoming State Archives. She uses museum and family photographs to put faces on some handsome frontier men and beautiful women. Esther Morris would not win a beauty contest, but she preserved her remarkable personal appearance well past middle age.

Americans may not learn much from history or we would not continue to make the same mistakes repeatedly. But I still believe history has much to teach us. We can learn a lot from Esther Morris's historic career, especially that the struggle for women's rights is a constant and never-ending battle.

WILL BAGLEY,
author of *South Pass: Gateway to a Continent*
(University of Oklahoma Press)

PREFACE

◆

D IVING INTO THE life of nineteenth-century Esther Morris, it is easy to understand her feelings of constraint and dissatisfaction. I found nearly all the information written about her personal life seriously flawed. She is most famous for a tea party at her cabin home in South Pass City. This fictional story has been renounced on all fronts, and yet it persists. This is a serious injustice to a woman whose life was spent seeking justice through abolition, suffrage, and as a judge. Esther's unembellished story is captivating and begs to be shared.

It has been a long bumpy road of nearly two-hundred-fifty years from the beginning of our country to reach this point of opportunity which today's women enjoy. Many women stand out along the path to suffrage and women's rights. Esther Morris is one of them.

One of eleven children, Esther was part of a large family, many of whom are mentioned in this book. I have created *Appendix B* showing each sibling, their children, and grandchildren for use as a guide.

Esther and her three sons corresponded for much of their lives with Esther's niece and the boys' first cousin, Frances McQuigg Stewart, known as Frankie. The letters were passed down in the family for two generations and were then donated to the Wyoming State Archives. Through these letters the reader can see Esther's life from her point of view. They reveal her personal frustration, humor, and anger. Her sons' letters to Frankie add depth to Esther's personality and daily life through their observations. Esther's story is further brought to life through original documents, extensive research, and photographs.

A multitude of depositions from an Illinois Supreme Court family divorce case shed even more light on Esther and her family.

I have modernized some of the spelling and punctuation in Esther's letters for easier reading. The letters of her sons are intact and speak for themselves as they reveal the different personalities of each writer. I used the traditional term "woman suffrage," though some contemporary writers now prefer "women's suffrage." When quoting, I deferred to the usage of the writer, even when it varied from the conventional.

I undertook this biography with three goals:

1. to correctly present the facts of Esther's life, debunking the generations of false information;
2. to understand the catalysts for Esther's actions throughout her long life; and
3. to give Esther Hobart Morris her rightful place in history.

KATHRYN SWIM CUMMINGS

Part One

"The Origin
of Things"

CHAPTER ONE

"She Wanted to Be Herself"

WOMEN WERE ALREADY touting equal rights and suffrage when Esther Hobart McQuigg entered the world on August 8, 1812.[1] The original thirteen colonies had become eighteen states, with Ohio the westernmost. James Madison was the fourth president. Lewis and Clark had returned from their Corps of Discovery Expedition across the continent only six years before. The second war with England, the War of 1812, had been fought for two months.

Even before the United States was born, Abigail Smith Adams became a link in the long chain of men and women determined to allow woman suffrage in the newly-formed United States. While John Adams was in Philadelphia working with Benjamin Franklin and Thomas Jefferson on the document declaring independence from England, Abigail was at home in Braintree, Massachusetts, running the farm and raising their children.

She created her own declaration in a letter to John on March 31, 1776, asking for the men to " . . . remember the ladies and be more generous and favorable to them than your ancestors. Do not put such unlimited power into the hands of the husbands. Remember all men would be tyrants if they could. If particular care and attention is not paid to the ladies, we are determined to foment a rebellion and will not hold ourselves bound by any laws in which we have no voice. . . ."[2]

Her husband, John Adams, did not listen. The other founding fathers did not listen—and equal rights for women remains a contentious issue today.

Abigail Adams was a contemporary of Esther's grandmothers, who encountered the same challenges in their homes in New England. Mehitabel Peck Hobart in Connecticut and Sarah Coburn McQuigg in New Hampshire saw their husbands off to the Revolutionary War, cared for their farms, and raised their children. But they could not vote.

In her book *Ladies of Liberty*, author Cokie Roberts defines the lives of these women. "Just getting through the day at the end of the eighteenth and the beginning of the nineteenth century would be challenging. Death was everywhere. The losses these women suffered are almost overwhelming. Every illness, every pregnancy—and they were perennially pregnant—every journey held the prospect of disaster. Still these ladies soldiered on with remarkable resiliency."[3]

Aside from war, revolution occurred in industry and in farms and homes. The founding fathers asked the women in their families to become more frugal and industrious and give up imports like tea and fabric from England. Men and women like Esther's New England grandparents took on the burden of more creativity and work. They provided food, clothing, tools, and farm implements for the family rather than accepting shipments from England.

Providing for themselves made the colonists self-sufficient. Both men and women grew more independent as individuals. Esther's grandmothers likely began a subtle shift in their perceptions about themselves and their roles in family and community.

Esther's father, Daniel McQuigg, was born in 1776. Her mother, Charlotte Hobart, was born in 1780. The 1800 marriage of Daniel and Charlotte created a built-in family dichotomy. Esther described both sides many years later in a letter to her niece Frankie, explaining, "Our grandfather Hobart was stingy to meanness, and our McQuigg grandfather was practical, so there has ever been a feud in the family."[4]

The pious Hobarts arrived in the new land in 1633, just thirteen years after the Puritans fled England on the *Mayflower*. Many Hobarts were preachers. One ancestor of Esther was referred to in a letter kept by the Massachusetts Historical Society from Increase

Mather to John Cotton: "He is quite close with a shilling and has a rather unfortunate disposition."[5]

The McQuiggs were quite another story. Esther's great-grandfather, John McQuigg Sr., and his wife, Mildred Lawson, were of Scots' ancestry, born in the north of Ireland. At one time, McQuigg Sr. escaped from a British press gang by jumping from one hogshead onto another. Esther's Scots-Irish grandfather, John McQuigg Jr., born on board a ship in 1740 when his parents traveled to America, had one foot in Ireland and one foot in America.

The McQuiggs were an argumentative lot. One McQuigg family legend recounted that McQuigg Sr. was a patriot, while his wife, Mildred, sided with the Tories. According to the story, during the Revolutionary War, four of their eight sons enlisted as Patriots and the other four fought for Great Britain as Tories.[6] No documents prove that eight sons existed or that sons fought on opposite sides; however, the family legend demonstrates the McQuigg temperament.

Esther's maternal grandparents, Edmund and Mehitabel Hobart, and paternal grandparents, John and Sarah McQuigg, left New England for Tioga County, New York, in the late eighteenth century. The Hobarts went to Spencer and the McQuiggs to Owego, eighteen miles away. Both grandfathers died before Esther's birth, but her grandmothers lived long lives. Their colorful stories were part of the fabric of Esther's childhood experience. Each lived until Esther was past twenty.[7]

At Esther's birth in 1812, New York City was the largest city in the new country with a population of more than ninety-six thousand. Philadelphia followed with more than fifty-three thousand. Spencer, New York, was located more than two hundred miles northwest of New York City.[8]

More than fifteen hundred miles west, the area which would one day become Wyoming knew only the Indians who had resided there for a thousand generations and a few hearty mountain men, like John Colter, George Drouillard, and Hugh Glass.

Esther Hobart McQuigg grew up on a large farm originally owned by her grandfather Hobart in the village of Spencer. The farm stood on an old Indian trail, which evolved into a road, running from Lake Cayuga to the village of Owego, situated on the banks of the exquisite Susquehanna River. The farm was located at what is now the junction of Ithaca Road and Fisher Settlement Road. Charlotte gave birth to eleven children, with Esther as the seventh.[9]

She watched her mother perform all the backbreaking tasks of caring for the family. They arose before daybreak. The men tended to the animals, and Charlotte prepared food for the family with the girls.

Pamela Goddard, former curator of Education at the Tioga County, New York, Historical Society, explains, "Cooking was done in a large kettle in the fireplace, and meals included baked goods, jam, and apple or berry pie by season. Meals were not named or defined, so in the morning, they took something to break the fast, such as beer, or cider with some bread, baked at home or in a large community oven. After the meal, the men worked outside, breaking in late morning for a light repast of more of the same. Later in mid-afternoon, the main meal of the day was stew, fresh fruits, and vegetables. More vegetables in summer, and more meat in the winter, when butchering was in season. There was a light supper at night."[10]

Daniel and the boys attended to the crops and the large animals and spent hours at the saw and grist mills. Charlotte and the girls cared for the smaller animals like goats, dogs, cats, and sheep. They did housework, prepared the food, and sewed the clothes. Each person may have had only one set of clothing, so mending was an ongoing chore. Young Esther helped make clothes and hats for the family, and she loved fashion. At one point the family owned a fulling mill which they used to cleanse wool before it was turned into fabric.

The women also worked in the kitchen garden, which was close to the house and furnished herbs, squash, and vegetables not grown as crops. Esther developed a lifelong passion for growing vegetables and flowers.

Of all the household tasks, laundry—constant work for the women—was the most relentless. They carried water from a well and then heated the water over a fire. The women scrubbed, rinsed, and wrung water from clothes, which were hung outside in the summer and inside in winter. This time-consuming task filled a whole day, usually on Monday, week in and week out.

Charlotte and the girls also pickled eggs, brewed beer and ale, churned butter, and made cheese. Herbs were distilled and made into domestic medicines like witch hazel, which was rubbed on their bodies to relieve pain. They made their own candles and at night, they spun cloth, sewed, and mended.

Grandma Mehitabel Hobart and Esther's mother Charlotte, strong Puritans, encouraged the McQuiggs to become a religious family. In 1810, Mehitabel served as one of the fifteen founding members of the Baptist Church in Spencer. Attendance at church became a significant part of Esther's life.

Her relatives encouraged her to become a missionary, "… but Miss Esther McQuigg declined, because she wanted to be herself," according to a report published after her death.[11]

In the McQuigg family, both brothers and sisters competed for position and sought the attention of their parents. Even though Esther was not the oldest girl, she was the standout leader of the female siblings. Her brother Edmund, seven years her senior, was the leader of all the siblings. Edmund, later known as E.H., and Esther dominated the others. Their personalities clashed and resulted in an antagonistic relationship that continued throughout their lives.

With the stern principles of the Hobarts and heartiness of the Mc-Quigg mind and body, Esther developed a strong work ethic. Years later, in a letter to her niece Frankie, Esther recalled the dreariness of daily chores, writing, "Our life is made up of day and night, winter and summer, labor and rest, and to get through that, you need to go out the other side. One is ever buffeting waves or beating winds."[12]

By the time Esther was thirteen, Daniel and Charlotte had been married for twenty-five years. Records show their hard work and years of intense labor brought them success. They lived on a seventy-acre farm with fourteen head of cattle, four horses, fifty-six sheep, and twenty-four hogs. At the time of the 1825 census, they listed thirty yards of flannel, forty yards of linen, and an unspecified amount of cotton cloth. They owned a grist mill and a saw mill.[13]

Tragedy struck in 1826 when Charlotte died of unknown causes at age forty-seven. Esther was only fourteen. This event effectively brought Esther's childhood to an end. According to Frankie's granddaughter Rosamund Day, Esther took over the care of her youngest sibling, her four-year-old brother George, who always held a special place in her heart.[14]

In the years following the death of their mother, the family began to scatter, with brothers John and Charles, both in their twenties, migrating to Ohio, and taking eleven-year-old Eliza with them. Twenty-year-old E.H. went a few miles north to Ithaca to clerk in a store.

Esther spent the six years following her mother's death on the family farm. The remaining family consisted of her father; her oldest brother, twenty-five-year old Daniel; his wife, Eleanor; and their two-year old daughter, Cordelia. Other siblings in the household were eighteen-year-old Jane, fifteen-year-old Jesse, twelve-year-old Mindwell, six-year-old Charlotte Susan, and four-year-old George. Seventy-four-year-old grandmother Mehitabel Hobart rounded out the family.

At fifteen, Esther was probably aware of the discussions of the new law in New York outlawing slavery in her state. She naturally embraced the topic of the abolition of slavery. By 1830 the cry for abolition resounded through the north. She attended the abolitionist-leaning Baptist church near the family homestead in Spencer.[15]

In 1831, Esther's older sister Jane married Alvah Archibald and moved to the nearby town of Owego. In March 1832, when Esther was twenty-one, her grandmother Mehitabel Peck Hobart died, probably from congestive heart failure. Recalling the event years later in a letter to Frankie, Esther wrote, "Grandmother Hobart died of dropsy at eighty years old. The drinking of liquor secretly is a family complaint as is fear which ever attends the secret that brands nervous diseases of all kinds."[16]

Death came again when a fierce cholera epidemic raged through the state of New York in 1833. This time, Esther's grandmother

Sarah Coburn McQuigg died in November, probably from cholera. Another catastrophe followed. Esther's father, fifty-seven-year-old Daniel, also died.

After her father's death, Esther's oldest brother, Daniel, now married with three children, inherited the family farm. Esther's older sister, Jane, and her husband, Alvah Archibald, made room in their Owego home for twenty-one-year-old Esther, nineteen-year-old Mindwell, and thirteen-year-old Charlotte Susan, as well as the baby of the family, George, who was then eleven-years-old.[17]

The McQuiggs were a quintessential American family. The eleven siblings grew up together in the same home but each found a distinctive life path. As the country grew, they spread across the land, several heading west.

CHAPTER TWO

"She Was a Great Favorite"

W HEN ESTHER AND her younger siblings moved in 1833, Owego, New York, was a thriving village of fifteen-hundred people on the banks of the Susquehanna River. The river—a super-highway of its day—supported many businesses like leather tanning and logging. Because of this, people were always coming and going. Esther often met interesting people in town.

The name Owego—derived from the Iroquois word *ahwaga*—meant "where the valley widens." In 1778, Owego, an Iroquois vil-lage, was burned to the ground by General James Clinton when he led the Continental Army to retaliate for the Wyoming Valley Mas-sacre at Forty Fort, Pennsylvania.[1]

The three McQuigg sisters, Esther, Mindwell, and Charlotte Su-san, and brother George settled into her their new household with the Archibald family: Jane, Alvah, and their son, Frederick, who was born in 1833. Two years after that, Jane gave birth to a daughter, Mary Jane, who lived only a year.

Esther continued sewing. She opened a millinery shop described in the newspaper as being "at the first door west of the bank upstairs."[2]

The move to Owego became an awakening for Esther in many ways. Her cheerful optimism helped her create a stable place for herself in town and at church. Her stance on abolition became even more passionate, and here, as she had in Spencer, she attended an anti-slavery Baptist church, Owego's First Baptist Church. The danger was even greater here. This congregation was twice mobbed for allowing a Quaker to preach on human rights. According to

Artemas Slack's birth is recorded as March 5, 1871. *(Author's Collection)*

the church historian, escaped slave, abolitionist, social reformer, and writer Frederick Douglass was driven out of town on his first visit to the church. Several years later, though, he returned and was allowed to speak.[3]

As the abolitionist movement grew, so did Esther's convictions. With deepening interest, she followed the activities of abolitionists including Quakers like James and Lucretia Mott, who refused to use cotton cloth, cane sugar, and other products grown with slave labor.

The year Esther moved to Owego, the American Anti-Slavery Society was founded in Philadelphia by William Lloyd Garrison and Arthur Tappan and led by Douglass. Other members included Susan B. Anthony and Elizabeth Cady Stanton, who would become known as important advocates of woman suffrage as well.

Esther was apparently contented at home. Her sister Jane was a quiet woman and Jane's husband, Alvah, was a hard-working man with a huge heart. Through the rest of his life he showered kindnesses on the McQuigg family many times.[4] However, the family suffered a great loss in 1836, when their always sickly sister Mindwell died at the age of twenty-one.

Always a reader, Esther found fertile ground for expanding her thoughts and actions. She subscribed to the *National Anti-Slavery*

Standard and the *Liberator* magazine. The *Standard* not only spoke for emancipation and suffrage for slaves, but suffrage for women. the *Liberator* was begun in 1831 in Massachusetts by William Lloyd Garrison. He once stated, "Our object is universal emancipation. To redeem women as well as men from a servile to an equal condition."[5]

The anti-slavery movement battled serious political headwinds. For example, U.S. President Andrew Jackson owned slaves. Twelve of the first eighteen presidents had owned slaves. Some held slaves during their time in office. When even the leader of the country owned slaves, ending the practice appeared to be impossible.

In Owego, the Pinney family lived next door to the Archibalds on Main Street. Rumors of the Pinney house being used as a station on the Underground Railroad ran through town. Hammon D. Pinney, just a year older than Esther, was thought to be a leader in the abolitionist movement. Because they lived next door to each other and shared similar views on the subject, Esther likely worked with him in support of this cause, although no documents exist to substantiate this.

The female suffrage movement gained momentum. In the 1830s and 1840s, Esther probably read British Mary Wollstonecraft's *A Vindication of the Rights of Women,* originally published in 1792, in which Wollstonecraft wondered why a man would want an uneducated person raising his children.[6]

Esther's visceral understanding of the true limitations and hardships of women came when she began her business as a milliner. She made hats for family and friends throughout her youth. Now, as a young woman operating her own business in Owego, she not only made money but interacted with many other women. Because women always needed hats, Esther enjoyed a prosperous and pleasant time while gaining insight into women's lives. Her shop was a sheltered place for women to relax and talk openly. She became increasingly aware of the numerous laws preventing women from enjoying many of the rights given to men. In New York, married women were not allowed to own, control, or inherit land until the law changed in 1848. Men controlled the children and the finances. A husband could desert his wife, take the children, and leave her no recourse. Not being allowed to vote prevented women from participation in the creation of laws ruling their lives. With no laws to protect their rights, they were essentially rendered helpless.

Esther realized that women's lives were, for the most part, hard and unfair. Esther's father, a responsible man, loved and cared for his wife and family. But her mother had worked hard, even within the shelter of a decent marriage. Esther now learned that if a woman was smart enough—or, more likely, lucky enough—to marry a good man, life could be a joyful experience, even with the hard work involved. If a woman did not marry well, however, life could be extremely painful.

In 1838, following the death of her brother Charles, Esther took her first long trip. Esther and her brother Daniel traveled to Rutland, Ohio, to visit their siblings John and Eliza. When Esther's brothers John and Charles moved to Ohio, John had settled in Rutland in Meigs County. Charles went on to Cincinnati in Hamilton County. By the 1830s, the thriving new city on the Ohio River drew many people from the east. They first came by steamboat and later rode the trains.

Although it is not known what occupation he pursued, Charles made money in Cincinnati. Other residents in town were preacher Lyman Beecher and his daughter Harriet. Harriet married Calvin Stowe there. Following their wedding in 1836, the Stowes moved to Brunswick, Maine. She later wrote a controversial book, *Uncle Tom's Cabin,* that not only affected Esther, but stirred others throughout the nation.

Esther's brother Charles died of consumption[7] in the spring of 1838, at the age of thirty-five. The young bachelor had realized death was eminent. To benefit all his siblings, he sent a legacy, consisting of money and land, to his brother John in Rutland.

John entrusted the funds, along with the land deed, to Esther and Daniel so they could safely take this legacy to their brother, E.H., in New York. E.H. was to give the money to siblings as needed.

No evidence remains concerning the value and details of the estate, but apparently the amount was sufficient to cause problems later. The use of that 1838 legacy caused sporadic family conflicts for at least fifty years, when Esther would find herself in the middle of the emotional troubles.

While staying in Rutland, Esther visited her sister, Eliza. Just three days shy of her fifteenth birthday, Eliza had married Joshua Wyatt Parker, a steamboat captain. They had two young daughters.

Returning to Owego from Ohio, Esther resumed her usual activities. But changes were occurring in town that would affect her life. By this time Owego had grown to 5,300 residents, demonstrating, in part, the need for improvements to the Ithaca and Owego Railroad, which had been built in 1834. Horses pulled the trains. The antiquated tracks were made of strips of cast iron attached to wooden rails. The New York and Erie Railroad was replacing the older company and, by the end of the 1840s, brought more modern capabilities, including locomotives powered by steam engines. Sometime after June 1840, a man named Artemas Slack arrived to work on the railroad from Illinois where he and his brothers had worked on the Illinois Central Railroad.

Slack, a native of Windsor, Vermont, had two brothers, Allen and Charles. Both studied civil engineering at Norwich University in Vermont, Allen graduating in 1938 and Charles in 1839. Although Artemas is said to have attended Norwich University, he is not listed in the alumni records. Allen worked on the Erie Canal before going to Illinois. The brothers purchased land along the Illinois railroad route. In 1840, the Slack brothers shared quarters in La Salle County, Illinois, along with another railroad employee. Allen was married in the spring of 1840 to Louisa Blanchard of New York City.

Charles Slack left Illinois and headed for California with a Norwich University friend. His friend returned, but Charles was not heard from again. Allen Slack went with Artemas to Owego, where they worked together as civil engineers on the New York and Erie Railroad. Esther's brother E.H. worked on grading the roadbeds.[8]

How Esther and Artemas met is not known, but they probably became acquainted during one of the local social activities common to courtship at the time. Pamela Goddard explained in an interview that hotels in Owego and nearby Candor often held dances in their ballrooms. Quadrilles, Virginia Reels and other country dances filled many evenings for people. Young people also often played cards and attended church picnics. Singing schools, where one person taught music and everyone sang along, were popular entertainment in that era. During the summer, activities focused around the river, and in winter, sledding and ice-skating became common pastimes.[9]

On December 15, 1841, Esther and Artemas were married at the Methodist Episcopal Church in Owego by A.H. Crandall. The ceremony cost five dollars.[10]

Following their wedding, Esther and Artemas settled in Owego. Esther gave up her millinery shop. Esther's close relationship with her sister, Jane, and Jane's husband, Alvah Archibald, continued. The family easily accepted Artemas. On October 2, 1842, Esther and Artemas became the parents of Archibald Artemas Slack, named in honor of Alvah Archibald. Though later in life, he would have an alternate first and middle name, he was always called "Archie" by Esther.

Esther's older brother, E.H., his wife, Eliza Jane Hall McQuigg, and the Slacks were part of the group of young people. Esther and Eliza Jane, connected by their strong feelings on abolition and women's rights including suffrage, deepened a friendship that would last a lifetime. During this busy time, Eliza Jane and E.H. had two daughters: Frances, called Frankie, was born in 1841, and Mary Elizabeth, called Libbie, was born in 1842. Esther grew close to both girls, but later shared her heart with Frankie through correspondence which continued for decades.

Tragedy struck Esther and Artemas when Artemas fell ill at only thirty-two. The nature of his illness is unknown, but by mid-April 1843, the family realized he would not recover. Artemas's brother Allen who worked on the railroad in Owego lent assistance. On April 22, 1843, Artemas, Esther, and Allen enlisted the help of

The upper image from Artemas Slack's will shows the second section which reads "I give and devise to my son Archibald Artemas Slack, all that piece and parcel of land. . . ." It records Archie's full name as Archibald Artemas Slack.

The seventh item reads: "I hereby appoint my said Wife & Alvah B. Archibald of Owega and my Brother Allen Slack, Executors of my last Will. . . ." The will also shows Artemas Slack's signature. (Tioga County, Nwe York, Records)

Owego attorney, Alanson Munger, to prepare a will and to handle business arrangements. Esther and Artemas sold some of his Illinois land to his brother Allen Slack. On April 24, Artemas made a will that left more land and the rest of his estate to Esther and their son. He named Esther, his brother Allen, and his brother-in-law Alvah Archibald as executors of his estate. Artemas died sometime in May 1843. He was buried in the Old Burying Ground behind the Presbyterian Church in Owego.[11]

> # A Card
>
> Mrs. Slack has resumed business at her old stand, first door west of the Bank up stairs, where she will be happy to see her friends and customers.
>
> May 18, 1843

Esther Hobart Slack, resumed her millinery business and announced it in the *Owego Advertiser* with "a card." This image was recreated from a low quality photocopy of the original newspaper. *(Tioga County Historical Society, Tioga, NY)*

Now Esther, a thirty-year-old widow with sole responsibility for seven-month-old Archie, was overwhelmed with grief. She also needed to make money because New York law prevented her from taking possession of the money Artemas had left her. She resumed her millinery work and advertised in the local newspaper.[12]

In February 1844, Esther mortgaged some Illinois land to her cousin Daniel Turner. Aside from the land in Illinois, Artemas also had business and property in Owego, which Esther was denied the right to access.

Esther was frightened and angry about this turn of events. Family members reported that Eliza Jane, Esther's sister-in-law and good friend, became "so incensed by the laws that she contacted Horace Greeley, publisher of the New York Tribune, in hopes that he could help." But he apparently did not.[13]

Esther's anger compelled her to go to Illinois where New York law did not apply, and there claim the land she inherited in Artemas's will. Off she went, with baby Archie in tow, heading west to begin a new life, or as she would later say, "a new pioneering experience." She gave an explanation in a later letter to niece Frankie, stating, "My husband sickened and died. I was obliged to go west and was too full of trouble to think much about others for at least two years."[14]

Artemas Slack's gravestone is at the Presbyterian Church Burying Ground
at Owego, New York. *(Author's Collection.)*

CHAPTER THREE

"Our Life is Made of Labor and Rest"

WHEN ESTHER ARRIVED in Illinois, in the spring or summer of 1844, the town of Chicago was eleven years old with a population of roughly eight thousand. Chicago's name evolved from the Miami-Illinois Indian name, *Shikaakwa,* translated in French to *Checagou,* and finally modified to Chicago. Illinois had been a state since 1818, but was still a beautiful, largely unsettled land until the completion of the Illinois and Michigan Canal in 1848, four years after Esther's arrival. Totally changing the northern part of Illinois, the canal connected Chicago on Lake Michigan to the Illinois River, terminating where the new towns of LaSalle and Peru—where Esther would eventually settle—were created. From those places, boats then continued down the Illinois River to the Mississippi River and then the Gulf of Mexico. Industry and people poured into Illinois, adding twenty-two thousand people to the population within a short period.

Possibly one of the men in the family accompanied Esther and young Archie on the trip west as other family members they could have visited lived not far down the Mississippi River.[1] Banking on the theory that women everywhere liked to have good hats, Esther worked at her millinery business.

Esther was in Ottawa, La Salle County, Illinois, in 1846 when she married John Morris, a merchant from Poland on February 17.[2] The book *Polish Pioneers in Illinois 1818-1850* states, "La Salle County had three Poles and possibly two others before 1850. John Morris, Aaron Neustadt, and a Mr. Oppenheim all list Poland as place of birth. They were all most likely Polish Jews."[3]

As Esther followed the issues surrounding women's rights, she saw the drama as it unfolded. Activists questioned women's subservience and also rallied around the movement to abolish slavery because that called attention to all human rights. Women wanted control over their own lives.

Esther was always aware of her lack of formal education. One of the books which could have sparked Esther's continued interest in women's rights was Margaret Fuller's *Woman in the Nineteenth Century*, published in 1845. Stressing education in all forms, Fuller wrote, "Today a reader; tomorrow a leader."[4]

In much of the nineteenth century, books and magazines portrayed women as most feminine when they were submissive to the needs and desires of the men in their family, whether father, brother, or husband. The men's obligations were to think out the right course of action when necessary and to take care of their womenfolk. For women, obedience was generally paramount.

Not every woman was unhappy with her life. But for women like Esther, whose lives had been disrupted by a family death or divorce, independent living was nearly impossible. Laws that withheld their rights offered few options for them to make lives as single women, as Esther experienced in New York when her husband died just a few years before.

After Esther and John married in 1846, they settled into the town of Salisbury on the Illinois River. The Illinois River became a part of Esther's daily life as the Susquehanna had in Owego. Salisbury was later incorporated and renamed Peru.

Although she was happily married, Esther read newspapers and magazines that carried articles about the rampant discontent that eventually resulted in the first Women's Rights Convention, which was held on July 19-20, 1848, at Seneca Falls, New York, very near her previous home in Owego, New York. Elizabeth Cady Stanton, the main author of the Declaration of Sentiments, read that document, which was inspired by the nation's Declaration of Independence, at the convention. Beginning with a statement that referred to the "absolute tyranny" of men over women, the document continued with fifteen points requiring correction before women could be considered equal.[5]

Among the sticking points Stanton listed were the facts that women were not permitted to vote and were denied rights that even the worst of men were allowed. She also noted that a woman could commit crimes if the illegal act was done in the presence of her husband. Stanton explained that a woman had to promise obedience to her husband, and he had power under law to keep her helpless and punish her when he felt it necessary. Women had no control over money, even money that they had received from their families when they entered into marriage. Stanton also remarked that women were limited in their careers; for example, she knew of no women doctors, preachers, or teachers of higher education.[6]

The Declaration of Sentiments was signed by sixty-eight women and thirty-two men. The Women's Rights Movement was officially launched that day at Seneca Falls. Each of the women and men who signed the document were links in the chain between Abigail Adams—who in 1776 urged her husband and the Continental Congress to "remember the ladies"—and the passing of the Nineteenth Amendment to the Constitution, which gave women the right to vote in 1920.

Author Ann Gordon writes that Elizabeth Cady Stanton practiced what she spoke about that day. She and her husband, Henry Brewster Stanton, may have been among the first to omit the word obey from their marriage ceremony.[7]

But Esther McQuigg Slack Morris was still learning about the Women's Rights Movement and was not yet a part of it. John Morris was providing well for her and Archie, and she was satisfied with her life. Their first son, John, named for his father, was born in 1849.

Esther soon endured another loss. Her youngest brother, George, died of cholera while traveling on board a ship. George, Esther's favorite sibling, had been coming home after seeking his fortune during the California Gold Rush. He was buried at sea off the coast of Mazatlán, Mexico, in November 1850.

John Morris's relative prosperity supported a comfortable home for Esther, Archie, and little John. They had two young Irish immigrant housekeepers who probably cooked for the household as well. Their house was also large enough to accommodate two male boarders. During the first election John became one of the aldermen from the second ward. Life was going well.[8]

While her interest in suffrage seldom waned, Esther was busy with her growing family. She gave birth to twins, Robert Charles and Edward John, on November 8, 1851. But soon her life would change dramatically.

Unknown to Esther at the time, events back at the family home of Esther's brother E.H. in Barton, New York, were unfolding that would have a lifetime impact on Esther and most of the women in the McQuigg family. Her sister-in-law and friend Eliza Jane Hall McQuigg and her daughters, Frankie and Libbie, struggled.

Eliza Jane, who endured a challenging marriage to Esther's brother E.H., had separated from him in 1846. According to family members, "E.H. was traditional and autocratic; Eliza Jane was unconventional, a woman ahead of her time. For example, she was a vegetarian, while he was a three-times-a-day meat-and-potatoes man. They also disagreed about educating their daughters. She wanted a full education for the girls; E.H. thought the basics were enough."[9]

During the late 1840s, Eliza Jane experienced turmoil, but she was not the only one. Many women of that era struggled. Women anchored the family and home, but few enjoyed any privileges in public life. Some were experiencing a growing discontent with their treatment.

Eliza Jane and Esther knew how difficult a woman's life could be. They both believed in women's rights and the importance of education for women. But while Esther accepted the responsibilities and limitations that marriage and child-rearing required, Eliza Jane appeared to refuse to accept any limitations at all. While she was still married to E.H., Eliza Jane traveled to Cuba as a nanny and later worked for months in New Orleans as an art teacher. She lived there with one of her sisters. In 1851, Eliza Jane left E.H. and their young girls behind.

Family members later testified in the divorce case that, according to Eliza Jane, "E.H. was a coarse man, and she did not love him, did not like him, did not respect him, and could not live with him." She confided she wanted to go where E.H. couldn't find her. Leaving her husband meant leaving her daughters, neither one of whom was yet ten years old. Under the law, they were the sole property of their father. Eliza Jane's decision created lifelong ramifications for the McQuigg family including Esther.[10]

Like Esther, Eliza Jane also closely followed the Seneca Falls Women's Rights Convention which took place only seventy miles from the family home in Owego, New York. Some of the history-making speeches deeply affected her. She set about preparing herself to live independently and earned a two-year medical degree in Syracuse in 1852.

She then struck out for San Francisco, took a steamer south, crossed the Isthmus of Panama, and boarded another steamer to San Francisco. In 1853, Eliza Jane changed her last name from Mc-Quigg back to Hall and immediately began work as assistant to a Dr. Bourne. The San Francisco *Daily Alta* reported, "Dr. Bourne is giving water treatments for all kinds of ills, including 'Isthmus Fever' and all diseases incident to the voyage. Dr. Bourne is assisted by Mrs. E. J. Hall, M.D."[11]

Around this time, Eliza Jane met the renowned feminist Eliza Farnham. They traveled together throughout northern California for several months, with Farnham speaking on suffrage and even going so far as to say women were superior to men. Eliza Jane's own strong feelings about suffrage solidified, and she made it part of her life's work. She and Esther reconnected, and she sent Esther a barrage of pamphlets and suffrage information throughout the years. Following her travels with Farnham, Eliza Jane returned to San Francisco. In 1854, unmarried Dr. Eliza Jane Hall gave birth to a son she named Charles Victor Hall.

—❦—

Back in Peru, Illinois, Esther's pleasant life had taken a turn for the worse. In 1852, an epidemic of cholera raged through the town, killing as many as six hundred people. Cholera was likely the cause of the death of Esther and John Morris's young son, John, during that period. Esther once again faced the almost overwhelming grief of losing a beloved family member.

Esther's grief-stricken husband, John, entered a downward spiral. During the 1850s, John began drinking more. He lost his business. He traveled, taking prolonged absences from home. He earned money through various endeavors that were mostly unknown to his family. During his travels, John bought and sold goods and gold stocks—that much Esther knew. Life was difficult when John was away, and John was difficult when he was at home.

Esther carried the full burden of educating the children, young Archie and twins Robert and Edward. She cared for her home and made do on the money John sent home. She supplemented those funds with her own earnings from hat-making and sewing. She stayed active in the community and in her church.

She made friends, like her neighbor Seth Paine. He was the independent kind of person that Esther was always attracted to, even as a young girl. People with freedom of thought and compassion for their fellow man were like a magnet to her. Paine and his wife, Frances, and their children were friends and neighbors of Esther and John in the early years of their marriage. Following the death of Frances, Paine married Almeria Winter and the new couple continued the friendship with Esther and her family.

Paine was a founder of the town of Lake Zurich in Illinois and later a founder and superintendent of the Women's Home at 189 Jackson Street in Chicago. That facility was home to about two hundred women who needed shelter, even though they were working.[12]

In 1849 Henry David Thoreau wrote *The Duty of Civil Disobedience*. Whether or not Esther read it, the book influenced the world around her. The 1850s were a time of dissension as storms of war gathered in the United States. During these years, Esther likely read Nathaniel Hawthorne's *The Scarlet Letter*, Herman Melville's

Moby Dick, Henry David Thoreau's *Walden*, and Walt Whitman's *Leaves of Grass*, which were all published between 1851 and 1855. *Uncle Tom's Cabin* by Harriet Beecher Stowe, published in 1852, sold one million copies within a year and was followed by *My Bondage* and *My Freedom* by Frederick Douglass. Esther's annual subscription to *The Atlantic* carried articles and stories by these and other of the best writers of that time, which increased her deep understanding of national and world issues and events.

The 1860 Federal Census listed John Morris without business and without funds. Interestingly, their money was listed next to Esther's name. The household in Peru consisted of John—when he was home; Esther; and the twins, eight-year-old Robert and Edward. No household help was listed.

Eighteen-year-old Archie was now attending school at Chicago University. Now known by the name he used in later life, E.A. Slack, he worked as a printer and resided as a lodger in the thriving city.[13]

—•—

Esther's correspondence with her niece Frankie, the daughter of E.H. and Eliza Jane, began in 1862. In one of her early letters, Esther described her oldest son, writing, "If Archie had not gone to Chicago to work, he never would have gone to the University. He felt he couldn't stay in Peru even if our schools were good, as there was no society here." She continued, explaining, "Mr. Morris was ashamed to have him a printer, but had not the money to educate him. I have acted more independently with Archie than I could have done if his father had been living and it has given me strength."[14]

Eliza Jane's nephew, Hervey Henry Hall, actually suggested Archie's life path as a printer. Hall had begun as a printer as well, first at the *Anti-Slavery Standard* and then going to work with Horace Greeley at the *New York Tribune*.

In her correspondence with Esther, Frankie sorted through her angry feelings about her mother's departure. In 1851, after Frankie's mother, Eliza Jane, left, Jane and Alvah Archibald came to the rescue again and cared for Frankie and Libbie at their father's nearby farm. The Archibalds, the children's aunt and uncle, had previously taken

Frances (Frankie) McQuigg and her father E.H. McQuigg pose for a portrait. *(Cliff Hall Collection)*

in Esther and three of her younger siblings after their father had died just six years following the death of their mother.

E.H. had no grounds for divorce in New York, so he searched for another venue. He chose Indiana because of more liberal divorce laws there, and then established residency in Indianapolis while selling land in New York. He tried to hide his assets and money from Eliza Jane, according to legal depositions. This went on for about two years until Alvah's health failed in 1853, and he and Jane left the farm in Barton to return to Owego. At about this time, E.H. began taking prolonged absences. Frankie and Libbie were placed in a boarding school in a nearby town for another two years while E.H. traveled and searched for another place for them to live. E.H.

Little Libbie McQuigg sits for a portrait with her mother Eliza Jane Hall McQuigg. *(Cliff Hall Collection)*

obtained a divorce from Eliza Jane in Indiana in 1854 on the grounds of desertion. He remarried in 1856, the same year his sister Jane Archibald died. Jane had considered E.H.'s lengthy absences to be harsh treatment of his daughters and never forgave him.[15]

E.H. then moved his daughters and new wife, Elizabeth Forman—another Libbie—to Flint, Michigan. Fortunately, Libbie Forman would be a wonderful stepmother to the girls, but the turmoil of separation and divorce was not yet over.

Eliza Jane returned from California in 1857. She came to Flint to claim her girls with the goal of getting them into good schools. But E.H. refused to allow Eliza Jane to see their daughters and a fierce battle ensued. According to information gleaned from family recollections and the divorce depositions, he finally told Eliza Jane she could take fourteen-year-old Libbie, because she caused too much trouble, but she must leave sixteen-year-old Frankie with him. Eliza Jane accepted the offer. She then went to Indiana and filed a motion to set aside the 1854 divorce.

The exact motivation for Eliza Jane's action is not fully understood, especially since E.H. had already remarried. One might guess she planned to then refile for divorce and gain custody of her daughters or perhaps gain financial benefits. A two-year battle with dozens of depositions sent from friends and family from New York to Indiana ensued with the matter finally decided by the Indiana Supreme Court in 1859. The dispute ricocheted throughout the McQuigg family and divided households as the men often remained loyal to E.H. while the women often supported Eliza Jane. The 1854 divorce was declared valid, and therefore, remained in force as originally decreed.[16]

Throughout her correspondence with Frankie, which began in 1862 when Frankie was twenty years old, Esther could only sympathize with her niece's pain. During Frankie's childhood Esther had no way of actually providing help and was overburdened with her own problems. She was unaware of all that had been happening in Frankie's life and with her parents. She later explained, ". . . I knew but little of their divorce. Trouble makes us all selfish."[17]

The emotional wounds incurred during those years affected all the McQuigg women and set the tone for many of Frankie's and Esther's letters. The scars deepened the resolve of many of the women to gain equal rights, beginning with suffrage. While the women in Esther's family realized that Eliza Jane's behavior was not always appropriate, they understood that many of her actions were reactions and believed the cause for her behavior was due, in part, to her lack of legal rights.

Esther worked to protect her children from as much family drama as possible. Her letters show her lifelong commitment to providing a pleasant, educational environment for her children. In

Young Robert Morris poses with his mother Esther Hobart Morris, circa 1859, Peru Illinois. *(Author's Collection)*

one later letter to Frankie, she wrote, "My children know little of the family troubles. They have other associations."[18]

During 1860, forty-eight-year-old Esther tried to move her family forward despite her husband's issues. Newspapers brought reports of the impending war between the states, increasing the worries Esther struggled to relieve.

By this time, she had lost many of her closest family members to death, but Esther stayed in touch with her remaining siblings, who were scattered across the country. Her sister Eliza and her husband, Joshua Wyatt Parker, lived in Dubuque—about 150 miles away, across the Mississippi River from Esther's home in Peru. They provided a close family connection, offering comfort to Esther and providing cousins for Archie, Robert, and Edward to enjoy. Esther's brother Daniel sold the family farm and now lived in the village of Brutus in Cayuga County, New York. Her brother Jesse and his wife, Mary Freeland, lived in Flint, Michigan, where E.H. and his new wife lived with Frankie. Esther's youngest sister, Charlotte Susan, married their cousin, Frederick Brown. They had three daughters: the oldest, Charlotte Elizabeth, known as Libbie; then Julia; and finally Jean. Esther grew especially close to this niece, Libbie Brown, as they shared their views on women's needs for more power in their lives.

Esther continued following the suffrage movement. She raised her children, and, like many others, dreaded war. Her resolve about her own needs strengthened as John's drinking continued, and he left home for long periods. The issue of suffrage and all the benefits that could result from women having more control in their lives was becoming a driving force in Esther's life.

CHAPTER FOUR

"I Had No Voice in the Matter"

Esther's family continued to experience upheaval while the United States headed toward war. The 1860 census reported 31.4 million people in thirty-three states and five territories and 3.9 million slaves, most of them in twelve states. In late 1860, South Carolina seceded from the Union, and soon six other states followed. The tension in the country was so great that Abraham Lincoln needed the security detail of Allen Pinkerton at his March 1861 inaugural in Washington, D.C. And then, the unimaginable happened, creating enormous change in the nation.

The broken nation exploded into war on April 12, 1861, when men of the newly formed Confederacy fired on Fort Sumter in Charleston Harbor. Four more states seceded. Any optimism for a short war soon dissolved.

The Civil War really began for Esther's family when Archie came home to Peru from Chicago University and announced he was enlisting. Esther later told her niece, Frankie, in a letter, "I would not consent to let Archie go, until he said he should die if he did not participate."[1]

On June 10, eighteen-year-old Archie Slack enlisted at Moline, Illinois, to fight for the Union. Enlistment papers showed his name as "Edward Archibald." Later military documents show his name as, "Edward Archibald Slack." For unknown reasons, he seemed to have set aside the name recorded in his father's will, Archibald Artemas Slack, and used Edward Archibald Slack, or E.A., from this point forward. He was a private in Company H, Illinois Nineteenth,

Archie Slack had alternate first and middle names, but Esther always called him Archie. This photograph circa 1861. *(Wyoming State Archives)*

recorded as six feet one, with light hair, grey eyes, and florid complection. He listed his occupation as printer. His birthplace was listed as Oswego, New York, but that was a bit off. He was actually born in Owego, New York, but another similarly-name town called Oswego was better known and the misspelling was a common error.[2]

The Nineteenth Illinois Volunteer Regiment began with four companies of Zouave cadets, popular for their colorful uniforms and precision drills. One-thousand men including Archie left Chicago. More volunteers were added, resulting in a total of ten companies and eighteen-hundred men, according to the history prepared years later by the Nineteenth Illinois Veteran Club.[3]

Esther, along with women throughout the nation on both sides, just wanted husbands, sons, fathers, and all men in their lives to return home soon and safe.

However, not only men went to war.

＝＝o＝＝

Eliza Jane was not the only unconventional woman in the Hall family. Her sister and Frankie's aunt, Susan Emily Hall, played her part in the great American disaster. Susan became a medical student at Elizabeth and Emily Blackwell's New York Infirmary for Indigent Women and Children, graduating in spring 1861. While living in New York City, Susan shared quarters with Eliza Jane and Eliza Jane's daughter Libbie. At the outbreak of the war, Eliza Jane and Libbie packed up and took the same long trek through Panama to San Francisco that Eliza Jane had taken fifteen years earlier. From that time on, Eliza Jane Hall, daughter Libbie, and son, Charles Victor Hall, made their home in California. Eliza Jane insisted Libbie change her name from McQuigg to Hall.

In June 1861, a mass meeting was held at Cooper Union in New York City where Dorothea Dix was appointed superintendent of nurses for the Union Army. Susan Emily Hall attended the meeting and then followed that with special training to become a war nurse. After she passed an examination and received additional practical training, she was one of the first women sent south "to assist the Union cause." Louisa Mae Alcott, a nurse also working for Dorothea Dix, based her book *Hospital Sketches* on this experience. She went on to write *Little Women.*[4]

Susan worked constantly as a nurse for the entire four years of the war. She served in Alexandria following the Battle of Bull Run, and at a number of other significant places, including Gettysburg, Nashville, and Murfreesboro.

Susan's health was permanently impaired. During a lengthy recovery period, she met her future husband Robert Barry, also recovering from his war wounds, at Dr. Jackson's Sanitarium in Dansville, New York. Both Susan and Robert received their Civil War pensions in 1887. Susan was rewarded for her four years of nursing service;

Susan Emily Hall, Eliza Jane's sister, made a name for herself as a Civil War Nurse. She was another exemplar for Esther. *(Office of Thomas F. O'Mara, New York State Senate)*

Robert for his combat duty and injury. Robert's pension was $12 per year.[5]

Frankie had wanted to become a war nurse like her Aunt Susan, but according to Esther's letters, Frankie's father dissuaded her from doing so. Dorothea Dix and the Civil War nurses fell under the jurisdiction of the United States Sanitary Commission. Frankie found the opportunity to contribute by dedicating herself to raising money and volunteers for the annual Sanitary Fairs.[6]

With war raging, reports of battles won and lost mounting, and death tolls rising, life went on for the family left behind in Peru, who anxiously awaited letters and word of Archie's well-being. What else was there to do but live and watch and wait? In September 1862, Esther wrote to Frankie, "My Archie is all right thus far, but things are such we do not know what will happen next." Commenting on Frankie's consideration of becoming a war nurse, Esther said, "If you cannot manage to endure defeat, don't undertake it."

As Esther reported to Frankie, John Morris was absent from home most of the time. Periodically, Robert, but more often Ed, joined their father in his travels. John spent months at a time in New York; he also traveled throughout the country, including journeying through the West. Esther shared her sadness and anger in a letter to Frankie, "I have heard from my husband. He will stay in the mountains so that he shall be freed from all responsibility in the family."

The national political scene and war compounded Esther's personal unhappiness.

Frankie wanted Esther to visit her in Flint, Michigan, but because of the war and a constant shortage of money, the time never seemed right. Even though Esther continued to make hats to supplement the funds John sent to her, there was never enough money. Esther revealed the distress she felt in an October 1862 letter to Frankie, writing, "I talk to you every day all to myself, and then Bob [Esther's son Robert] puts in a word as he knows my attempts to visit you. What a quarrelsome time we have had, and Bob finally said, 'I don't care, I will go to Uncle Ed and live with Aunt Libbie and see cousin Frankie anyway.' My dear Frankie, how I wish we could spend the winter together with nothing to do but grow strong. I expect Mr. Morris back next week and the election will be over in more ways than one. I expect the conservative vote to carry Illinois."[7]

Esther and Frankie were Republicans, and at that time, Republicans were liberal. Support of the anti-slavery movement was both liberal and radical. Democrats held more conservative views. The women were disappointed when Esther's prediction about the election of 1862 proved true. The conservative Democrats who ran for the House of Representatives carried Illinois. However, Esther soon came to terms with the results. She wrote to Frankie again in March 1863, explaining, "My health is good and if I am not entirely successful, I am happy with life. As far as the war is concerned, I am submissive to the purveyors. There is no use rebelling against them."[8]

In August 1863, Esther told Frankie again how much she would like the younger woman to move to Peru and revealed something of her financial situation, stating, "I do not own my house. I rent and have plenty of room for you. Mr. Morris has not been home and since he don't write himself I don't know where he is. I'm not getting rich at any rate."[9]

In October 1863, Frankie shared her own emotional distress with her aunt. At age twenty-one, Frankie still reeled from the separation and divorce of her parents, which had been finalized just three years before. She also suffered from the absence of her mother, Eliza Jane, and her sister, Libbie, both now living in California. Esther responded with compassion and understanding, writing, "When we find our own words coming from the mouth of another speaker on the same subject and on the same day we feel like we commune in some mysterious way. I often find myself either reading something I want you to know, talking to you, while alone, looking into those great sad eyes of yours. I am sorry indeed to hear of their weakness, but they have taken in so much for one so young. Let them rest a while. I truly believe if you do not change your train of thought you will not live out half your days. Little Bob has written you a number of letters but would not feel satisfied and did not send them."[10]

Robert, in part, likely acquired his mother's concern with good handwriting. Ashamed of her own handwriting—at times an illegible scrawl—Esther prodded the boys to write well. Robert, at nearly twelve, worked to become a careful scribe. Robert's twin, Ed, did not care much for study but had a more than adequate hand. Their older brother, Archie, not only had a fine script but also was a budding journalist.

Archie had traveled throughout the South with the Nineteenth Illinois Volunteer Regiment as the soldiers faced the challenges of the war. The regiment left Chicago on July 12, 1861, with 911 men. More men joined them along the way. Archie was attached to Company H, also known as the "Moline Rifles," a unit of ninety-six men. Company H fought in the Battle of Murfreesboro in Tennessee, July 13, 1862. Next for Archie came the Second Battle of Murfreesboro, also known as the Battle of Stones River, December 31, 1862, through January 1, 1863. Archie's company fought in the Battle at Chickamauga in Georgia on September 18 through 20, 1863, which was a significant Union defeat with the second highest number of casualties in the war.

The Illinois Nineteenth then joined the Union Army of the Tennessee, commanded by General William Tecumseh Sherman. Archie fought under Sherman during the Battle of Missionary Ridge in Chattanooga on November 25, 1863, which forced the Confederate Army into Georgia.[11]

Archie remained in Chattanooga until at least May 1864, when he began his correspondence with Frankie, to politely decline her invitation for him to visit.[12]

Reflecting her love of nature, Esther shared in April 1864, "What a difference the sunshine makes. I begin to feel quite cleaned up." Then, "I have a letter from [your] Aunt Charlotte [Susan Brown]. Mr. Morris was in Owego."[13]

In June 1864, Esther's twenty-one-year-old niece, Libbie Brown, suffering from ill health, traveled twelve hundred miles from Owego to stay with her aunt in Peru. Libbie, one of Esther's younger sister Charlotte Susan's daughters, brought radical thoughts on women and their place in the world. She provided books and pamphlets from the East which were a welcome addition to Esther's library. The younger woman's assessment of the way things should be, along with her tenacity, provided Esther many opportunities for conversation and laughter. A strong supporter of women's rights, Libbie later worked for Susan B. Anthony. Libbie and her sisters, Julia and Jean, all left home as young women.

Libbie dazzled Esther's twins, Robert and Edward, who would turn thirteen on the upcoming election day in the fall. Many of the young men of Peru stood in awe of this sophisticated young woman from the East.

On July 3, 1864, Esther, in her plainspoken language, described Libbie in a letter to Frankie, "Libbie Brown has come, and she has order enough to command a regiment or a retinue of servants. What a pity such talents should be lost in a woman just at a time we need generals so bad." Further, she explained, "This week Lib is in the middle of a flirtation. Lib is smart and selfish like the rest of us, but the one quality which does not belong to all the family in general I think will help her out. She is very affable to the beaux." Esther also gave details in the letter about fixing up her house, perhaps in honor of Archie's return, and evidently because she had received money from her husband. John "bought a new side board, a set of plates, and a set of china for the table. I papered and painted the kitchen," she wrote. She had also purchased a new carpet and replaced carpet in several of the rooms. She admitted that she only read "when I am too tired to work." She mentioned some of her recent reading materials, including *The Atlantic*.

She finished the thought on a tart note, writing, "If it was not for fixing, what would we women do. I suppose I should do as men do, sit down and find fault with others."

Frankie must have been working for her father, probably at the lumber company, or another one of his businesses, because in the same lengthy letter, Esther offered practical advice that displayed her understanding of the relationship between Frankie and her father as well as her grasp of the younger woman's rights. Esther advised, "If you stay with your father, you have a right to a salary as if you taught school, and a vacation to reconnect yourself. You can be sick or disagreeable as you think best, and I would say while he gave talk to the money, take it into your own hands and ask for it. Self-protection is the first law of nature and who should care for a person who does not care for themselves. I don't get anything unless I demand it, coax it. . . . I do my own work for the last year and looking first rate. It's one year since Mr. Morris was at home but will be here the first of the month."[14]

Soon after, Archie came home. He spent a few days with Esther, Robert, Edward, and Libbie before leaving for Chicago, where he mustered out of service on July 9, 1864. Archie was one of the fortunate men who had not been injured physically; however, as with many soldiers, he suffered from psychological wounds. When Archie enlisted, Company H had four officers. One died at Andersonville Prison in Georgia, one went missing at Chickamauga, and the other

Archie enlisted to fight for the Union as a private in the Nineteenth Illinois Volunteer Regiment which had begun with four companies of Zouave Cadets.

two mustered out. The company had eighty-three privates, acquired seventeen recruits, and had one cook. Of these, sixteen men were transferred for various reasons; nine died; two were captured; two deserted; and thirty-four were discharged because of injuries. Archie was one of thirty-seven men who mustered out on July 9.[15]

Esther's world revolved around her sons and, of the three, firstborn Archie was perhaps the most independent and self-sufficient. His letters display his intelligence and ebullience and reveal that he was articulate, ambitious, and persistent, and that he worked to improve himself. These attributes, in addition to his attractiveness and his height, possibly opened doors for him.

Archie returned to school in Chicago and on September 18, 1864, wrote to Frankie about his recent visit to New York City. He had treated himself to the trip following his release from the service. He wrote, "I went out to Central Park again. I rambled through 'The Ramble,' and rode around the lake. I viewed the city from the steeple of Trinity Church. I went to the beautiful home for the frail perishable wealthy citizens of New York, Greenwood Cemetery. What a change it was to go from this assembly of graves to the busy scene of the Navy Yard where 8,000 bodies flit around actively engaged in building huge gun boats, iron clads, mounting master cannon and manufacturing destructive missiles all, for the purpose of slaying their fellow creatures."

In one short sentence, Archie hinted to his cousin of the deterioration of the relationship between Esther and his stepfather, John. He wrote, "Mother has some idea of coming to Chicago to live and when she does will send for you to come and make us a visit.[16]

At Chicago University, Archie was listed in the officers of the school as the historian. He joined the Phi Delta Theta fraternity and was named in the alumni roster as a journalist with the *Chicago Sun*.[17]

With the war still ongoing, Camp Douglas—considered the Union's Andersonville, a notorious Confederate prison—located next to the university, held more than seven thousand Confederate prisoners of war. Archie continued his correspondence with Frankie on November 11, 1864, wherein he told her that the university officials had feared that the institution might be taken over by the Confederate States Army because of its possible use as a fort. Students offered to help the Union soldiers guard the university, and Archie commanded the volunteer unit.

Evidently Ed had been staying in Chicago with Archie, who continued the letter with, "My father visited Ed and I three weeks ago. It happened that he came at the right time to hear my first attempt at debating. Ed got homesick and I let him go home to see his mother."[18]

The twins turned thirteen on November 8, 1864. This was also Election Day, when some feared Abraham Lincoln would lose the election for his second term to General George B. McClellan. Lincoln worried that he might lose for many reasons; one was that an incumbent president had not been re-elected since 1832. Nine presidents in a row had served only one term. Some predicted that war casualties would also turn voters against Lincoln; sixty-five thousand Union soldiers died during the summer of 1864.

In the Morris household, war-weary Esther and niece Libbie Brown, both Republicans, favored Democrat McClellan. Of course, their allegiance didn't count because John was the only who could vote. The boys were too young, and neither Esther nor Libbie had the right to vote.

On October 3, 1863, Abraham Lincoln's Presidential Proclamation had created Thanksgiving Day—a national holiday to be celebrated the last Thursday in November.[19]

On that holiday, November 24, 1864, Esther—sad and lonesome—began a letter to Frankie. She wrote, "I sometimes feel this body of mine is always going to bother me. Do not come if I do leave it. I find that I am getting old and lazy. I think a good deal and do but little." Esther went on to answer Frankie's questions about some family history, including a snippet about her uncle Rodney Hobart. She wrote, "He lived to be 90, but never done any work after he was 40, but sat in a great chair lined with sheep skin and read Swedenborg and argued against orthodoxy. Your father would like Uncle Rodney. I have been to the Congregational Church and a radical Abolitionist sermon." Obviously distraught from these thoughts and memories, Esther concluded with, "That has me as . . . I do not write anything I expected to say, so I'm going to go to bed."[20]

After she recovered from her distress, Esther revealed more of her thinking to Frankie. Resuming the letter on December 6, she confessed, "I went to bed and wondered why I stopped writing. I see now why it was. When I came to your father, I felt me different. I believe he can't help it. It is the same with Mr. Morris and Mr. McQuigg [Frankie's father, E.H.]. The former thinks the country cannot be saved only through the old constitution and the Democratic Party. The latter looks to the Presbyterian Church for a passport to heaven. I embraced them both early in life and like many other forms, I have chosen better platforms. Not that they didn't do well at the time, but new occasions and a larger family enlarged my arrangement."

At a crossroad in her life, Esther revealed her lack of feeling for John, but her interest in national events brought her back to the recent election. "Like you, I felt that I wanted a change in our government, but the majority have decided for Lincoln. I had no voice in the matter, so I feel no responsibility in the decision. I sometimes think I feel a little like the Democrat, I had no hand in making this war and I shall not be drafted." She went on to speak of John with disdain, writing, "Mr. Morris came home from New York quite sanguine McClellan would be elected. He talked large and thought small, but he felt quite crest fallen when he found he was beat." Her humor was demonstrated with, "As McClellan had resigned, John thought he had better follow suit, so, he donned his hat and started for New York."

She continued, "And now to the next generation, as I look to them for the union of the United States. The bones of our nation are so broken, and it is often reported the backbone has been broken, which is always fatal. We should move on from the past suffering which can only be remedied by forgetting or by our passing away."

She concluded with a sentence that indicated her gloom at the time, writing, "I have a long winter before me, but it will soon pass. I am certain that adversity makes us strong if we can only live through it. I say, do all the good you can while you do live and be as comfortable under the circumstances as you can, and when we come to die, we can say we have tried to do our duty and are not afraid to die."[21]

On March 4, 1865, President Lincoln officially began his second term. In his inaugural address, he expressed his desire to "bind up the nation's wounds" and "to do all which may achieve and cherish a just and lasting peace among ourselves and with all nations."[22]

President Lincoln's Burial Service was held at Oak Ridge, Springfield, Illinois, May 7, 1865. The engraving is based on a sketch by Thomas Hogan. *(Library of Congress)*

The Morris household returned to routine, evidenced by a March 1865 letter from Robert to his cousin Frankie. He wrote, "Today is Sunday. It is beautiful weather. The steamboats are up the river. Edward and I go to the free school, where there are some girls. We like it very much. Cousin and I have been a walking this evening. I'm learning violin and studying German."

On a more serious note, he explained, "Father is in New York the past five months. Archie is in Chicago. I do not know what I will do when Cousin Libbie goes away. You do not know how much I would like to have a sister. Ed says he does not write because he has nothing to say. He and I send much love."[23] Whatever unhappiness Esther experienced over the winter of 1864–1865, she continued to try to give her children as normal a childhood as possible.

The war officially ended on April 9, 1865, when General Ulysses S. Grant accepted the surrender of General Robert E. Lee in the parlor of the McLean home in Appomattox Court House, Virginia. With the war over, the country could begin to heal. Celebration on some fronts was in order but short-lived. Only five days after the official end of the war, President Lincoln was shot at Ford's Theatre. He died the next morning, on April 15, 1865.

Businesses closed and flags flew at half-mast in honor of the deceased president. His body was taken to the White House and then lay in state at the Capitol rotunda. On April 21, the funeral train traveled from Washington, D.C. to Springfield, Illinois, passing tens of thousands of Americans who lined the route to pay their respects. He was buried at Oak Ridge Cemetery in Springfield on May 1, 1865.

The Emancipation Proclamation that had been created by Executive Order was signed by President Lincoln on September 22, 1862. This order became effective on January 1, 1863, and was finally ratified as the Thirteenth Amendment on December 6, 1865, seven months after his death.

After thirty-five years of hoping and working for abolition, Esther must have been overjoyed.

CHAPTER FIVE

"Difficult the First Time Trying"

Marital difficulties, along with raising the twins and working to produce money from making hats and clothing, took a toll on Esther's health, Archie reported in a letter to Frankie written in May 1865.

"Mother has been very sick during the past month, but is now slowly recovering," he told his cousin. "Father went home and stayed a few weeks and returned to New York City last week. As soon as mother was able to get out of bed she attempted to write to me but her strength failed and Ed finished the letter. She said, 'write to Frank and tell her to come and make us a visit and tell her when you will have a vacation.' You can see what a good mother I have who, while confined to her bed with sickness is planning for my happiness."[1]

He wrote to her again in June, explaining, "I decided some six months ago to spend this summer at home, and now that mother is in poor health, I cannot think of doing otherwise. Therefore, it is settled that I shall not see you for an indefinite period."

He continued, telling her, "There is something else which I wish to say to you which I would have reserved till we met if there was any immediate prospect of it. When I returned from the army my soul was contaminated with the associations of camp life. In a word, I was demoralized. I flattered myself then that army life had made no inroads upon my morals, however much it might have injured others, and that I was capable of resisting temptations in any form. It is a divine truth that in our strength we are weak."[2]

When he wrote again in July, he revealed a little more about his mother. He told Frankie, "Your kind letter came to hand via Peru, after being peeped into by Mother. I expect her to make me a visit by the coming Friday. It is possible I may prevail upon mother to establish head-quarters here. She is already prepared to make a movement, but father's adhesiveness has yet to be over-come. He is still in New York but will start for Colorado next month."[3]

By this time, the relationship between Esther and John had apparently dissolved to the point of Esther openly discussing separation with her son. Archie, although obviously in favor of such a move, recognized the lingering connection between the two.

The next month, Esther wrote to Frankie of her plans to go to her husband. "Mr. Morris has written me to come to New York and spend the winter," Esther told her niece. "If I can find someone to leave the house with I will do so. Archie has been making arrangements to go to school this winter. I expect to leave Ed with him while Bob will go East with me. He wants to go by way of Flint and see Aunt Libbie, Uncle Ed, and you. Cousin Libbie Brown wrote me that she would be in New York City this coming winter."[4]

However, Esther did not go to New York for the winter. When she wrote to Frankie in January 1866, she gave more details about John, who had remained in New York, and she also spoke of his work. Esther wrote, "He has not made a very much of a sale this past year, only does enough to keep us alive, but he is expecting to do better as the result of the new possibility of gold. He is interested in a company that is the Park Mining Company. He has confidentially struck in it, but is waiting for it to disclose dividends. Ed went to John in New York about Thanksgiving. He stopped to see cousin Libbie, but is with his father at present. Ed is bashful, and I thought it would do him good."

Esther also shared her enjoyment of the writings of Gail Hamilton, whose works she admitted to liking better than those of Harriet Beecher Stowe. Hamilton was the pseudonym used by Mary Abigail Dodge, who wrote about women's equality.[5]

Esther allowed fourteen-year-old Robert to include his own note to Frankie. He alluded to the increasing tensions in the family, stating, "This term I am studying arithmetic and algebra, German, grammar and Latin. We are also studying bookkeeping. Mother and I keep house all by ourselves. Edward and Archie write often. Mother and I enjoyed Christmas and New Year's very much. You asked me if I took the Young Folks Magazine. I do not but some of my school mates do and I can get them. Mother takes the Weekly Republican and Atlantic Monthly and the Banner of Light and she gets considerable other books so I have plenty to read."[6]

In March 1866, Esther felt more positive about her life and future as she reported to Frankie, "This spring looks very pleasant to me; in fact, I have not felt so hopeful for years."[7]

Whatever made Esther so optimistic in March had obviously dissipated by May. Both Esther and Frankie reached crossroads in their lives at about the same time. Esther considered whether she should leave her marriage, while Frankie mulled over leaving her father's home.

Esther tried to comfort Frankie, writing, "My Dear Little Chicken, I have been watching and wondering how long before your shell would break, because I am too old to nurse infants. Now dear Frank, nothing would give me more pleasure than to take you into my own arms and hold you to my heart of hearts until you feel strong in the magnetism of self-reliance. You have only to give one good cram and you would be a leader instead of a follower."

She offered some advice to her niece, suggesting that she come to Peru or else perhaps St. Paul, Minnesota, or St. Louis, Missouri, because these were places where Frankie had family. Esther also dispensed a bit of her life's philosophy, writing, "We all want influence or affection to stimulate us to action."[8]

Esther's first crossroad had created her decision to leave New York for the unknown rather than stay with the familiar. She had taken Archie and moved to Illinois. Now she wondered whether to stay in an unhappy marriage or take her twins and try to make a life on her own.

Esther also shared her thoughts about her brother E.H., Frankie's father. She wrote, ". . . He has good qualities to attract one and he disguises his selfishness under a cloak of benevolence for his own good. I really think he deceives himself." She continued, "I do believe I have to contend constantly with the same complexity. I love my children and would like to have them with me and take my sons. But as you say, do it my own way. In that I differ from the rest of my family and I think it is owing more to what had to do with the millinery business that cured me."[9]

Esther's referral to the millinery business reflected her fear of striking out on her own. She had heard many sad stories from other women, and in addition, remembered her own difficulty of working to support herself and her child in a man's world.

Esther expanded her thoughts. She explained, "When we are old we do not need more experience, and do not gain strength. But when we are young we will follow anything, rather than to sit still. We gain strength physically by walking and we have the benefit of knowledge from our early education. What is the point of that if we do not make use of it?" She went on, "Everything is difficult the first time trying. Did you ever hear of a child that walks or talks without first trying? Just as we women are told to shut up and lean on our husbands, the very thing they do not hear one word of. The only time I was ever lost was when I kept quiet."[10]

At this time few jobs for women existed. Men still dominated the rights and jobs. Even clerical and teaching positions had not yet opened up to women. If a woman was lucky enough to marry a good man who lived a long life and retained the ability to support the family, life might be good. A poor choice in a husband could result in limited opportunity to care for herself and her family. No laws protected her.[11]

Esther continued, "In early life I had no parent to control me and I think it is worse to do just enough to keep me from doing for myself. I was too young to worry or might have done so. I think the paternal feeling is almost an insanity in our family. Your father's is all due to selfishness and he is tyrannical."[12]

John McAuley Palmer is shown on the frontispiece of his 1899 book and Malinda Ann Neely Palmer's portrait is from the Illinois First Lady Collection. *(Illinois State Library)*

Esther and Robert continued to "keep house all by ourselves," as he had told Frankie, while Archie studied in Chicago. Archie graduated from the university in 1866 and returned to Peru for the summer. That fall he moved to Fulton, Illinois, to study at Soldier's College, and he wrote a letter to Frankie. He told her, "Outbursts with mother [over the summer] served to unfit me for a congenial fellowship with present associates who are just commencing to climb the indifferent ladder of human knowledge. I have quit reading of the thoughts of men and have commenced to interest myself in their actions. By the way I heard Fred Douglass, [the famed abolitionist] last Monday evening."[13]

The arguments with Esther took a toll on Archie. His discomfort increased as he was highly displeased with the Fulton college. When the 1867 spring term ended, he decided not to return. Neither did he want to return to Peru, so he accepted a classmate's invitation to work as a printer in Carlinville, Illinois, a decision which turned out to be life-changing.

Frances (Frankie) McQuigg, the recipient of many of Esther's letters, posed for a portrait at about the time of her wedding to Damon Stewart. *(Cliff Hall Collection).*

Archie's classmate was a relative of John McAuley Palmer, a lawyer and highly decorated Civil War general. Archie eventually became friends with Palmer and his large family. Palmer was married to Malinda Neely. Her sister, Sarah Neely, would play an important role in Archie's life.

The Palmers had taken Malinda's siblings into their family when her mother died of cholera in 1852. When Archie arrived in Carlinville in 1867, the Palmers were a family of sixteen. Sarah Neely was twenty-six.[14]

Although she had hoped to become a teacher after a visit to relatives in Iowa, John Palmer did not want women in his family to

Captain Damon Stewart was a Civil War veteran and a long time friend of Frances (Frankie) McQuigg. In 1867 he became her husband. *(Cliff Hall Collection).*

work, so Sarah returned home. During the Civil War Sarah's oldest brother was wounded at Shiloh and a younger brother spent a year in the notorious Andersonville Prison.[15]

Archie became friends with Sarah and wrote to her when he returned home to Peru to contemplate his future. John McAuley Palmer was elected governor of the state of Illinois in 1869. The large family, including Sarah, moved into the governor's mansion in Springfield.

In Flint, Michigan, in the fall of 1867, Archie's cousin Frankie married her longtime friend Captain Damon Stewart, a man seven years her senior. He had enlisted at the outbreak of the Civil War and had been wounded at Williamsburg in 1862. Stewart was captain of Company K of the Twenty-third Michigan Infantry. He served until the end of the war.[16]

Damon perhaps understood well the losses in Frankie's life, as he lost his father at age thirteen and a sister when he was seventeen. Both of his brothers died in the war. Twenty-four-year-old William died at the Battle of Jonesborough, Georgia, and eighteen-year-old Richard died at the Battle of Resaca. The brothers died within ninety miles and four months of one another. Because he was the oldest and only surviving son, Damon cared for his mother, Lucy. She would live with Damon and Frankie, and Damon would come to know Esther and her family well. According to Frankie's granddaughter, "Damon was a loveable man, and he and Frankie had a very happy marriage."[17]

While Frankie was settling into her life, both Archie and Esther were ready to turn the page and start new beginnings.

CHAPTER SIX

"More Light She Craved"

Twenty-five-year-old Archie returned home to Peru. Six months in Carlinville set his mind to consideration of his future. His stepfather, John Morris, had also returned, having dealt in gold and mining speculation for a time. On January 29, 1868, the *Chicago Tribune* carried a lengthy article about the Sweetwater Gold Rush and told about South Pass City in the area that would become Wyoming Territory:

> The headquarters of the Sweetwater mines is situated on Willow Creek, twelve miles north of South Pass Station, on the old overland mail route. It was first laid out in October 1867. It now has eighty houses and eight places of business, including a very good store. Seven hundred persons are wintering here, awaiting the approach of spring to resume operations. The Western Union Telegraph Company have made arrangements to build a telegraph line next spring to connect this place with the Overland Line. It is confidently asserted by many that a population of twenty to thirty thousand will throng hither next summer, and that South Pass City will experience a much more rapid substantial growth than Cheyenne City.[1]

The two men became excited about the possibilities of taking a trip to the new gold rush region. Archie's eagerness mirrored that of thousands of men who dreamed about the possibility of adventure and striking it rich. Archie and his stepfather decided to team up and take the twelve-hundred-mile trek to South Pass City to look for gold.

However, in her letters, Esther later said that John hid his drinking from the family by being absent from them. She may have spoken of leaving him. His absences showed he was as unhappy in the marriage as Esther was, and his drinking may have escalated at this time.

Esther resolved to maintain the status quo in her marriage and await events. At that time, the West was like a foreign land. The family most likely educated themselves as best they could about the region as they planned John and Archie's spring foray.

In April 1868, John and Archie left to find riches while Esther and the twins moved east to New York City to await word from the men.

By this time, the population of New York City had grown to more than 800,000. Gas lamps lit the downtown streets. The first elevated train was in operation, and Alfred Beach was experimenting on the first underground tube for what would become the subway.

In contrast, the largest city in the West was San Francisco with 149,000 people.

Esther's new beginning included settling herself and her sixteen-year-old twins, Robert and Edward, with cousins Libbie and Julia Browne. Although they had been born in Owego, the young women now lived in New York City. Once they were accommodated, Esther traveled to Owego for extended visits with other family members. The twins found jobs in New York City. Robert worked at Calhoun, Robbins & Co., selling notions; Edward, too, seems to have worked regularly.

Esther's niece Libbie, the young activist who stayed with them in Peru four years before, had grown into a twenty-four-year-old New York sophisticate. Born Charlotte Elizabeth Brown, she had changed her name to the more stylish Elizabeth Hobart Browne and chose to be known as Lib. Both sisters, Lib and Julia worked in the packing department of a firm that sold homeopathic pharmaceuticals.[2]

By May, Esther grew worried about John and Archie because she had not heard anything from them since they left for South Pass City. As often occurred whenever she wrote to someone other than Frankie, she did not trust the legibility of her own handwriting to convey such an important message, so this time she asked Robert to write a letter to Frankie. Esther thought that John and Archie may have written to her in care of Frankie. Robert said that Esther had enjoyed visiting the Owego relatives but she "would now like to remain with us some time to come. We wish much to have her for we have learned to appreciate a home by our separation. Edward is well, but very anxious to go to his Father."[3]

By July, Esther had heard from the men, and Robert told Frankie, "Father's and Archie's first letters were somewhat discouraging, as the surface gold was not abundant, but since, they have written more favorable. They were both well as it is now some time since we received a letter from them, we look for one daily."[4]

Frankie's husband, Damon Stewart, visited New York and was so impressed with Robert that he offered him a job in one of his stores in Flint, Michigan. In September, Robert left New York for Flint to take up his duties in Damon's business. He would live with the Stewarts.

Lib and Julia Browne also made new beginnings. They paid a visit to the office of *The Revolution*, a weekly newspaper on women's rights and the official publication of the National Woman Suffrage Association. The association was formed by Susan B. Anthony and Elizabeth Cady Stanton. Stanton and Parker Pillsbury edited the newspaper, while Anthony handled the business aspects of the paper. *The Revolution* was located in an office at the *New York World*. Both Lib and Julia impressed Stanton and Anthony who hired them as clerks. Lib soon became Susan B. Anthony's private secretary. Lib worked for Anthony until the newspaper ceased publication in May 1872, and they remained friends.

The Revolution acted as a voice for the National Woman Suffrage Association, with a circulation reaching three thousand. The content addressed previously forbidden subjects such as sex education, rape, divorce, domestic violence, and discrimination against working women. The articles emboldened women to develop higher opinions of themselves and their places in the world.[5]

Financing for *The Revolution* came from wealthy eccentric George Francis Train, and the financial editor of the *New York World*, David Melliss. Train was an entrepreneur who organized a

The Revolution was the voice for the National Woman Suffrage Association where Esther's nieces worked with Susan B. Anthony, Elizabeth Cady Stanton, and Parker Pillsbury. *(Library of Congress)*

clipper ship line routed from New York around Cape Horn, taking passengers to San Francisco. He helped organize the Union Pacific Railroad and Credit Mobilier. He traveled the world during his 1870 U.S. presidential campaign and made two other such trips, later claiming Jules Verne used him as the model for Phileas Fogg in his landmark book, *Around the World in Eighty Days.* Train's secretary, his cousin, George Pickering Bemis, traveled with him. Lib's sister Julia met and married George Pickering Bemis who had also traveled with Mark Twain through the West and played a prominent part in

Twain's book *Roughing It.* They were married on June 8, 1870, in New York City, during the time she worked at *The Revolution.*

As 1869 dawned, though, Esther's family was scattered around the continent. Archie and John were outside the "states" in distant South Pass City. Esther and Edward lived in New York City, and Robert remained in Flint, Michigan, with Frankie and Damon Stewart.

Esther found life in New York City, where she had lived for ten months, only deepened her beliefs in woman suffrage. Her long-smoldering yearning for suffrage and equal rights for women turned into a flaming passion.

Esther probably visited the offices of *The Revolution* and met Susan B. Anthony as Lib worked with her daily. Certainly her daily exposure to Susan B. Anthony's philosophy through discussions with Lib and Julia and her reading of the latest in suffrage news and exposure to Anthony's speeches, stiffened Esther's resolve to fight for suffrage whenever and wherever she could.

Esther Morris sat for a portrait in an outfit embellished with lace and fancy buttons. *(Wyoming State Archives)*

CHAPTER SEVEN

"LAND OF UNBELIEVABLE HORIZONS"

THE CIVIL WAR CHANGED the United States, and people struggled to adjust in diverse ways. Many fled westward to begin again, taking with them their prejudices along with visible and unseen war wounds. Immigrants arrived from around the world. Many of them looked for a new home or sought adventure and hoped to find riches.

Many Indians resented the invasion and fought to preserve their land and centuries-old way of life. The resulting dilemma was described by Wyoming historian Dr. T.A. Larson, "The first white visitors to Wyoming found roving bands of Indians: Shoshonis in the west, Crows in the north, and Cheyennes and Arapahos in the southeast." He continued, "The Shoshonis and the Crows welcomed the whites and made friends with them, although the Crows continued to steal horses from both red men and white men without discrimination. The Sioux, with occasional help from the Cheyennes and Arapahos, caused endless grief in the period 1853-1877."[1]

Two men helped in the settlement of the area surrounding South Pass City: Eastern Shoshone Chief Washakie and mountain man and guide Jim Bridger. The men were born within a few years of each other at the turn of the nineteenth century, and each played a large part in changes to come. They became fast friends.

Born in Richmond, Virginia, and later living in St. Louis, Jim Bridger headed west around the age of nineteen, working as a trapper for William Ashley.

According to historian Henry Stamm, Bridger and Washakie trapped together for about ten years along the Snake and Green

Rivers. In 1843, Jim Bridger and his partner established Fort Bridger, a crossroads on the Oregon Trail, California Trail, and the Mormon Trail.[2]

As a trapper and guide employed by fur trading companies, Jim Bridger joined in nearly all the annual rendezvous of mountain men between 1826 and 1840, three of which were held near the area that would later become known as South Pass City. In 1850 Bridger married Mary, daughter of Chief Washakie.[3]

"Chief Washakie probably began his long association with whites during his adolescence and grew into adulthood leading a dual role, one with white trappers, and one with Shoshones." Washakie's Shoshone tribe participated in most of the mountain men rendezvous.

Stamm asserts that Chief Washakie knew enough English to communicate, but more importantly, he understood that the westward expansion of the United States was inevitable. A feared warrior in his youth, Washakie developed a pragmatic approach to whites moving west. He became a friend to Brigham Young, leader of the Mormons, who worked to increase settlement around the west. Washakie's desire to keep his land for hunting created his willingness to help establish the Wind River Reservation. He was baptized in the Mormon church in 1880, and in 1883, baptized again into the Episcopal Church by missionary John Roberts.[4]

With the construction of the Transcontinental Railroad, Cheyenne—the future capital of Wyoming—was created and famously identified as a "Hell on Wheels" town. Such towns were not stationary, but moved as the railroad progressed, although many such settlements, like Cheyenne, became permanent after a time. Periodically, according to historian Stephen Ambrose, the caravan that followed the railroad workers would plant itself in a spot for as long as it took to build the track from one town to another, with towns created along the way. Most men who built the railroad were "battle-scarred veterans of the Civil War. The vicissitudes they suffered while building the railroad were nothing new to most of

Jim Bridger and Chief Washakie both frequented the South Pass area and were longtime friends. *(Wyoming State Archives)*

them. The big tent of the 'Hell on Wheels' town gave them a place to blow off steam after a long hard day's work. The tent moved as the end of track moved. It could be taken down and set up again in a day. Depending upon the location, the population numbered two thousand or so, and the big tent was a hundred feet long and forty wide. There was a long bar, gambling tables, and the band played, day and night. Fair women in light and airy garments mingled with the throng."[5]

In the spring of 1868 a man traveling to the gold country saw the new town of Cheyenne about the same time as Archie and John Morris, as they went on their way to South Pass City. James Chisholm was a Scotsman who immigrated to the United States during the Civil War. He was on assignment for the *Chicago Tribune*. He penned a letter on March 27, 1868, which years later appeared in a history of South Pass, describing his impressions about Cheyenne to family members back home. He wrote, "Scarcely eight-months-old, it is already a compact, well-built city full of good hotels, spacious stores stocked with wares of every kind. It is full to the brim, all day alive with the murmur of trade and traffic and all night still more alive with murmurs of a less attractive kind." His bleak conclusion was, "The black sheep outnumber the white. There is no such thing as friendship, no hospitality. Tis all a rough battle for gain."

An article by Chisholm, printed in the *Tribune*, spoke of the "floating population, mixed, consisting of miners, mule drivers, bull whackers, gamblers and a sprinkling of eastern men on their way to the mines. The former class are a rough, noisy set, who can throw themselves outside of more whiskey than you can imagine."[6]

Newspapers appeared in every new town along the railroad. Nathan Baker published the first issue of the *Cheyenne Leader* in 1867.

One of the most unusual newspapers of the territory, the *Frontier Index*, was a traveling press that followed the railroad and printed the news from Hell on Wheels towns. When the railroad crews moved their camp, the printing press moved, too. The masthead of the *Frontier Index* read, "The Motto of This Column: Only WHITE MEN to be Naturalized in the United States. The RACES and SEXES in their respective spheres as GOD ALMIGHTY created them. We oppose the privilege of voting being extended to Negros, Indians, and Chinese."[7]

Arriving in South Pass City in May 1868, Archie and John, as well as hundreds of other miners, did not find gold as readily or easily as they had been led to believe. Historian Mike Massie explains, "Despite their disappointment, they [Archie and John] eventually purchased mining and business property, including the Mountain Jack, Grand Turk, Golden State, and Nellie Morgan lodes, hoping to make a profit through mining and speculation."[8]

In the town under construction Archie found work. He and his stepfather settled in and made friends such as Richard and Janet Sherlock, who had come to South Pass City from Salt Lake City. Janet was a Scottish immigrant. Archie and John saw a good deal of the Sherlocks. In an interview with Grace Hebard in 1920, Janet

Janet Sherlock Smith was an early resident of South Pass City where she knew the Morris family. *(South Pass City State Historic Site)*

Sherlock Smith said, "Mr. Morris and Mr. Slack lived in South Pass before Mrs. Morris came."[9]

The building of the Transcontinental Railroad increased the interest and the need for Wyoming to separate from Dakota and create a territory of its own. On July 25, 1868, the new Wyoming Territory was created from parts of Dakota, Idaho, and Utah. South Pass City became the county seat of Carter County which was re-named Sweetwater County in 1869. Since it would be nine-and-a-half months before the new government appointees of Wyoming Territory arrived in Cheyenne, a loose government structure prevailed. Residents were chosen to fill government positions, but, as historian Marion Huseas explained, "county officials continued to play musical chairs with the various government positions."

Huseas recounts the following stories. On December 18, 1868, Archie was appointed constable, and when a man named Barry refused to turn over election returns, Archie went after him and handed the returns over to the court. Barry was fined $12.20. Another time, Archie arrested Sheriff Houghton by order of Judge Kingman. The latter had questioned the sheriff about some cattle that were in controversy. Houghton refused to answer, and Kingman issued a warrant for his arrest. After twenty-four hours, a personal friend of the judge and sheriff persuaded the sheriff to answer questions, and the judge ordered the sheriff released.[10]

Around this time, Archie acquired the nickname "Colonel" because of his service in the Union Army. The nickname stayed with him throughout his life.[11]

While in South Pass City, Archie matured and hit his stride. He joined in local affairs finding many ways to care for himself and John, whose drinking was increasing. Archie became the authorized agent for the J.W. Anthony Lumber Company. This was a brilliant move on his part because of all the building projects occurring in the town. He provided lumber for cabins and businesses under construction. His business sense was demonstrated because he learned to file liens against properties for unpaid bills.[12]

Winters at the elevation of about eight thousand feet were long and often brutal. Many miners fled the area during the winter of 1868–1869 and headed to new mines in Cottonwood, Utah, and other places. In the spring of 1869, South Pass City was rejuvenated with miners returning, and building resumed.[13]

After spending the winter in South Pass City and watching the spring resurgence, Archie and John concluded the town might make something of itself. Now that the railroad was complete to Green River and a stagecoach made daily commutes from near there to South Pass City, they sent for Esther and Ed to join them with plans for Robert to follow from Michigan in a few months. By the time Esther and Edward arrived, the Transcontinental Railroad was complete. The golden spike had been placed at Promontory Summit in Utah on May 10, 1869. When she arrived in South Pass City a few days later, Esther's dream of having her family together again was about to come true.

Part Two

"THE HIGHER PLAIN
OF HUMAN RIGHTS"

Esther and Ed took the train from Omaha, Nebraska, to near Green River, Wyoming. Then they took a stage to South Pass City. This photograph shows Green River in 1868. *(Wyoming State Archives)*

CHAPTER EIGHT

"Pleased With This Country"

F OR ESTHER AND ED, the two-thousand-mile journey from New York to South Pass City probably felt arduous as well as exciting. At Omaha, Nebraska, they boarded the Union Pacific Railroad to a small stop called Bryan, about fifteen miles west of Green River, Wyoming.

Alex Benham's Sweetwater Stage Company ran a four-horse Concord coach daily between Bryan and South Pass City, a trip of one hundred miles. The trip took about fifteen hours on a good day. The ticket cost $20. Historian Todd Guenther points out, "in May 1869, the stagecoach likely would have been delayed, perhaps bogging down in mud. May around South Pass City is late winter, not spring."[1]

The stagecoach ride was undoubtedly thrilling for seventeen-year-old Ed. After a couple of hours sitting on a hard board bench while the coach bounced over rugged terrain, even Esther, who loved new experiences, probably would not have enjoyed herself. When the stage finally rounded the hill and headed down into the large ravine where South Pass City was located, the weary travelers saw the rugged mining town which was to be their home. The stagecoach stopped in front of the hotel on South Pass Avenue.

All around the travelers, dogs, and horses wandered freely. Horse-drawn wagons delivered goods and picked up shipments. Guenther describes the scene, "Every day people gathered around to witness the stagecoach as it thundered into town. This was their contact with the states. The stagecoach brought people, packages, newspapers, and letters filled with news and gossip. The streets were awash with mud. Manure and garbage contributed to the awful smell in the air. The very nature of the mining town made it a temporary place. People had no better solution to handle garbage than to dump it outside."[2]

Some residents undoubtedly watched in surprise as Esther stepped down out of the coach to the muddy road. Few women came to the mining town, and Esther, at fifty-six, was older than most. Almost six feet tall, she surely appeared imposing, self-assured, and dignified.

⸺•⸺

Coincidentally, some of the men appointed by President Ulysses Grant to create and run the government of Wyoming Territory arrived in Cheyenne within days of Esther. Territorial Governor John A. Campbell of Ohio, Territorial Secretary Edward M. Lee of Connecticut, and Chief Justice John H. Howe of Illinois arrived on May, 7, 1869. Justice John Kingman of New Hampshire arrived on June 11. Other appointees were Associate Justice W. T. Jones of Indiana and Church Howe of Massachusetts who was named United States marshal.[3]

Wyoming Territory had been created July 25, 1868. After President Ulysses S. Grant's inauguration almost a year later, on March 4, 1869, he made the territorial government appointments.

Governor John Allen Campbell, born in Salem, Ohio, had served in the Civil War on the staff of Major General John M. Schofield, a friend of Grant's. During the war, Campbell was promoted from lieutenant to brevet brigadier general.

Connecticut-born Territorial Secretary Edward Merwin Lee had moved to Michigan and enlisted in 1861 in the Fifth Michigan Calvary. He served with George Armstrong Custer, fought at Gettysburg, and was breveted a brigadier general for gallantry. He spent a year in Libby Prison at Richmond, Virginia. Military historian John Robertson explained more about his background, stating, "Lee had practiced law and had been in the Connecticut Legislature in 1866-1867. He had lectured throughout the east in the postwar period." Both Campbell, thirty-three, and Lee, thirty-one, were bachelors when they arrived in Wyoming.[4]

Justice John Kingman, shown in about 1864, was one of Esther's most vocal supporters. *(Courtesy David M. Morin)*

Each one of these well-educated, influential men from the East would touch Esther's life. Justice John Kingman befriended Esther and became her most vocal supporter. Kingman had suffered the death of a daughter during the war and lost his wife in 1866. He, like Esther, came to Wyoming Territory to build a new life for himself and his remaining children.

Soon after the arrival of the territorial leaders, various city and county governments were organized. In May, Governor Campbell named Cheyenne the temporary capital of the territory and home of the First Judicial District Court. In June, the second court was created in Laramie, and the third was established in South Pass City. Esther's son Archie Slack was appointed clerk of the Third Judicial District Court.[5]

The Morris cabin has been reconstructed at the South Pass City State Historic Site. *(Author's Collection, 1994)*

Upon arriving in South Pass City, Esther's family moved into a 24' x 26' log cabin that Archie had purchased on Lot 38 near the town's eastern edge. Willow Creek flowed along the southern boundary of their lot, and the Carissa Mine sat on the northern rim above their home. Willow trees lined the creek, and aspens grew on the hills.[6]

Like most mining towns, South Pass City had been built quickly without much planning and with little consideration of durability. Abandoned mines were filled with garbage and covered with dirt. Many cabins, like the one Archie purchased for the family, had been built by speculators. The cabins, most of them built of logs set on the ground with no foundations, did not last. As time passed, the cabins melted like butter into the ground.[7]

Frankie's husband, Damon Stewart, had loaned Esther the money to get from New York to South Pass City. Esther wanted to write to Damon, but as usual, her poor penmanship and grammar

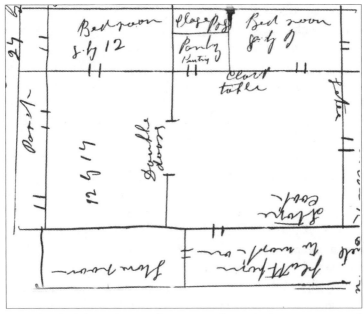

Esther sketched their cabin in a letter to Frankie. It had a main room and a cooking room with bedrooms on the side *(Wyoming State Archives)*

made her uncomfortable writing what she considered important letters. She asked Ed to write the letter for her, and she dictated: "I was very sorry I could not send the money from Peru for the bill of goods purchased of you, but Mr. Stenfield disappointed me." Then Esther shared the clever negotiation tactics she'd used with her former landlord, "When I told him [Stenfield] Edward and me would be compelled to stay with him until we got money to go, he took enough money out of his business for us to go to South Pass." Esther continued, "My only regret when I think of you and Frankie is that you are not at liberty to come to South Pass to live. I know Frankie would enjoy our clear dry atmosphere while you would re- alize your ideal of a shanty amongst 300 or 400, which I counted yesterday while standing on a rocky high eminence overlooking the town. As for the gold, one might as well question there being lumber in Michigan as gold in Wyoming. It may be possible, it may be in- fatuation, but I am more than pleased with this country."[8]

In June, Esther received a letter from Frankie's sister Libbie, who lived in San Francisco with their mother, Eliza Jane. Twenty-six-year-old Libbie, still hurting from her father's callousness, contemplated her first trip to Flint, Michigan, to see her father, E.H., since 1857. At that time, E.H. had instructed Eliza Jane to take Libbie because she was troublesome. Sisters Frankie and Libbie planned to see each other, in Michigan, for the first time in twelve years. Libbie asked to stop over with Aunt Esther in South Pass City on the way.

Esther's reply demonstrated her ability to come directly to the point. On June 22, 1869, she wrote, "My Dear Niece, I am just in receipt of your letter. I just arrived too busy to write and know but little of the country, but thus far am pleased with what I do know."

She gave her niece straightforward advice. "Now to the main subject about your going East. I am decided that you should visit Frankie and your father. Should you go on an Emigrant Train [providing rough one-way travel for incoming emigrants], which is not necessary, I said to your father that he should send you money to come with, if he never gives you another dollar. I have re-read the great portion of your letters that you have written over a year. I see you are both prejudiced and spirited. The first will not make you wise nor the latter make you happy and neither is worth securing."

She continued, "You speak of going there as a gratification. I can only say should you go there, make yourself useful and agreeable, both, and they will be more than gratified. It is my opinion that all will be thankful. Should you wish to return after a pleasant visit, you will find me ready for a visit. But should you go there bitter and angry, you will meet with those that can handle such weapons as well as yourself; for when McQuigg meets McQuigg there comes the fight which you must have learned without another encounter."

She further explained, "Thus far the Halls [referring to Libbie and Frankie's mother] and the Formans [E.H.'s second wife Libbie] have not conquered, for your father is as sharp as ever. Perhaps I have cut the clothesline in what I have written. If so, consider this the end of it. I would like to hear from your mother but would much rather see her."

And she declined to accept Libbie's visit, in part because of the lack of available space, writing, "I shall not expect you here on your way East as we have hardly room for ourselves and I know Mr. Stewart [Frankie's husband, Damon] has prepared a place for you. I was in hopes you would have been there before Robert left. Should Archibald go East as he intends to do in the fall, I hope he finds you a pleasant and agreeable girl instead of a sharp cross old maid. I shall be pleased to have you return with him. From your Aunt Morris."[9]

Esther later explained more in a letter to Frankie, writing, "She spoke about stopping on the way to see me. I wouldn't want that." Esther spoke of the financial reality in South Pass City, saying, "It would cost her at least forty dollars back and forth to the railroad and had she got here with scarcely a place to lie down, no place to live clean, short of money and costing ten dollars a day for poor living, and only grub at that. I told her that you had every accommodation."

Esther followed with the advice, "If she made herself agreeable she would have a pleasant visit. I did say that Betty Forman [Libbie Forman McQuigg, stepmother of Libbie and Frankie] had the same man for a husband that your mother had, and you had the same father and our family do not grow amiable as they grew old. If Archie would go east this fall and she had not become a cross old-maid, he would like her to come here with him. I will send you a diagram of my cabin and you will see that I have a place for you."[10]

Robert finally joined the family in South Pass City in July. As Esther told Frankie, he became very ill. "He was not well, complained of being sleepy, short of breath with no strength until he came down with the Typhoid Fever. It ran fourteen days, and he was in a critical condition but came out all right with only a fifty-dollar doctor bill. . . .The doctor says this climate brings out whatever is in the system and all diseases are acute."

She continued, "Robert has fleshed up and getting fat and has been employed by Archie as Deputy. They are both very busy. If Mrs. Odele and Perrmon are still in Flint tell them to come out

Robert included this sketch of their South Pass City neighborhood in a letter to Frankie. It says "log houses with dirt roofs." *(Wyoming State Archives)*

next summer and bring their blankets and take a cabin and see the rocks that God made mountains of."[11]

When Robert recovered, Archie put his brother's education and superior penmanship skills to work. He hired Robert to clerk for him at the district court. Esther's insistence that Robert master the written word had proven worthwhile. He had further enhanced his value as a deputy clerk by following Libbie Browne's advice to learn shorthand.[12]

Aside from his responsibilities at the court, Archie was still working as the agent for J.W. Anthony's Lumber Company and complemented his position by acquiring a sawmill located about four miles from the family cabin. Ed worked as a bookkeeper there for Archie.

Esther's ability to contribute to the family income was limited. The rough mining town was no place for a millinery business. She probably made some money sewing and mending. The family held interests in several small gold mines, but none were producing. It appeared John had no consistent work and as his drinking increased, his attitude deteriorated.

In November Robert wrote as part of a description of South Pass City, "Twenty-five feet is all the law allows one man to preempt [in South Pass City streets]. The houses are most all built of hewed logs and about the same plan, square with four rooms, two bedrooms, front room, and kitchen."

He also sent Frankie a drawing to illustrate his words, explaining, "The following is a sketch of our neighborhood. We live about the same distance from our stores as your father does in Flint. We find it very convenient as the office is in town and the lumber yard is at the house."[13]

This 1869 Cheyenne street scene shows the Rollins House, a "Bazaar of Fashion," a jewelry manufacturer, a merchant-tailor shop, and the Herman & Rothchild store selling staples and drygoods. (*Wyoming State Archives*)

CHAPTER NINE

"LIKE ALL THE LIBERAL PAPERS"

SEPTEMBER 2, 1869, was the day set to elect the delegates to the first Wyoming Territorial Legislature. A contentious newspaper announcement in the *Sweetwater Mines* newspaper the year before, on May 30, 1868, demonstrated the town's political atmosphere. It read, "A Call!!"

Historian Massie explained the newspaper article, "clearly warned that only those Democrats who 'repudiated the Reconstruction policy of Congress, negro suffrage, and the principles espoused by the radical Republican party. . .' should attend." Justice of the Peace James Stillman was one of the speakers. Attendees supported a resolution that "condemned the 'Radicals' in Congress for forcing Black suffrage on the Southern states," Massie stated. "Chairing the meeting was a Southern Democrat from Virginia—William Bright."[1]

In the ensuing year little had changed. As a lifelong "radical Republican" with strong feelings in favor of abolition and woman suffrage, Esther would have been horrified by the tenets of the local Democrats' meeting.

Predictably in the 1869 election trouble erupted at the polls. Massie states, "Drunk and armed with revolvers, several South Pass City residents, gathered near the precinct polls at Noyes Baldwin's store, added further excitement to the election by vowing to prevent the town's Blacks from voting. Expecting trouble, United States Marshal Church Howe traveled to South Pass City and led several Blacks to the polls, where they cast ballots in relative peace."[2]

Not surprisingly—as shown by the 1868 Democrats' meeting—all those elected in September 1869 throughout the territory were conservative Democrats.[3]

A CALL!!

A Grand Democratic Mass Meeting will be holden at South Pass City, on the Thirty-first day of May, 1868, to nominate a Delegate to the National Democratic Convention. All good and true men, who repudiate the Reconstruction policy of Congress, negro suffrage, and the principles espoused by the Radical Republican party, and who are in favor of equal and exact justice to all sections of the Union, are respectfully invited to participate.

J. M. Thurmond,	H. A. Thompson.
W. H. Bright,	C. H. Stuart, M. D.
W. D. Matheny,	P. A. Gallagher,
Jeff. Standifer,	E. D. Hoge,
Jas. W. Stillman,	Jno. M. Neall,
R. Bell, M. D.,	Jas. S. Lowery,
John Temple,	N. Baldwin,
John R. Murphy,	James Smith,
	N. Vice.

The *Sweetwater Mines* newspaper announced a Democatic meeting in contentious language, demonstrating the town's political atmosphere. South Pass City was then a part of Dakota Territory. *(Wyoming State Archives)*

The national uproar over suffrage began in the East and gradually advanced west. *The Revolution* led the way. The *Cheyenne Daily Leader* wrote in October 1868, "There are few of our weekly exchanges that we peruse with more interest than we do *The Revolution. . . . The Revolution* is bound to win."

Women were traveling through the West on speaking engagements. One was a nationally known suffragist, twenty-six-year-old Anna Dickinson. Larson explains, "After reading about her in an Omaha paper, Nathan A. Baker, in his *Cheyenne Leader*, proposed in June, 1869: 'Let's try to get her here.'"

In Cheyenne, on September 24, 1869, Dickinson, introduced by Territorial Secretary Lee, addressed an audience of two hundred fifty. Larson wrote, "The *Leader* reported that when the 'celebrated

William H. Bright and his wife, Julia, were strong supporters of Woman Suffrage. Bright was elected the first president of the Wyoming Territorial Legislative Council. *(Wyoming State Archives)*

lady' stepped out on the train platform for a breath of air, she was 'surrounded by a crowd of staring mortals. She sought refuge in a passenger coach. She was then subjected to an enfilading fire from the eyes of those who succeeded in flattening their noses against the car windows. . . . Anna is good looking.'" In subsequent articles, Larson explained, "the *Leader* called Anna 'the female humbug,' one who lectured for the love of money and notoriety, and 'the pepper' of the woman's rights movement in contrast to 'the vinegar,' Susan B. Anthony."[4]

Mark Twain humorously remarked on her speaking abilities in a letter to San Francisco's *Alta California* newspaper. He wrote, "She did her work well. She made a speech worth listening to. Her sarcasm bites. I do not know but that it is her best card. She will make a right venomous old maid someday, I am afraid."[5]

Wyoming's people, like those in other western territories, longed for statehood. With a population of less than ten thousand in 1869, Wyoming had far to go to meet what was considered the federal requisite of a sixty-thousand resident minimum. Larson wrote, "Ever since the Northwest Ordinance of 1787 had stated that parts of the Northwest Territory might be considered for statehood when a population of sixty thousand had been reached, that number had been regarded by many people as sufficient for statehood."[6]

Many men thought this was a strong impetus for passage of woman suffrage, arguing that giving women the vote would encourage more women to move west. The theory was that with more women, more men would follow, therefore expanding population numbers.

The suffrage discussion, along with Esther's unbending views on women's rights, led her new friend Janet Sherlock to describe her years later in an interview with historian Grace Raymond Hebard as "a strong-minded woman, but not as mannish as she looked. Mr. Morris, her husband, was a Jew and a Democrat, although she was a radical Republican." Sherlock went on, "Public women and politics were always in her mind. She talked about Susan B. Anthony and spoke of her often, quoted her and she seemed to have gotten her inspiration from Miss Anthony." Sherlock was not as complimentary about John, saying, "Morris, her husband, drank and played cards, [later] kept a saloon, played auction pitch, a game for drinks which kept him tanked up all the time with the other old toppers."[7]

Esther brought Frankie up-to-date on her current view of the issue in an October letter. She wrote, "We got a copy of the Citizen. Accept my thanks. I shall keep the family well posted on the woman's question. But I have all their rights here and a dozen or two more I might have if they were here. We have ten young lawyers and doctors who keep track. Damon would like it here first rate."

She continued with more mundane matters. "Archie put up the tenements, but Mr. Morris did not like either of them well enough to finish off to live in, so he put up another expecting the money from Peru." However, she went on, explaining why money would not be arriving from Peru. Archie and Robert only earned money when court was in session. She wrote, "There have been three or four criminal cases, so there is an extra session called and Archie and Robert say in two weeks or sooner I shall have the money to pay Mr. Stewart."

Although the family was "busy as bees" preparing for winter, she reported splendid weather and how the extra court sessions would help family finances. "Edward is keeping books for the sawmill about four miles from here. He had Archie's pony to ride out on, but one morning he got up and the pony was not to be found. There has been a party of Indians in the neighborhood and the box that Robert shipped from Peru with about one hundred dollars-worth has not reached us yet.

"My health was never better. I do all my work. I have a good washing machine the boys bought me and when I get the money I will get me a sewing machine. We're all wearing out our old clothes, yet I feel very contented here."[8]

She also reported that rather than work at mining that summer, they found paying jobs, but she spoke of their mines, writing, "We have an interest in nine ledges with one between thirty and fifty feet deep and shall go deeper as we can spare time and money to do so. We have scarce rain here, so the men can work in the mines all winter."

Esther also mentioned her old friend from Peru, Seth Paine, stating, "He is the founder of the working women's home in Chicago and the correspondent of the Tribune in Chicago. He is stopping with us for the present. I like all the liberal papers that are sent to him."

She continued, "We are happier than we have ever been before together. I have only one thing that really troubles me and that was to pay Damon."[9]

Esther wrote of the extra session of court without elaboration, obviously keeping the disreputable side of their mining town from her niece. The truth, as told by C.G. Coutant in his *History of Wyoming*, was that, "Drinking, gambling, and excitement growing out of business relations resulted in a number of deaths." Five murders were documented in South Pass City in 1869.[10]

Although one might be tempted to think that Esther's family, tucked away in South Pass City so far from the more civilized

In 1869, E.A. "Archie" Slack was a young man on his way up in South Pass City. *(Wyoming State Archives)*

regions of the country, was isolated, they were not. With such a large extended family and their old friends and acquaintances coming and going, the family members—who also made new friends—were by no means lonely during that summer and fall of 1869.

However, women accounted for only twenty-four percent of the population in South Pass City. Esther kept busy caring for her home, for her men, and for her house guests. She visited new friends in town and took long walks. In the evenings, she wrote letters and played cards with family and spent hours reading.[11]

The fresh mountain air of South Pass City exhilarated Esther, and so especially did the freedom from societal restriction she found there. Her independent nature was reflected in her choice of liberal friends like John Kingman and Seth Paine. Lib and Julia Browne, the nieces Esther and the twins stayed with while in New York City, kept her informed regarding current national suffrage events. Both young nieces still worked at *The Revolution* with Susan B. Anthony in New York City. Thanks to Frankie's mother Eliza Jane, Esther received a steady flow of suffrage flyers from San Francisco. She shared this information with whomever would listen. Many men in South Pass City, including Esther's friend, District Court Judge John Kingman, also supported woman suffrage. Her husband John, though, was not one of them.

Archie succeeded in South Pass City. He was well-educated. His strong character and exuberant personality attracted opportunity. His drive and enviable work ethic helped make his efforts lucrative. J.W. Anthony's lumber yard was the only one of any size in the area, and Archie did well as the authorized agent. Historian Huseas reported, "Slack sold window sashes, doors, joists, and boards of various sizes, including extra-width for wagon boxes and door panels. He also kept 100,000 shingles in stock at all times."[12]

Nathan Baker's *South Pass News* carried front-page advertisements of hotels and restaurants on South Pass Avenue that showed South Pass City thriving at the time. The City Hotel, run by Mrs. C.D. Chapin, advertised "the best and choicest eatables the market affords." The Eclipse Hotel, run by S.W. Shulock, advertised "meals at all hours" with a single meal costing seventy-five cents. Shulock charged $12 per week for boarders. The California Restaurant on Price Street offered board at $6 per week and fifteen meal tickets for $10. The Empire Hotel and Restaurant offered "rooms furnished with imported spring cots." Board there was $2 per day or $13 per week. Single meals cost seventy-five cents.[13]

Archie's younger brother Robert Morris spent the months from November 1868 until July 1869 in Flint, Michigan, working in Damon's store and living with the Stewart family. Robert turned seventeen in Flint on November 8. He had become accustomed to having things his own way at home, but when he arrived at the Stewart home, Frankie was eight months pregnant. Frankie's and Damon's first child, Hobart, was born on December 6, 1868. Damon's mother also lived in their home. Suddenly, Robert became just one of many busy household members. These changes undoubtedly proved challenging for him.

Robert Morris always maintained a close relationship with his mother, Esther. *(Wyoming State Archives)*

After arriving back in South Pass City and allowing time to pass for reflection about his experiences with the Stewarts, he wrote to Frankie. On November 17, 1869, he explained, "When I left you last July I felt I was relinquishing a certain good for an uncertain hope and when I think how pleasant and comfortable you made me, I feel guilty I did not show myself more grateful for your kindness. It is said, 'we are never satisfied' which I have often thought, but it is a wrong way of viewing things when we have so much around us to enjoy if we would only think so. I look back over my eight months' residence in Flint with so much to improve myself and enjoy and feel ashamed that I was not more satisfied and contented and allowed some little thing to make me feel miserable."

Robert also referred to Frankie's husband, writing, "Mr. Stewart has often thought how foolish I acted, and I think so myself, but hope I may never do so again with a good and kind employer. Frankie, you may not understand why I write this. It is because I am grateful to you and Damon and do not want you to think different."

In addition to his contrite words, Robert added family news, "Archie left us Wednesday November 10th for the East. He will go to Chicago, St. Louis, Carlinville, and Springfield." Robert wrote of Archie's plan to visit Sarah Neeley while in Springfield. But he said, "I am sorry Archie will not be able to make you a visit, his time is limited as Court commences in about a month and he will have to be here."

He continued, writing, "I wish you could come to these mountain tops for a season. I know it would do you so much good as there is such a buoyancy of feeling in this dry invigorating atmosphere. Everyone says they feel better here than in the states. Most all have the mountain fever or a touch of it before they become acclimated."

Although he recently had suffered from typhoid, Robert apparently made a quick and full recovery. He explained, "I have never enjoyed such good health in my life or knew how to appreciate a genuine good appetite. One of the first changes newcomers remark is they never were so hungry in their lives and that seems a general complaint of all who live here."

He gave a lengthy description of his thoughts about the mountains, expounding, "I was not as greatly impressed by the Rocky Mountains as I anticipated. What they call the range of mountains a few miles north of us are not much higher than the mountains along the Hudson River, but they give their elevation at eight, nine, ten, and twelve thousand feet. Their elevation is given from sea level and we are eight thousand feet high before we see their base."

And Robert gave Frankie an optimistic and detailed description of the town and area, explaining, "South Pass has grown very much since I have been here and the Sweetwater Mines including three towns four miles apart, [South Pass City, Atlantic City, and Miner's Delight] has doubled its population this summer and there seems no longer a doubt of this being a rich gold country. Capital is now largely invested, and many new companies are now being organized in the east. Everyone is sanguine as to next season and large stocks of goods are coming in and stored away for next spring trade. There are 12 groceries here and all other business is largely represented."

Robert's continued, "I think it would be hard to form any idea of the appearance of this place, it is so different from a town in the states. Imagine a gulch or ravine four or five hundred feet wide with steep rocky hills three, four and five hundred feet high on all sides and you have the location of South Pass City in the center of the gulch."

He included some details about crimes as well, writing, "Gamblers and roddies [sic] saloons are very plenty here, and exciting dog fights a common Sunday amusement. Last court there were sixteen criminal cases tried which shows the state of society. Last night a man was shot and not expected to live, that's nothing as such things are very common."[14]

Local violence seemed almost routine. A population of seventy-six percent male, many of whom had been through a brutal war, probably contributed to this. Although other factors such as isolation and the abundance of risk-takers in a gold mining community likely played a part.

Despite living in a town with rampant disorder, residents were unwilling to provide money for a jail. Huseas reported that following arrest, prisoners were housed in the back room of the Houghton and Cotter Store. Bars on the windows and a strong front door, along with a jailer, kept prisoners contained.[15]

Both Esther's and Robert's letters mention Indians, but neither of them elaborated. Coutant's writings show there was a bloody response from the Indians on the invasion of their part of the world. Coutant wrote, "On August 20, William Skinner and George Colt were killed on the north bank of the Big Popo Agie. Mr. Camp was killed on that day near Hot Springs. On August 21, the Jeff Standifer party of seven men were attacked on Big Wind River where Lehman and two others were killed. On September 20, John G. Anderson was killed near Miners' Delight and his three yokes of cattle taken. A man by the name of Latham, while chopping wood on Atlantic Gulch, was killed. Henry Lusk was wounded, and his band of horses taken."[16]

This photograph, taken near South Pass City in 1870, shows Chief Washakie's encampment of Eastern Shoshone Indians. *(Wyoming State Archives)*

In 1869, whole town was on alert for Indians. Guenther explained in an interview, "When miners went out to dig for gold they went in threes. One to dig and two to stand guard."[17]

In Robert's November letter, he spoke about possible additional businesses, writing, "I was glad to have you recommend the agency of sewing machine for it has put me on the lookout for agencies. Archie will get me the agency of building paper and I think it will be just the thing to sell in this country. Next spring, I will see about sewing machines. I would this fall, but do not think I could do much this winter." He wrote about his work and expressed his joy at the receipt of the law books he and Archie had ordered, stating,

"I am attending Archie's business, lumber agent and district clerk and have all I can do. The United States Records 45 books arrived three days since. They cost one hundred and fifty dollars and their monster size and elegant binding make my office look very dignified, especially the desk."[18]

CHAPTER TEN

"Suffrage Is No Child's Play"

The first Wyoming Territorial Legislative Assembly met in the capital, Cheyenne, from October 12 through December 10, 1869.

The Assembly consisted of a Council—now known as the Senate—with nine members and the House of Representatives with thirteen members. Historian Larson explains, "Unhappy with their pay of only four dollars per day, the legislators appropriated an additional six dollars per day for each member and twelve dollars for the presiding officers."

During the first meeting on October 12, South Pass City miner and saloon keeper William H. Bright was unanimously elected president of the Council.[1]

Bright was not a political novice; he had learned how things were accomplished from living and working in Washington, D.C. He was born in Virginia in January 1827. Following his father's death, his mother Betsey [Elizabeth] married George Minott Kendall on September 3, 1853, in Washington, D.C. Kendall worked as a clerk in the post office, and his brother, Amos Kendall, a member of Andrew Jackson's Kitchen Cabinet, was a founder of Gallaudet University and also served as Postmaster General. William H. Bright worked as a policeman and bricklayer. He lived with his mother, stepfather, and brother in Washington until he married Julia A. Stewart on September 22, 1862, in the District of Columbia.[2]

Huseas writes, "Julia was an attractive, intelligent woman. She had a large collection of books which she loaned out freely. Mrs. Bright had the reputation of being a woman of literary taste and attainments."[3]

Bright's 1863 enlistment papers in the Union Army stated "William H. Bright, 36, bricklayer." Bright worked in the office of the Chief Quartermaster in Washington, D.C. in 1864, an experience which likely honed his future political savoir faire. After the war, William and Julia moved west. Their son, William Jr., was born in 1868 in Salt Lake City, Utah Territory. While in Salt Lake City, Bright served as a special agent in the Salt Lake Post Office Department. Following the birth of their son, William and Julia moved to South Pass City. William owned a share in the Cariso Mine.[4]

Historian Tom Rea explains that during this initial 1869 session of the Wyoming Territory Legislature, the lawmakers "passed a law guaranteeing that teachers—most of whom were women—would be paid the same whether they were men or women. And they passed a bill guaranteeing married women property rights separate from their husbands."[5]

Larson describes the process: On Friday, November 12, the woman suffrage bill was brought forward. William Bright temporarily stepped aside as president, announcing "he would introduce a bill for woman's rights," and he did, on November 27.

As introduced, the bill would have given women the right to vote at the age of eighteen. On November 30 the bill was passed in the Council, without change by a vote of 6-2, with one member absent.

Ben Sheeks, the young lawyer from South Pass City, argued against the original bill in the House of Representatives. He offered two amendments: one giving 'all colored women and squaws' the right to vote and the second lowering the voting age from twenty-one to eighteen. His second amendment was adopted, and the bill passed with a vote of 7-4. After the Council had accepted the amendment the bill was transmitted to Governor Campbell on December 6, 1869.[6]

The final bill, approved on December 10, 1869, read:

> Be it enacted by the Council and House of Representatives of the Territory of Wyoming:
>
> Sec. 1. That every woman of the age of twenty-one years, residing in this territory, may at every election to be holden under the laws thereof, cast her vote. And her rights to the elective franchise and to hold office shall be the same under the election laws of the

territory, as those of electors. Sec. 2 This act shall take effect and
be in force from and after its passage.

Most of the lawmakers thought Campbell would veto the bill.
Massie writes, "The lobbying efforts of Secretary Lee, Chief Justice
Howe, Mrs. Amalia Post, Mrs. M. B. Arnold, and Judge Kingman
who presided over the third judicial district and lived in South Pass
City, convinced the chief executive to sign the legislation. Besides
citing the country's tradition of fairness and equality, Campbell
later noted that women were as capable as men in exercising the
good judgment required to vote. He also commented that women
who own property must be taxed, making woman suffrage necessary
to ensure fair representation in the creation of tax laws."[7]

The December 10, 1869, entry in Campbell's diary states:
"Signed large number of bills. . . . Was in Secretary's office signing
bills until 12 p.m. when I went to ball given to me and Legislature.
Wrote to Secy. of State—Signed Woman Suffrage Bill."[8]

Several reasons are put forth for the passage of the ground-
breaking suffrage bill in Wyoming Territory. Among them are the
need for increased population to qualify for statehood and the
subject of race in the West. The U.S. Congress had passed the Fifteenth Amendment to the Constitution in February 1869, and it
was on its way to ratification by the states. Black men would soon
be enfranchised.[9]

Guenther clarified, "The order of acceptance in the West was
white males, white females, Hispanics, Indians, Blacks, Chinese."
Larson provided insight about William Bright's thoughts on the
matter, writing, "The reasons given on various occasions by Colonel
Bright, who introduced the bill, was that he thought it right and
just and that if Negroes had the vote, as they did, women like his
[Bright's] wife and mother should also have the right."[10]

The *Cheyenne Daily Leader* carried a gaudy snippet on its front
page on April 28, 1870. "Women who want to vote will be interested
to know that the following speech, delivered in the Wyoming legislature, was the clincher that caused the passage of the Act which accorded them the right to vote. A member arose and said: 'Damn it,

if you are going to let the niggers and pigtails vote, we will ring in the women too.' And they were immediately 'rung in.' – Ed."

Massie wrote, "Attempts to pass woman suffrage legislation in a few states and in Congress failed, leading many advocates to believe the first woman suffrage bill would probably be adopted in a territory, where a majority vote of the legislature and the governor's signature were the only requirements for passage."[11]

Larson observed, "No other Wyoming law has received so much favorable attention down through the years. Susan B. Anthony, great national suffrage leader, said at Laramie in 1871, 'Wyoming is the first place on God's green earth which could consistently claim to be the land of the Free!'"[12]

Soon after Wyoming Territory passed the suffrage bill, Robert Morris wrote to his cousin Lib Browne. His letter of December 27, 1869, caught the attention of Susan B. Anthony and Elizabeth Cady Stanton, who published it on January 13, 1870, in *The Revolution*. Robert's letter demonstrates the importance of *The Revolution* and the suffrage vote to the Morris family, as well as the high regard in which they held William Bright:

> Dear Revolution, There have been many representatives of Woman's Suffrage in the legislatures throughout the United States, but the first successful legislator of the cause is William H. Bright of Wyoming Territory, and a brief sketch of him may interest your readers.
>
> Mr. Bright returned to his home in this place a few days ago, and Mrs. M. and myself, as the only open advocates here of Women's Suffrage, resolved ourselves into a committee and called on him to tender our congratulations and thanks for his services in our behalf as well as for all true lovers of equal rights.
>
> We found Mr. Bright in a comfortable log cabin with his good wife and little son. We met with a cordial reception, and he expressed himself pleased that there were some persons here who endorsed his views on Woman Suffrage. Mr. Bright is about thirty-five years of age, [his actual age was forty-three] is a strong man, rather tall, with a frank, open countenance, which his name describes most truly. He is truly an original man, was born in Virginia, where in his early life he had not the benefits of a free school, and his parents were not in a condition to give him an education, and although he writes

This photograph identified as being taken in 1870 at South Pass City is the only dated photograph of Esther at the Wyoming State Archives. Ever the milliner, Esther seldom had a photograph taken without a hat. *(Wyoming State Archives)*

and is well-informed he says, "I have never been to school a day in my life, and where I learned to read and write I do not know."

In regard to Woman's Suffrage, Mr. Bright says, "I have never thought much about it, nor have I been converted by a woman's lecture or newspaper, for I never heard a woman speak from the rostrum and never read The Revolution. I knew it was a new issue and a live one, and with a strong feeling that it was just, I determined to use all influence in my power to have the bill passed."

The Wyoming legislature have made many laws for our territory, but Woman's Suffrage is looked upon as the most liberal, and therefore, the most appreciated. It is a fact that all great reforms take place not where they are most needed, but in places where opposition is weakest; and then they spread until they take up all in one great principle of right and become universal; just so, it will be with Woman Suffrage.

Wyoming has been the first to lead the way and there is probably no state in the Union where women have more freedom and are less deprived of their rights, and certainly there is no territory where there are as few; and I join Horace Greeley in urging the girls to come to this higher plain of Human Rights, as well as to have a home in our high, clear, mountain atmosphere. [The letter was signed] R. C. M.[13]

About that same time, Esther wrote to Frankie, but only a fragment of her letter survives. She stated, "Robert wrote an article in The Revolution. Suffrage is no child's play and not likely it passes in Colorado."

Esther also added a little colorful information about South Pass City, explaining, "I have been to nice size balls and we have a place where we dance every week and girls are so scarce, I am obliged to dance with half a dozen men. It is first come, first serve."[14]

CHAPTER ELEVEN

"I Feel I Am A Citizen"

SILENCE ANNOUNCED the coming of winter in South Pass City. Through the summer, sounds of miners and machinery, men at work, the pounding of horses' hooves as the animals pulled wagons, and the daily rumble of the stagecoach filled the atmosphere. And then, suddenly activity stopped when many miners departed for mines in milder climates like Cottonwood in Utah Territory. Many South Pass City stores and a few saloons closed. The town went into its quiet time.[1]

Many people left, but the Morris family spent the long, cold winter of 1869-1870 in South Pass City. The constant wind, which blew some warmth through the small valley in spring and summer, drifted snow in winter with no sign of stopping. Even a dusting of snow was snatched up in the howling wind and pushed at night against the east side of the buildings. Two inches of snow might cover the ground in one spot, yet three feet away ten-feet-tall drifts piled up. In South Pass City, locals categorized the seasons into "early winter" which arrives in October and November; "mid-winter," which lasts from December through March; and "late winter" which includes April and May. Spring, summer, and fall all take place in June, July, August, and September. Residents in the mining town then and now must constantly reckon with the force of winter.[2]

During the winter of 1869-1870, Esther was still optimistic about her new life. She wrote an unusually difficult to decipher letter to Frankie in late January 1870. For a woman with five living siblings, she penned a telling comment, "I never expect to see any relatives, except you, Hobart, and Damon. I have a nice little room for you. I wish you were here now. I like our weather, our water, and we get good milk. I think if we can plant vegetables that stand the frost and get growing before the great freezing comes, we can have as good vegetables as grow in Canada or Michigan. I will try and get an early start."

She remarked on Archie's return from Illinois. "Archie came home without a wife. [Now] he and a group of about 30 have gone down into the valley on a buffalo hunt to last three weeks. They will go about one hundred miles."

Showing the family's lifelong interest in books and literature, she added, "Archie brought us many books. Ed takes the 'Star Spangled Banner.' We get the 'Wyoming Tribune' and the 'South Pass paper.' Archie brought in 'Gates Ajar,' [Elizabeth Stuart Phelps, later Ward, 1869], Renan's 'Life of Paul,' [Joseph Ernest Renan, 1869], and about a dozen other books. Lib sends us 'The Revolution.' I got two new dresses and Archie brought me material for sewing."

Shifting to a pensive tone she ended. "I am sitting at a window watching the snow melting like spring. While the country looks old as hills, everything we have done is new. In part I feel that I am a citizen and would go back to the best state in the union and not be a crazy girl."[3]

South Pass City Justice of the Peace James Stillman had resigned in December, possibly in protest over actions taken during the legislative session. It fell to the County Commissioners to appoint a replacement. The governor's newly-appointed Sweetwater County Board of Commissioners was composed of Chairman John W. Anthony, Archie's employer; Nathaniel Daniels, a miner and editor of the South Pass News; and John Swingle, the owner of the Miners Exchange Saloon in South Pass City.[4]

The commissioners began a search for Stillman's replacement. This created the opportunity of a lifetime for Esther. When Esther's interest in the opening became apparent, her friend Judge John Kingman supported her bid to become justice of the peace. She gave credit to him later in a letter stating, "It was our district judge,

Hon. John W. Kingman, who proposed my appointment as a justice of the peace and trial of women as jurors."[5]

In February 1870, Esther walked from the Morris cabin through the biting cold air to the Miners Exchange Saloon to fill out her application for Justice of the Peace of Sweetwater County, Wyoming Territory. Historian Guenther shared, "The average height of a Wyoming miner was five and half feet; Esther was nearly six-feet tall and every inch a dynamo. As she strode down the street, miners jumped out of the way. Entering the saloon was a brave act in itself, as in those days cultured women did not go into a saloon, and in more structured cities, would even cross the street rather than pass in front of one. The saloons stank. The men seldom bathed. They did heavy labor, rode, chewed tobacco, drank and threw up right on the floor of the saloon."[6]

The commissioners knew Esther and expected her visit, but when she arrived, her bearing and audacity likely left them momentarily taken aback. Esther must have been filled with purpose and resolve. The chance to apply for a man's position with a man's wages was something twenty-year-old Esther McQuigg in Spencer, New York, could not have imagined. Now, fifty-seven-year-old Esther Morris grasped the opportunity with both hands.

Words from a man who knew her, W. E. Chaplin, paint a picture of Esther. "She looked like a leader. Esther Morris was a large woman, almost six feet tall and one who would attract attention in any company. She had a head and face that indicated strong character, positive will, and dominating spirit. With her boys what she said was law. This fact was noticeable by all who knew them."[7]

The commissioners considered and debated Esther's application. Following their decision, on February 14, 1870, Chairman John Anthony wrote:

> I had the honor to preside at the meeting of the county commissioners of Sweetwater County today when a petition and application were presented by Esther Morris, wife of John Morris, for the office of Justice of the Peace for said county. One of the board, by name of [Nathan] Daniels, voted for it, John Swingle voted

Esther Morris's handwritten Oath of Office was also signed by Archie who was the Clerk of the Eighth District Court. (*Esther Morris Collection, Wyoming State Archives*)

against it, and it was left to me as chairman to decide. It put me to my trumps. The lady is in every way qualified and considering everything, I voted for it and ordered her to file her bonds and be sworn into office, and the clerk, [Esther's son Archie], to telegraph to the world that Wyoming, the youngest and one of the richest territories in the United States, gave equal rights to women in actions as well as words. You can make this public or not, as you feel inclined. I don't think it will hurt us if the world knows.[8]

Commissioner Nathan Daniels wrote to Robert and Edward in 1914 stating: "The commissioners then went to Gilman's Saloon for a drink before dinner: Your father was there and I said, 'John come up and join in a drink with us as we are about to celebrate the election of your wife as justice of the peace. We have given her the appointment and done all we could do. All she will have to do to be J.P. is to qualify and give bonds making her the first woman justice of the peace in the U.S.' Your father said, 'Well as you boys have done my wife and family the honor, I will accept your invitation to drink and then go home and break the good news to Mrs. Morris.' Your mother, I must say was a true woman's rights advocate and come nigh being a duplicate of Miss Susan B. Anthony as any woman I ever knew."[9]

Mike Massie tied the story up, "With her $500 bond in place, secured by Archie and G.W.B. [Alphabet] Dixson, her application was submitted to the new governmental officials in Cheyenne, and Esther's appointment was soon approved."[10]

Esther received from Cheyenne a certificate and a letter dated February 17, 1870, signed by Acting Governor Edward M. Lee:

> To Mrs. Esther Morris, South Pass City, Wyoming.
>
> Madam, I have the honor to transmit herewith your commission as Justice of the Peace for the County of Sweetwater, Wyoming. Should the same accept you will please take and subscribe the oaths endorsed thereon. Also, execute the within Bond and oath and file both papers with the County Clerk of Sweetwater, W.T. I congratulate you on being the first judicial position ever held by a woman. Please notify this office of your acceptance.
>
> > Very respectfully,
> > Your obt. Sev. Edw. M. Lee,
> > Secretary and Acting Governor Wyoming Territory.[11]

She wrote her Oath of Office, in much neater handwriting than many of her letters, and Archie, as the District Court clerk, must have been brimming with pride when he swore in his mother as the first woman in the nation to hold judicial office.

Larson's research revealed: " . . . three women were commissioned justices of the peace [in February 1870]. Only one of them, Mrs. Esther Morris, is definitely known to have served. . . ."[12]

Esther's certificate, dated February 17, 1870, corresponded with another significant date in her life. It was exactly twenty-four years after her marriage to John Morris.

Esther, happy for the additional income for her family, understood the historic nature of her appointment, and felt that the swearing-in, done by her son Archie, made the event especially meaningful.

This certificate appoints Esther Morris as Sweetwater County, Wyoming Territory, justice of the peace. (*Wyoming State Archives*)

Each member of Esther's family most likely saw her appointment in a different light. Archie and Robert continued to be proud and supportive; John was routinely derisive; and Edward, perhaps rather oblivious and wrapped up in his own life, tended to lean toward his father's feelings in all things.

In addition to the honor of holding an office, the very act of voting for the first time possibly outranked all other considerations for Esther. In South Pass City, according to her January letter to Frankie, Esther had learned to think of herself as a "citizen," which to her meant she was viewed as equal to the other citizens, i.e. men. And now, her belief had been reinforced by the resounding February events.

CHAPTER TWELVE

"Let Alone a Justice of the Peace"

THE DOCUMENTS SURROUNDING Esther's appointment and her beginning duties as justice of the peace contain apparent conflicts. Esther's appointment was approved by the commissioners on February 14, 1870. Her certificate and letter from Acting Governor Lee were signed February 17. Her handwritten oath of office was dated February 25.

The confusion arises with the dates entered in the official docket book Esther purchased to record her cases. The first case on page two in new docket is dated as coming before her on February 14, 1870, the day the commissioners approved her appointment. Esther likely heard her first case before she was certified by the state and before she signed her oath of office.

The defendant was her predecessor, James Stillman, who had refused to turn over his own court docket. With most of the town watching, Esther began her duties as justice of the peace.

Esther's first docket entry recorded the arrest of James Stillman for refusing to return his docket to the courts:

> "No. 1: Information subscribed sworn to and filed Feb 14. 1870. Warrant issued and deliv^d to S. Jackson Constable Feb 14. 1870. Def^t appeared upon return of Warrant Feby 15. 1870 and asks for adjournment until next day. Trial resumed Feb 16 1870. Plss asks leave to amend warrant. Not granted. Deft. Moves to dismiss the case in informality of warrant: Motion sustained.
>
> No 2: Information subscribed sworn to filed Feb 14 1870. Warrant issued and delive^d to S. Jackson Constable Feby 14 1870. Def^t appeared upon return of warrant.

> Def[t] moves to dismiss on grounds of insufficiency of war-
> rant. Not sustained. Moves to quosh the proceeding on
> the ground of no jurisdiction and informality of infor-
> mation. Motion sustained.[1]

Using a trial date of February 17, Massie explains; "Upon a motion by Stillman's lawyer, Mrs. Morris agreed to postpone proceedings for the remainder of the day in order to allow the defense attorney enough time to prepare his case. When court was reconvened. . .the defense attorney correctly noted that the warrant for Stillman's arrest was not completed correctly, Morris sustained his motion to dismiss the case, but then immediately issued a new warrant to begin the proceedings again. Finally, the defense attorney claimed that Esther did not have the jurisdiction to try the case because, as Stillman's successor, she had an interest in the docket's return. She agreed and dismissed the case."[2]

The *Wyoming Tribune* of April 26 summarized the events. After stating Acting Governor Lee's appointment of Esther Morris met with general approval, the article continues, "Her first court was numerously attended and the proceedings were characterized by a high degree of judicial decorum and dignity. The case brought up for adjudication was intricate and involved many nice legal points. Sharp legal counsel in either side made all sorts of motions, and indulged in all kinds of argument peculiar to the craft; but when the trial was ended she rendered a decision strictly in accordance with law and equity and which would be sustained by the Supreme Court of the United States if brought before that tribunal."

The article continues with, " To that city [South Pass City] belongs the high honor of holding the first judicial tribunal in history presided over by a woman."[3]

The next entry in Esther's docket shows the second person to come before her as case No. 3 on February 21 and was followed by a case on February 25, the day she swore her oath.

On March 3, Robert wrote to his uncle, E.H. McQuigg and E.H.'s wife Libbie, Frankie's father and stepmother. He explained, "You are informed by the papers, that your sister Esther has been

Esther's docket, written by her clerk and son Archie, shows her first case as being *The Territory of Wyoming vs James W. Stillman*. (*Wyoming State Archives*) appointed Justice of the Peace and I am glad to say Mother is very well pleased with her new position and has the support of our best citizens and Wyoming Press."

He wrote that Esther was being accepted by attorneys and that he would serve as her clerk: "I have just finished reading "Eminent Women of the Age" [James Parton et al, 1868]. And when I think of what the first advocates of Abolition and Woman Rights had to endure of public ridicule and much worse were sometimes rioted, scorned and hissed at, the way of their followers now seems comparatively very smooth.

"Mother has the prospect of considerable business as most all of the legal profession here offered to bring her their cases. I am her clerk and since the appointment have employed all my leisure time in studying the law for forms used in our new business."

Robert's letter moved on to family and social matters: "Archie returned home six weeks ago. He did not bring a wife, but I am quite certain he has one picked out, but you know all such things are secrets.

"I have not told you what pleasant dancing parties we have had all winter every Thursday evening from eight to twelve o'clock. They are delightful affairs and why shouldn't they be with a good hall good floor and four musicians, but I regret to mention the fact there is but one single young lady in town and she has a host of gentlemen admirers."[4]

Esther seemingly took everything in stride. She did not mention her first few cases when she wrote to Frankie on March 7, but instead spoke more about her feelings and South Pass City. She told Frankie, "You say you expect to hear about our suffrage associations. We do not need them out here. A lady saw your mother's name in a Los Angeles paper as president of a suffrage association.

"We had a fine winter here. . . . The business has been brisk all winter. Buildings going up and shafts going down."

Thinking of her journey from New York to Wyoming Territory she reminded Frankie, "I am much happier here than I was last year at this time with the long journey and the uncertainty before me. Now with my family all together and all doing as well as could be expected, while I have done better, for I didn't really expect to be a citizen, let alone a justice of the peace. I received a letter from brother Daniel on the subject."

In addition to earning money at court, Esther continued to earn money from her sewing. "I have a Doty washing machine and expect a Singer sewing machine in about two weeks. One of my neighbors has a fluting machine [a machine that created intricate pleats similar to ruffles in fabric] so you see that I am working."[5]

Newspapers from New York to Hawaii printed an article which also appeared in the *Milwaukee Daily Sentinel* on March 24, 1870, titled, "Justice in Skirts." The report stated, "The following is extracted from a letter to a young lady by her cousin in Wyoming (a lad of fifteen) son of Esther Morris, Esq, one of the newly appointed justices of the peace in that territory. 'You are informed by this time that your Aunt Esther Morris is a justice of the peace, and if not yet one of the 'eminent women of the age,' she is the first woman who has ever exercised the judicial power, at least on the American continent.'"

The article continues with more of the same information as was included in the letter Robert wrote to E.H. He also wrote a near duplicate to his cousin Lib for *The Revolution*. She probably forwarded it to news outlets. The March 24 letter in the article ends with this sentence: "Those who will finish the grand reform of equal rights, will no more realize the hard work, self-denial, and suffering it required, than the polisher who has glazed the statue which has employed so many days' hard work in quarrying and chiseling the rough marble to a beautiful form."[6]

Robert followed this missive a few days later with a letter to his cousin Charlotte Converse, from the Hobart side of the family, who lived on Esther's childhood farm in Spencer, New York. This time, Robert used his company's letterhead.

He copied much of what he had written to his cousin Lib, but added: "If you will take the New York World you probably read the correspondence describing Mother's first court. It was in some respects an untruthful statement, at any rate and as much as the correspondent dared to write. He is a neighbor of ours, but not very friendly for the reason that brother Archie last spring was appointed United States District Clerk and he was one of the applicants for the same appointment."

He continued with an update on family, "Business here is good and improving every day. I am still employed in a dry goods store but will leave the 1ˢᵗ of May to assist Archie. He is in the lumber and powder business, and with his office, has more than he can attend to. Edward is clerk at the sawmill four miles from here and is doing well."[7]

Robert's comment on the newspapers refers to the press coverage that began on April 2, describing Esther's first day on the bench. *Frank Leslie's Illustrated Newspaper* reported, "Mrs. Esther Morris, one of the new justices of the peace in Wyoming, is fifty-seven years old. On the first court day, she wore a calico gown, worsted breakfast-shawl, green ribbons in her hair, and a green neck-tie." The *Milwaukee Daily Sentinel* added, "Mrs. Esther Morris is . . . the mother of three sons, and although she writes for *The Revolution*, she never lectures." The *Sentinel* then also repeated the information about her calico dress. [8]

With its famous tongue-in-cheek, *Frank Leslie's Illustrated Newspaper* added, "The People of Wyoming don't know whether to call their female judge a Justicess of the Peace, or a Justice of the Peacess."[9]

In an undated letter, which was probably written in early April, Esther reacted to the commotion in the press. She shared her thoughts with Frankie about the Stillman case and Stillman himself. Esther suspected he might have had something to hide in his docket and possibly used other reasons for not turning it in.

"My head is about level, yet notwithstanding the newspaper notoriety, my first case was one in which mercy was necessary as he was a drunken justice with a wife and babies. I was appointed to fill his place and he did not want to yield his books to a woman and I penned a clean docket to begin with, and not to be his successor. So, one must run the gauntlet, and I did not fear for my past record. It does belong to men to take care of women. I have ever been engaged in men's work, so this will be nothing new to me, for I like it. I earn one dollar for recording a deed; eight dollars for a [unreadable].

Esther's handwriting was indeed hard to decipher and possibly kept her letters from being used by researchers for years. (*Wyoming State Archives*)

Still, I think drunks will settle their quarrels rather than be brought before a woman."

.Reviewing the situation she shared, "Archie has a nice office and does seem as everything is confirmed for me to take the place. The Governor sent me word, he knew if I accepted the office and commission appointed me before word would get there. The telegraph to Chicago and Boston, the same day that my commission came. [It appears Esther learned of her approval at the same time it was reported to the rest of the country.] Mr. Morris acted about as your pa would have done if it was you. [Likely with sarcastic disdain.] Archie is pleased and so is Robert, all trying to assist me all they can."

After a lifetime of adjusting to circumstances, Esther remained self-possessed, her sense of humor intact: "I shall take things as they come, even if I should be President of the United States, but really, I do have too much to do things well. But I shall be reinforced after while by volunteers."

Continuing with the reality of keeping house in a cabin she added, "It has not frozen in my pantry all winter, so do not dread the winter as expected." [10]

In this letter Esther refers to fifty-two-year-old James Stillman as a "drunken justice." Her poor opinion of Stillman was at least partially the result of her friendship with his wife, Emma. Twenty-year-old Emma Stillman gave birth to twin sons in South Pass City just two months after Esther's arrival. It is probable Esther assisted Emma with the birth of her twins. When Emma's twins were christened, twins Ed and Robert Morris were named godfathers. In an interview on her eighty-sixth birthday, Emma Stillman Philbrick provided more details of her life in South Pass City. Stillman treated his wife abominably. Between her abusive husband and the constant fear of Indian attacks, she finally left South Pass City in June 1870. [11]

Historian Huseas wrote that James Stillman told the town his wife had run off with Shakespeare, the billiard parlor owner, and the court put their sons in the care of Sisters of Charity in San Francisco. Shakespeare was in South Pass City to appear in Esther's court in September. Federal Census records add to the story. Emma Stillman was reported in South Pass City with her husband and two sons on June 2. She then fled to her mother's home in Scipio, Utah. She and her sons were reported there on June 17. Rather than running away with a man, she ran to the protection of her mother. [12]

Esther's pragmatism is reflected in her next letter, written on April 10. This letter highlights her wit and fascination with life, whether labeled good or bad: "Dear Frank, your seeds reached me alright. I made a hanging basket and put it in the window, and this morning the cabbages are up. We have a snow storm every night,

J. Emma Wilson Stillman Philbrick married James Stillman when she was nineteen. (*Wyoming State Archives*)

and it goes off the next day. We have no rain. But we had an Indian raid. I will send you the paper, so you can see that we have our excitements. Archie went after the Indians. Every day brings some new excitement and it is possible we may have an Indian war, but I expect to stay if we do."

Esther mused at the newspapers' interest in her dress: "Did you feel bad about my calico dress? The girls in Owego did, so will tell you I wore my black empress cloth, still a nice calico would have been very suitable. [George] Wardman wanted me to appear as a feminine leader. He is only one of pa's [John's] dirty politicians. It has gone the rounds and will show the reputation of the family and will hurt no one, unless it would be Jesse's wife and Aunt Libbie.

Archie wrote a short biography [explanatory letter] to put a stop to all the talk and inquiries, and I sent it on to most of the family. But it is all over here and has become a matter of business. Just now business is dull, still we look forward to a busy summer."

Some family members were apparently upset by the snide remarks in the news reports. Archie wrote to several relatives to try to calm them, but Esther, as usual, put the matter aside and carried on with her life.

She concluded with a request for more seeds, writing, "You done so well [with the last seeds you sent] I will enclose the money for five more papers of garden seeds. One parsnip; two beets, one early turnip beet, one long one; and two radishes; one early turnip radish and one of long radish."[13]

Many in town stood strongly against suffrage and opposed women being seated as jurors. One of the most outspoken opponents to woman suffrage was South Pass City attorney Benjamin Sheeks. In addition to having worked to block the vote on the territorial bill, he made life difficult for Esther during her tenure as justice of the peace. He tried several cases before her. During his appearances in her court, he challenged her and did not treat her or the court with respect.

According to items in the 1920 collections of the Wyoming State Historical Society, he was credited with saying, "Woman never knows what she wants and is never satisfied until she gets it."[14]

However, a letter written in 1920 by Sheeks to Wyoming historian Hebard related a complimentary story about Esther. He wrote, "I remember one case in particular where the atty. [sic] on the other side persisted in pettifogging until I became exhausted and put him out of the room; I returned and apologized and offered to submit to any punishment she might inflict for the contempt of court. She merely remarked she thought I was justified—Yet, Mrs. Morris and I were never exactly what you would call friends. She was too manish [sic], if you will excuse the expression, to suit me."[15]

Sheeks's law partner in South Pass City, Parley Williams, spoke of Esther as mannish, articulate, well-spoken, non-combative, and thoughtful.

The passage of the December 1869 suffrage bill included women being seated on juries. According to the book *History of Woman Suffrage, Volume III*, "The first term of the District Court, under the statutes passed by the first legislature, was to be held at Laramie City, on the first Monday of March 1870. When the jurors were drawn, a large number of women were selected, for both grand and petit jurors.

The uproar was reported throughout the country by newspapers, and the county attorney sought the assistance of Wyoming Territorial Supreme Court Chief Justice John Homer Howe. After consulting with Justice John Kingman, Howe replied, 'Their husbands were more pestered and badgered than the women, and some of them were so much inflamed that they declared they would never live with their wives again if they served on the jury. They will have a fair opportunity, at least in my court, to demonstrate their ability in this new field. I hope they succeed, and the court will certainly aid them in all lawful and proper ways."[16]

———o———

Esther and Robert made passing comments in their letters regarding Indian issues in South Pass City, but the reality was much more precarious than they indicated. For example, on April 9, 1870, the *South Pass News* carried the story of young Frank G. Irwin. The report stated, "After being attacked by some Indians he thought friendly, he walked about a half-mile toward town on his own, and then a man named Ward saw him and carried him the rest of the way. Dr. Harrison removed the bullet and three arrows, but Frank's injuries were severe, and he did not survive."[17]

Frank Irwin's father was a doctor himself, who became the Indian agent on the Wind River Reservation.

Indian raids were big events in South Pass City, but the *South Pass News* took the opportunity to make a humorous jab at the new women's rights: "The women take a lively interest in the Indian campaign. We observed two of them carrying refreshments to one of the pickets, the day before yesterday. Our women are now voters and jurors, but not yet warriors. We have learned of no instance of any of them shouldering a musket and marching to the front. Our streets present a very quiet appearance now so many men being absent upon the Indian hunt. Those remaining are nearly all organized into a company for home protection, or to reinforce the party who have gone out if it should be necessary."[18]

Among other activities in town, Esther could hear this large gathering from her cabin. Marion Huseas adds the story of a chilling visit from a band of friendly Shoshone to South Pass City: "Chief Washakie and his Indians passed through the area this time every year. One time there were approximately 1,500 Indians in camp on the plateau just above the town and south of it. Each night they held a scalp dance at which young Indian women danced with a Sioux scalp on a willow reed. The dances lasted three or four hours. They had primitive instruments, and a large chorus of women chanted through their teeth while the men shouted. The Shoshone were friends of the South Pass City residents, but there were others causing constant fear."[19]

Stamm explained, "During this time Shoshone Chief Washakie walked a delicate tightrope, working with the white leaders to maintain peace by living and farming on the Wind River Reservation. He lived in a log home rather than a teepee. His children attended school on the reservation. He maintained Shoshone customs by taking his children on buffalo hunts and later led Shoshone bands into war against the Sioux and Cheyenne with the U. S. Army."[20]

In the wry humor of the time, on September 13, 1870, a short snippet from *South Pass News* reported that Archie was about to be married: "Honorable William H. Miller, Judge Jones and E.A. Slack, Esq., were among the departures by Friday's coach. Mr. Miller goes to practice law in Cheyenne, Judge Jones goes to Congress and Mr. Slack goes to be married. Will people never agree as to what constitutes happiness? Almost never!"

CHAPTER THIRTEEN

"ONLY LADY AT THE DEMOCRATIC MEETING"

WHILE ESTHER WAS performing her duties as justice of the peace and making a home for her husband and sons, Archie and other men of the Sweetwater Mining District confronted the Indians in the area.

In 1870 the East was a different world than the Wyoming Territory. John D. Rockefeller and others founded the Standard Oil Company in Ohio. The same year, Georgia—the last former state in the Confederacy—was readmitted to the Union, finally reuniting the United States. The Fifteenth Amendment to the Constitution had been ratified, legally preventing states from denying the right to vote on grounds of "race, color, or previous condition of servitude." Tenements in New York City accommodated the wave of immigrants, but poor sanitary conditions and extreme poverty made living conditions onerous. In contrast were the mansions built along New York City's Fifth Avenue. For part of the country, what was to become known as the Gilded Age had just begun.[1]

The United States Census Bureau reported 38,558,371 residents in the states and territories. New York City had a population of 942,292, and San Francisco showed 149,473 residents. Los Angeles, then the home of Frankie's mother Eliza Hall and her two grown children, Libbie and Charles Victor Hall, reported a population of 5,728 residents.

Along with her duties as justice of the peace, Esther was offered the additional task of postmistress of South Pass City. Following a review, however, she could not accept the offer, "because according to postal law, no married woman could hold the position."[2]

Esther's extensive reading kept her aware of the politics in the town, the territory, and the nation. The upcoming Wyoming election was her first opportunity to vote and have a say in issues important to her.

On September 6, 1870, election day, Robert penned another newsy letter to Frankie. "Business is now much better than it has been during the past few months," he wrote, "and the Indians have not troubled us for some time. There is more gold taken from the mines now than any time previous, and the prospects of those who remain are very encouraging."

He continued the long letter, explaining, "Archie now owns a saw mill and is doing a good business. The government is building a military post [Fort Stambaugh] for four companies a few miles from here and we hope henceforth to be well protected from Indian depredations.

"I am Archie's deputy clerk and do all his writing. The June term of court lasted almost two months and I have had more to do this past summer than ever before.

"Today is election day and our District Judge, Hon. William T. Jones is running for delegate to Congress on the Republican ticket, and although far superior to his opponent it is feared he will be defeated, as the Democrats have been largely in the majority and are thought to be so now."

Her proud son testified to Esther's demonstration of leadership: "Night before last Mother was the only lady at the Democratic meeting, but last evening when Judge Jones spoke, most of the ladies in town were present. His speech was very fine and eloquent, in addressing the ladies. He said he was for Wyoming's men and women, that he had been opposed to woman suffrage, but since he had given it serious thought and had heard such noble women as [Lib Browne's friend] Anna Dickinson and Olive Logan lecture, he was convinced and was in favor of women voting."

Esther's interest in fashion appeared undiminished even in the rough town. Robert wrote, "Mother says when you write to Frankie, tell her: 'From what I have earned as justice of the peace, I have been able to buy for myself material for a velvet cloak at twenty-five dollars a yard, and handsome lace trimmings and also a black silk alpaca dress besides having what spending money I wanted since I have had the office.' Mother thinks the office pays well for the little work it requires. A new justice will be elected today. Mother did not care to run for the office for she has had much glory from it.

"There are three ladies running for office in Laramie County on the Republican ticket for county clerk. It is surprising to note how public sentiment has changed in this little community in regard to women voting. You hear no open sneering about it as at first, and many have become open advocates."

He then switched from politics to love, "Archie leaves for Springfield, Illinois in a few days and will be married at Governor Palmer's [mansion] to Miss Sarah Neely, a sister of Mrs. Palmer and a lady about his age."[3]

There was some truth in Robert's assertion that Esther was not running for election as justice of the peace because she had "much glory from it," but there were likely deeper reasons. She no doubt found it exhausting to work in the court and also do all the cooking, housework, sewing, mending, and all the other chores required to keep the family running smoothly. Housekeeping improvements since her childhood, such as a woodstove and her Doty wringer washing machine, made housework easier than before. Even so these tasks took most of the day.

With Archie leaving to be married and Robert taking on extra duties in his absence and Ed busy, Esther would have no help at all with what Robert refers to as "Mother's domestic duties." As usual with Esther, family came first.

On that election day of September 6, 1870, at the age of fifty-eight, Esther Hobart Morris appeared at the Baldwin Building in South Pass City, Wyoming Territory, to joyfully cast her first vote. After enduring a lifelong struggle, she finally had a say in the political and legal structure under which she lived. Becoming the first woman to hold judicial office in the United States, followed by casting a ballot, likely provided a sense of achievement beyond her highest expectations.

Two days after the election on September 8, Robert wrote again to Frankie, "I did not mail my letter, for I thought you would be interested to hear how the ladies succeeded in voting. At South Pass

Seventy-year-old Eliza Gardner Swain, often referred to as Louisa Swain, of Laramie, Wyoming, was the first woman to vote in a general election. (*Wyoming State Archives*)

City, there were eight women voted and I assure you they received the utmost courtesy at the polls. A number voted at Atlantic City, and at Hamilton, 8 miles from here, 13 women voted including all there were in the place.

"What the women want, who did not vote, is a little enlightenment from such as Anna Dickinson, Olive Logan or Mrs. Stanton, and they will then appreciate the high privilege which Wyoming alone can give. From the returns, Judge Jones has been elected delegate to Congress. I have not learned yet whether the ladies who ran for office in Laramie County were elected. Mother holds her office until the 1st of November."

Returning to the family news of the moment Robert shared, "Archie leaves on the stage in the morning for Springfield, Illinois and will return by the 1st day of October when court commences. I pressed some wild flowers with the intention of sending you some, but they have faded so much, I came to the conclusion not to send them for they would be no example of the bountiful flowers we find here. As to forest leaves, there is no kind of lumber in country, but pine and cottonwood. Two weeks ago, Mother walked in from Archie's saw mill, a distance of eight miles and was but little fatigued. Her health is very good."[4]

Robert neglected to mention that in Esther's stead—ironically—James Stillman ran for the position of justice of the peace and was elected. Following the election, Esther continued her work as justice of the peace to complete the two months left in her term.

The *Laramie Daily Sentinel* reported a historical fact of the election. "Mrs. Louisa A. Swain, a lady seventy years of age, walked up and deposited her vote, it being the first here, and probably the first ever deposited in the world by a lady at a general election. Mrs. Swain is an old lady of the highest social standing in our community, universally beloved and respected, and the scene was in the highest degree interesting and impressive."[5]

Most women of the time did not become involved in politics. Opposition to woman suffrage came from both men and women, explaining the low female turnout Robert reported in his letter.[6]

As women voted in Wyoming, Susan B. Anthony, with assistance from her secretary, Esther's niece Lib Browne, pushed the point home in the September 8, 1870, edition of *The Revolution*:

> "Woman has now nearly unlearned that fulsome doctrine that there is no higher aim in life than to sell herself to the highest bidder. Woman has now nearly unlearned the creed that she is the toy, the pet or the slave of her husband. She believes herself, not his superior, but his equal, and claims for herself, not superior, but equal rights. She desires also to have a voice in the affairs of government which she is annually taxed to support. She claims this—no more.
>
> I am a woman. I do not claim that my sex is, without exception, fitted for any loftier posts than they presently occupy. I do not claim that they, having been educated to their present condition, would become another. Yet I do claim that these same weak, perhaps trifling, frivolous women, over whom I assert no superiority,

can be fitted by education for positions equal to those occupied by men.

Oh, you wise men of today, do you remember the fond mother who reared you belongs to this sex, whose rights you oppose; and do you reflect that in choosing a mother for your children, she too is one of them? Therefore, **I cry out, elevate her! And when the time does come, for come it will, when man and woman stand on equal footing, then, and not till then, can America truthfully wave her flag and prate of liberty!**"[7]

A significant visitor arrived in South Pass City just after the election of 1870. Photographer William Henry Jackson produced the only-known photograph of South Pass City during Esther's time there. Jackson was part of the Hayden Survey, a government survey of the Rocky Mountain region led by geologist Ferdinand Hayden. In 1870, the group traveled through central and southwest Wyoming Territory. According to the *South Pass News*, the survey team arrived in South Pass City on Thursday, September 8, 1870.[8]

With a budget of twenty-five thousand dollars for the expedition, all Hayden could offer Jackson was to pay his expenses—no salary. "Jackson would have to be content with the satisfaction of making a significant contribution to understanding the West. And, of course, with the adventure of exploring the largely uncharted wilderness."[9]

Most of Esther's work as justice of the peace included acknowledgments of deeds, mortgages, agreements, and other papers. She presided over trials involving misdemeanor cases, and once, she officiated at a civil wedding ceremony. She was possibly correct in her assessment that men chose to settle arguments themselves rather than go before a woman judge.

One of Esther's more humorous cases on September 22 made the *South Pass News*. According to Esther's docket, James Haas was transferred from James Irwin's court in Atlantic City, because Irwin was a witness for the prosecution.

"Mr. Haas, of Atlantic City, was arraigned, on Friday last, before Justice Esther Morris, on the charge of assault and battery on an idiotic young man named Pope, who, when called upon the stand to sustain the complaint, said he was ignorant of the nature of an

The Hayden Survey Party largely followed the Oregon Trail through Wyoming and arrived at South Pass City in September 1870, where photographer William Henry Jackson took at least one photograph. Ferdinand V. Hayden is seated at the rear of the table. William Henry Jackson is standing on the right with his hand on his hip. (*U.S. Geological Survey Photographic Library*)

oath. The evidence showed that he had been somewhat severely chastised with a willow switch, at least the Justice thought so, and Haas was fined $25 and costs." According to her court docket, Esther ordered he stay committed until the fine was paid.[10]

Stories about Esther and John circulated. John's drinking caused many difficulties for her. It was said that John Morris made such a scene in Esther's court she had him arrested or she had him jailed for violence against her. No evidence in Esther's docket shows that John was brought into her court. John was clearly emotionally abusive but did not ever appear in her court. Pride alone would have prevented such a public display of private pain.

A much happier circumstance occurred when Archie married Sarah Neely on September 22, 1870, at the governor's mansion in Springfield, Illinois. Prior to the wedding, Sarah had lived in the John and Malinda Palmer household, which was always large and busy. John Palmer had been elected governor of Illinois in 1869 and the family moved from Carlinville to Springfield. In the 1870 census the Palmer household listing included Governor John W. Palmer, his wife Malinda, six of their children, and Sarah and Ellen Neely. Three sisters, wards of John and Malinda, also lived with the family. The family had two servants and a gardener, creating a household of sixteen.

According to Sarah's and Archie's daughter Hattie, whose recollections were published in the *Annals of Wyoming* in 1927, "Sarah dreaded parting from her sister Ellen, so near her own age they were often taken for twins, but perhaps the hardest wrench was in leaving her small nephew, Louis Palmer, whom she idolized." Archie and Sarah went to St. Louis on their honeymoon and then returned home to South Pass City to live in their cabin home next door to Esther.

Hattie reported Sarah's encounter with the Indians, writing, "The Indians in the vicinity of South Pass City at that time were supposed to be friendly, too much so perhaps, as I have heard my mother tell about the uncomfortable feeling it gave her when they flattened their noses against the window-pane and peered in at her while she was occupied with her household tasks."[11]

Archie's wife, now Sarah Frances Slack, known as Sallie, was well received in the male-dominated Morris family. Robert wrote a glowing report in his November 1, 1870, letter to Frankie, stating, "A few weeks have passed since we received your kind congratulations and now that our new sister has been with us some time, and we have become acquainted, it is a pleasure to inform you we like her very much and feel she will be to Archie, a most loving and devoted wife."

Robert, obviously pleased with Sallie, wrote, "Frankie, I think you would like your new cousin very much. She is not as intellectual as my cousin Frank [Frankie], but in two things very much like her. That is, she is very quiet and accomplishes a great deal without attracting much notice. As I have no good picture to send you of our sister Sallie, I will describe a little of her appearance.

'She is just about Cousin Libbie Browne's size, as tall as my mother and weighs 105 pounds. She resembled no one I have ever known and is very unlike our family, having black hair and eyes. She is not pretty, nor homely and is decidedly stylish."

Esther and Archie's cabin shared a yard backing up to Willow Creek. "Archie lives in the cabin adjoining ours and our doors are only five feet apart. Enclosed I send you a photograph of Archie, taken while he was east, and is the best photograph he has ever had. Archie did not come home in time to attend the first week of the October term of court and the duty all devolved upon me. I succeeded in giving satisfaction to the judge and lawyers, and now have full charge of the office; Archie having resigned in favor of a Mr. Wiswell and I am his deputy.

"Father has been in the house two weeks with a severe attack of rheumatism, but is not much better. Mother sends love and says, 'Tell Frank my office is over.' Next South Pass paper I will send you Mother's obituary from office. Give my love to Uncle Ed and Aunt Libbie and write soon."[12]

Esther's term ended with her final case on October 31, 1870. During her time in office, she had ruled on thirteen criminal cases and fourteen civil cases. None of her rulings were overturned. The point had been made. Esther successfully proved a woman could competently serve in public office. At the end of her term, she turned over her docket to James Stillman who had been elected as justice of the peace.

As 1870 ended, news came of two untimely deaths in Esther's extended family. Twenty-one-year-old Charles McQuigg, son of Esther's brother Jesse, was shot in a hunting accident in Flint, Michigan, and nine-year-old Willie, grandson of her brother Daniel, died in Weedsport, New York.

On December 24, Robert recalled the year's events in a letter to his uncle, E.H. McQuigg and E.H.'s wife Libbie, Frankie's father and stepmother. "Charles McQuigg's death was a dreadful misfortune, and I felt from my innermost soul for Uncle Jesse. A Letter from Uncle Daniel last evening informs us of the death of his grandson, Willie Davie. It is indeed very hard to bear our misfortunes when death takes from us those whom we love, and are so full of promise, and we have to bury then with all our hopes."

Robert's descriptions then provided a snapshot of their life in the fading town. He wrote, "Business is very dull here this winter. The new mines at Cottonwood near Salt Lake City and other new discoveries have attracted a great many from here, and our population has decreased nearly one half. But, we do not give up, and think the country will come out right and prosperous.

"I cannot say the decline in business affairs has affected us much for it has thrown considerable business in our hands that others have left. The county clerk and ex officio register of deeds has gone east and I am his deputy and will hold the office until next spring, if not longer.

"Archie resigned as district clerk and Mr. Wiswell, his successor in office has appointed me his deputy and I now have full responsibility of the office. Between the two offices I will have all I can do, earn good salary, besides I learn a great deal about business laws and transactions."

Then Robert revealed additional income: "Mother's holding the office of justice of the peace placed a great many bill notes in her hands for collection and I acted as her collector and succeeded so well that I now have most all the bills and notes for collection of parties who leave here.'

Robert gave a report on John Morris. "Father has had the rheumatism for six weeks and two weeks ago, went down to Wind River Valley, thirty miles from here, to try the hot sulphur springs [Present-day Thermopolis, Wyoming]. I received a letter from him yesterday and he is entirely well and says he goes in bathing every day. Does it not seem strange when the temperature is one degree below zero here that 30 miles north of here and 3,000 feet lower that it is quite warm and pleasant, as I am informed, and barely any snow falls all winter.

South Pass City, Wyoming Territory, was photographed during its boom days by well-known photographer William Henry Jackson in 1870 as he traveled with the Hayden Survey Party. (*U. S. Geological Survey Photographic Library*)

"Father is staying at a military post near the hot springs and there is a tribe of 3,000 or 4,000 Snake [Shoshone] Indians there preparing to settle down in civilization. The government is erecting saw mills, grist mills and other buildings and next spring will set the Indians to farming 2,000 to 3,000 acres of land [on the Wind River Reservation]."

Then Robert concluded with an update on Archie, "Archie still owns the saw mill, and this last fall has sold the government 100,000 feet of lumber for military buildings [at Camp or Fort Stambaugh]. The cost of manufacturing lumber is 20 dollars a thousand and sells for 40 dollars a thousand. Most all other goods sell proportion-ately, with the exception of groceries, for competition will not allow grocery men to make over 50 per cent."[13]

In the nineteenth century people who drank as much as John were known as 'habitual drunkards.' Hydrotherapy was in common use for the treatment of habitual drunkenness, and the springs at Thermopolis were available to help with John's 'rheumatism.'[14]

Although Wyoming Territory was the first government to allow suffrage and Esther served her term as a "female first," the mood in her former home of Illinois was shifting in favor of suffrage. Frances Willard and members of the Illinois Woman Suffrage Association traveled to the capital, Springfield, to convince members of the Illinois Constitutional Convention to include universal suffrage in the proposed document. Buoyed by petitions to the General Assembly, which favored female suffrage, Willard declared, "The idea that boys of twenty-one are fit to make laws for their mothers is an insult to everyone."[15]

In 1870 Illinois passed two laws allowing limited suffrage to women, but full suffrage was not granted there until 1920, when Illinois became the first state to ratify the Nineteenth Amendment.

CHAPTER FOURTEEN

"Labored in Faith and Hope"

As justice of the peace Esther experienced euphoria at bringing home a man's wages, earning a grander sum than she ever had making hats. At the same time, however, her relationship with John became more difficult.

She shared a few details with Frankie in a January 1871 letter, "When I look back and see how much has happened that people could not grasp, and see them standing in the same old tracks, not so much as getting a new idea of what is going on around them. I suppose the time will come when I too refuse any move and be unwilling to have changes."

She continued, stressing Archie's life-long love of philosophy: "I have lived a very busy life since I left you both in body and mind. Archie, Robert, and myself have had everything to call us out, have been able to use all we know, and at the same time, learn all we could. Robert now occupies the office of Deputy District Clerk. Archie has the steam saw mill and this winter has done all he could in the printing office. He has been reading all the time he could get, in Herbert Spencer's Philosophy. Robert is studying shorthand for reporting. I done a good deal of sewing this winter for myself."

Esther's letters to Frankie were beginning to be more forthright about her soured relationship with her husband, "Mr. Morris has acted the part of critic. When there was credit, he ridiculed and when it was paid, he sneered because it was not more, and between both, he has sat around doing nothing, sometimes mad. He had to go the hot springs, so Bob and I had a good time."

Then Esther revealed an unusual opportunity, "I have been so busy with my family, that I had not thought of myself until I received a letter of invitation to attend the Washington National Convention from Mrs. Hooker with my express paid. The time was short, and I was so unprepared it was impossible to go, but it made me feel that I should be ready."

She ended with her thoughts on Sarah, setting the tone of their relationship. "Archie's wife is a sensible little lady. She is not a reformer naturally as has had no education in that line. Archie needs a house helper more than anything else. You should not be surprised at anything you hear as this is not a stand still town, and not a place to take root in. Now write me all you want me to know. All this to yourself. Anty Morris. Love to Damon."[1]

Esther wrote to Isabella Beecher Hooker when she declined the invitation to attend the January 1871 National Woman Suffrage Convention in Washington, D.C. Hooker, one of the main figures at the function, was the half-sister of Harriet Beecher Stowe, author of *Uncle Tom's Cabin*. Hooker, raised in Cincinnati, Boston, and Connecticut, founded the Connecticut Woman Suffrage Association and was a cowriter of Connecticut's first property law for women.[2]

Robert probably penned the letter for his mother. She reported her experience as a justice of the peace—something deeply significant to Hooker and others. So much so, in fact, that the letter was published in the *Chicago Tribune*.

> My Dear Mrs. Hooker:
>
> After this long delay, I would return many thanks for your kind letter, your sensible report, and more than all, for the strong right hand of fellowship.
>
> So far as woman suffrage has progressed in this Territory, we are entirely indebted to men. To William H. Bright belongs the honor of presenting the woman suffrage bill; and it was our district judge, Hon. John W. Kingman, who proposed my appointment as a justice of the peace and the trial of women as jurors.
>
> Circumstances have transpired to make my position as Justice of the Peace a test of woman's ability to hold public office, and I feel that my work has been satisfactory, although I have often

regretted I was not better qualified to fill the position. Like all pioneers, I have labored more in faith and hope. I have assisted in drawing a grand and petit jury, deposited a ballot, and helped canvass the votes after the election and in performing all these duties I do not know as I have neglected my family any more than in ordinary shopping, and I must admit that I have been better paid for the services rendered than for any I have ever performed.

In some thirty civil actions, tried before me, there has been but one appeal taken, and the judgment was affirmed in the court above and in the criminal cases also before there has been no call for a jury.

My family consists of a husband and three sons, all of whom have been more ready to assist me in the performance of my official duties than in my domestic affairs.

My term of office expired November first, and I sent you a paper with an account of a supper given by the new officers and notice of my retirement from office.

She shared her opinion about women's equality in Wyoming Territory. In what was possibly the most valuable part of the letter for Hooker and others, Esther explained:

My idea of the woman question in Wyoming is that while we enjoy the privilege of the elective franchise, we have not been sufficiently educated up to it. The election here, and agitation of woman's voting, has caused us to think, and has placed us far in advance of what we were, and I now think that we shall be able to sustain the position which has been granted us.

I have had the pleasure of reading one of your tracts, and would be pleased to receive a few for distribution, for I think your views on the woman question are such as will convince those who are open to conviction.

Hoping that I may in no distant day have the pleasure of a more intimate acquaintance, I remain your sincere friend, Esther Morris.[3]

Esther was unable to attend the conference. Famous suffragist Susan B. Anthony traveled from California to Washington, D.C. to attend the convention, and stopped in Cheyenne, Wyoming Territory. Anthony recorded her visit in her diary on January 5, 1871: "I saw

Church Howe, Governor Campbell, Mr. Arnold & others. Joy that woman suffrage was & is saved in the Territory. I called at Mrs. Post's [Amalia Post, who was a strong advocate for women's rights in Wyoming Territory] and she went to the Depot with me. At 1:30 train was off and at first class speed, and oh what joy in all faces."[4]

History of Woman Suffrage, Volume II, summarized that the Third Annual National Woman Suffrage Convention was held at Lincoln Hall in Washington, D.C. in January 1871. Attendees included Lucretia Mott, Elizabeth Cady Stanton, Susan B. Anthony as well as Amalia Post of Cheyenne, Wyoming Territory. Amalia Post read Esther's letter aloud at the convention. Speakers included Isabella Hooker, Stephen Douglass and Victoria Woodhull. The record commented in a footnote, "Mrs. Esther Morris, a large, fine-looking woman, administered justice in that territory [Wyoming] for nearly two years and none of her decisions were ever questioned."[5]

The *New York Herald* reported on the Universal Franchise Convention stating: "Wyoming was heard from through an epistle from Esther Morris, Justice of the Peace in that paradise of female voters, in which she pays a tribute to her husband and three sons, all of whom she states rendered her efficient service in the discharge of her official duties."[6]

The *Chicago Tribune* published Esther's letter to Hooker, writing, "The following letter was written by Mrs. Esther Morris of South Pass, Wyoming, the first woman Justice of the Peace in America, and read before the Woman Suffrage Convention in Washington, D.C.[7]

Many newspapers—from *The Guardian* in London to newspapers in Memphis, Tennessee, and Corvallis, Oregon, and West Yorkshire, England—carried short pieces on Esther. They ranged from. "Mrs. Esther Morris, Justice of the Peace of Wyoming has retired from office after credible service." To, "Mrs. Esther Morris, Justice of the Peace of Iowa has temporarily retired from the bench to nurse her baby."

With Esther basking in recognition, the long-simmering difficulties in the Morris marriage and within their family finally came to a head and resulted in violence. Esther may have found the events too embarrassing to write about even to Frankie, but other records of significant incidents reveal the pain that all members of the family suffered. Esther, Archie, and Robert lost patience with John and decided to make him accountable for his actions.

On April 10, 1871, Archie filed a complaint against John in the court of H.A. Thompson. Ex officio Justice of the Peace J.A. Breman heard the case. The complaint was listed as replevin [claim and delivery], and stated that "John Morris did commit upon E.A. Slack, the Theft of goods and chattels." John was arrested and taken to court where both Archie and Robert testified against their father. The docket states, "It was decided and adjudged that the right of property is in Plaintiff and that Defendant pays the costs of the suit amounting to $4.05."[8]

Regardless of the trouble, Esther's sons continued to thrive. Robert was still employed as Deputy Clerk, planning a career as a stenographer. Drawing upon his love of books, and the knowledge that there were still many book-hungry miners living in town, he began a small book business. A.B. Conaway, editor of the *South Pass News,* noted on April 12: "Robert Morris, never behind the times, received another large installment of magazines, periodicals and newspapers by yesterday's mail. Robert's literary emporium is becoming one of the permanent institutions of the country. Don't forget to call when you wish anything in this line."[9]

Soon after, Archie joined C.J. Coles as editor of the local newspaper. The *Wyoming Tribune* reported on May 20, 1871: "The South Pass News has changed editors. Mr. Conaway retiring and E.A. Slack late clerk of the third district court taking his place. We hope E.A. will make his fortune. His first number contains considerable interesting reading concerning Indians, farming and mining, and an account of the 'head' with which the editor was threatened." The first masthead to show E.A. Slack as editor appeared in the May 24 issue.[10]

On June 7, 1871, Esther appeared in court. J.A. Breman again heard the case. The title of her complaint was, "Criminal Charge of Assault and Battery." The docket stated that she "accuses John

Morris of the crime of Assault and prays that a warrant be issued for his arrest. Warrant issued, but not served, the matter being settled between the parties."[11]

This was surely not the first such incident, but after twenty-seven-years of marriage, Esther had finally reached her melting point. However, once again, she stepped aside and agreed to try to work things out with John.

At this time, Archie's wife, Sarah, was pregnant, which added a new dimension to Archie's life and his future. After becoming the editor of the *South Pass News* in May, he purchased the newspaper from C.J. Coles in June and became a newspaper publisher. Nathan Baker reported in July, "We glean the following item of interest from the South Pass News, which paper, under the new management of Mr. Slack is assuming much more interest as a local paper than formerly." Archie used an up-to-date Gordon press to print the news.[12]

Across the country in Owego, New York, Esther's niece Lib Browne (Charlotte Elizabeth), married Levi Chatfield in June 2, 1871. Chatfield was thirty-five years her senior and had been speaker of the New York State Assembly in 1848. They met while Lib worked at *The Revolution* with Susan B. Anthony. Lib's sister Julia and her husband, George Pickering Bemis, moved from New York to Omaha, Nebraska. During the suffrage push of 1871, Lib's friend Anna Dickinson traveled throughout the Midwest on her speaking tour.

Esther's August 1871 letter to Frankie reflected on motherhood and also evaluated her life decisions as she faced the final break in her family. She did not directly speak of the painful events of the past few months, but she was likely feeling humiliated with her pride shattered. "My Dear Niece, I was glad to hear from you, as Robert has said a number of times, why does not Frankie write? I would tell him you had both hands full. You are busy with two children. No mother has much time to think of those at a distance, our hands are full of work.

"I often think of how much happier a mother is that lived her own girlhood life cultivating herself so that she is ready to be a mother and give herself back to her children."

Esther went on to tell of a relative who lived in a difficult situation. It had been years since she spoke so openly about her increasing unhappiness with John. "I often think so of Mr. Morris when we differ so much in organization. There is much loneliness. It may be well for the next generation, but a great cross to the present. It's like a revolution one has to pass through anarchy for the reward.

We have had much experience in our mountain life. I have felt the full value of my pioneering in Illinois to my children. I have given them liberty. We have passed through the excitement of settling a new territory and the speculation of mining everything down to a matter calculation."

Shaking off her sadness she gave an update on South Pass City. "Saloon gamblers have mostly left the country. Business is very dull and most of our miners too have gone to other diggings to find riches, give over their lives, or return to the states satisfied with less gains and more comfort. Archie and Robert have done well, but not as well as the state of the country will admit. But it is still possible.

"Archie may return to Illinois late this fall as he has an offering for a wider field of work at than present. Robert has all that he can or ought to do and of the kind that is giving him good experience. Ed has grown stout and is enjoying a frontier life. Mr. Morris waddles along and spends his time about like your father but has not struck pay streak yet. We have two large English cows.

Returning to her continued discontent she penned, "All past legislation has been in favor of woman subjection to men backed by all religious ceremony and when she is freed by law her helplessness and ignorance are like dead weight. Life is a struggle from the bottom to the top."[13]

But soon, the struggle of life also provided great joy. Sarah gave birth to Esther's first grandchild, Charles Henry Slack, on October 26, 1871.

Life then handed the family another challenge in the form of fire. Archie printed the last issue of the *South Pass News* on October 31. A fire at the print shop ended Archie's career as a publisher in South Pass City. There was never another newspaper in the town.[14]

Archie's printing press survived the fire and is on display at the South Pass City State Historic Site. (*Author Collecction*)

Archie soon ended his stay in South Pass City. In December, he headed for the larger town of Laramie to begin again. He took the materials that he salvaged from the fire with him. Because of severe winter weather, he left Sarah and infant Charles in Esther's care. The *Wyoming Tribune* reported on Archie's progress in November. "Mr. Slack, formerly of the South Pass News, intends starting a daily paper at Laramie City. 'Taking coals to New Castle' we should say." By late December, Archie was listed as the proprietor of the *Laramie Daily Independent*.[15]

In Laramie, Archie prepared a place for Sarah and Charles to join him when the snow in South Pass City cleared enough for them to make the trip safely.

The Second Wyoming Territorial Legislature assembled in Cheyenne in November 1871. One of the bills under consideration was House Bill 4, an act to repeal woman suffrage. House Speaker Ben Sheeks, who had practiced law in South Pass City and who had appeared in Esther's court, moved the bill forward. After some lengthy discussion in the House and additional careful consideration by the Council, the bill passed 9-3 in the House and 5-4 in the Council. On December 4, 1871, lawmakers sent the bill to Governor Campbell for his signature.

But Campbell vetoed the bill. In his veto statement, he wrote, in part:

> For the first time in the history of our country we have a government to which the noble words of our magna charts [*sic*] of freedom may be applied, not as a mere figure of speech, but as expressing a simple grand truth, for it is a government which derives all just powers from the consent of the governed.
>
> We should pause long and weigh carefully the probable results of our action before consenting to change this government. A regard for the genius of our institutions, for the fundamental principles of American autonomy, and for immutable principles of right and justice, will not permit me to sanction this change.[16]

The women of Wyoming Territory retained their right to vote.

—o—

With Archie gone and Sarah and Charles leaving soon, Esther realized that her South Pass City experience was over. This created a dilemma. John made it clear he was not leaving South Pass City. Ed would not leave without his father. Esther did not want to stay with John, but she questioned whether she should leave him here to die without her. She had always known that Ed was much closer to his father than to her, and if she separated from John, in a way, it meant she would lose Ed too.

Additionally, she faced the same old problem. With no way to make enough money for herself, where would she go? What would she do? How would she live?

Above: The first phase of the Wyoming State Capitol, completed in 1868. (*Wyoming State Archives*)

Left: Until they were able to move into the new Capitol, the First Territorial Council met at this building at 17th and Ferguson (now Carey). (*Carrie Chapman Catt papers, Bryn Mawr College Library, Special Collections*)

Part Three

"I Do Not Withdraw from the Woman's Cause"

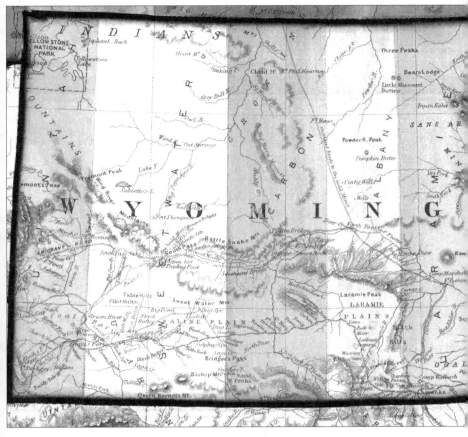

This 1872 map of Wyoming at organization shows the five counties running the entire distance of the state from north to south. From the left, they are Uinta, Sweetwater, Carbon, Albany, and Laramie. South Pass City as well as Green River were in Sweetwater County. Laramie was in Albany County. Cheyenne was is Laramie County.

CHAPTER FIFTEEN

"I Am Recognized Wherever I Go"

THE TEMPORARY ANSWER to Esther's dilemma came in the form of an invitation from Frankie's mother, Eliza Jane Hall, to visit San Francisco and Los Angeles, California. In January 1872 Esther wrote to Frankie, "It makes one almost believe in fate and you will, when I tell you I'm about to pioneer again to California. I should have gone three months ago. It has been too cold and white the last month. We were snowed in. As you have lived north, you know something of snow. It has been up to the second story, but the roads are now often clear of snow. Soon we will get Sarah out. Archie went to Laramie to publish a daily paper when the baby was two weeks old, so they could not go with him and have been with us all winter. She goes to the railroad with me."[1]

In Ottawa, a town near Peru, Illinois, a long, backhanded article appeared in the newspaper:

A WYOMING JOKE:

How the wags served Mrs. Judge Morris'
Husband – A wife Committing her Spouse.

Everybody was satisfied with the new justice, and the new justice with everybody. One day however, the wine of bitterness was mixed in her cup of bliss, and notwithstanding her womanly and wifely feeling, she was compelled to drink it. Her better half who was now in charge of the domestic department of the firm had previous to his retirement to the sweets of domestic life, occasionally taken a social glass with his friends.

Taking advantage of this weakness, some friends waited upon Mr. Morris one day and, having made Mr. Morris drunk, led him

Though history has been critical of Esther's stern appearance, had she been a male justice of the peace this unsmiling portrait from the side would probably be considered a traditional professional pose. *(Wyoming State Archives)*

into a breach of peace, then hastened to the Esquire's office and lodged a complaint with her honor against her honor's 'liege lord and master,' that used to be, and demanded a warrant for his arrest.

After giving the prisoner a Caudle lecture, as amended by the laws of Wyoming, her Honor imposed the usual fine, and required the prisoner to give bonds to keep the peace; upon which the court gallantly offered to let him go, and Mr. Morris vanished."[2]

This article, not intended to be taken seriously, also stated that John pleaded with Esther to go home and nurse their baby and make the beds.

Obviously still unable to admit the actual events of violence Esther responded to Frankie, "You ask me if it was true that Mr. Morris was brought before me for trial. It was some time after you wrote before I saw the article you spoke of and it was sent from Illinois most likely got up by some of Mr. Morris' friends. A man is not allowed to be the judge of his wife, much less a woman of her husband. It would not be a legal proceeding; neither do women nurse their child after they are fifty-five."

She attempted to explain her tolerance of John, "Mr. Morris was very well satisfied with woman suffrage while it was a democratic measure, but when the republican party adopted it, he was as down on woman suffrage as he was on negro freedom. He's about like your father in politics. He drinks whiskey, but can stand more, and as I am more or less dependent on him, and I don't know what to do about it. I have never regretted coming here. You will hear of me from California."[3]

The weather improved and roads eventually cleared. Esther, Sarah, and the baby took the fifteen-hour stagecoach ride to the train stop near Green River where they caught the Number Four train east to Laramie as first- or second-class passengers. The Number Seven, an emigrant train, also ran the route regularly but it transported the very poor. It offered no services, and passengers sat on benches in the boxcars, attached to the freight train. Esther and Sarah were no doubt relieved to have a choice.

Esther remained a short time in Laramie to help Sarah get settled. Then she reversed direction and headed back west to California. The Union Pacific train left Laramie at two in the afternoon on one day and, after fifty-five stops, arrived in Ogden, Utah, three days later. At Ogden, Esther changed trains and boarded a train of the Central Pacific Railroad. And then, after three more days of travel, including sixty-three stops, she finally arrived in San Francisco.[4]

Esther spent several weeks in San Francisco. The city had grown since the California Gold Rush of 1849–1850. The population was now nearly 150,000. She visited Eliza Jane and Eliza Jane's sister

Susan Emily Hall Barry, the former Civil War nurse, and her husband. Eliza Jane was active in the suffrage movement in both that city and in Los Angeles. Some of her responsibilities included organizing conventions and receptions. Esther attended the 1872 American Suffrage Association Convention and was the guest of honor at a reception held by the California Central American Woman Suffrage Committee.

Historian Larson mentioned the informal event held at Pacific Hall on February 12, 1872. He quoted the *San Francisco Call's* reporter as writing:

"Mrs. Morris, Ex-Justice of the Peace. . . is a matronly looking woman, past middle life, yet much younger looking than her actual years. Her face and head indicate the possession of a strong individuality of character and great firmness. Her manners are those of a courtly, self-possessed woman, full of natural dignity and ease, while her conversation clearly shows that she is possessed of more than an ordinary share of shrewdness and correct appreciation of human nature. Her manner of speaking off-hand, ready, and at times brilliant. . . .

With reference to her own appointment and success,

. . . she never felt that the office was above her capacity,

. . . She had never studied law, except in transacting her own affairs, but had found little difficulty in comprehending the cases coming before her."[5]

In March, Esther left San Francisco for Los Angeles. What a long eventful journey it had been from her birth in the 1812 village of Spencer, New York, to her visit to Los Angeles, California, in 1872. After more than a half-century of hard work and strife, during this visit, Esther relaxed, basking in the California sun and enjoying her accomplishments.

She found that Frankie's sister Libbie Hall had matured since 1869 when she had chastised Libbie in a letter, referring to her then as "prejudiced and spirited."[6]

Esther relished the opportunity to become reacquainted with Libbie and her home. Libbie, now a schoolteacher, labored to improve the beautiful property she owned with her mother. Eliza Jane's son (Libbie's half-brother), sixteen-year-old Charles Victor Hall, also lived there.

In a long March 27, 1872, letter to Frankie, Esther revealed her elation, "I am now in Los Angeles seated at Libbie's table writing. What a dream my life is. I often wonder if it is me. It must be, for I am recognized wherever I go.

"I had a very pleasant stay in San Francisco and saw your mother two or three times a week. She is at that period of life where she would not be likely to enjoy very good health. [Life expectancy was about 58 years at that time.] But there are times when she looks almost as when I first saw her, pretty and agreeable. I can see more than ever how little she is fitted for her daily routine of housekeeper. How much she needs the comforts of home and how anxious Libbie is for a pleasant home for herself and I do think she will succeed in time in making one for herself, and then she can make one for her mother.

"They have a beautiful piece of land and the water is near, well irrigated, with orange orchards and trees. Libbie is now engaged in digging a well on her place so that she can irrigate around the house. She put in a garden of vegetables. Everything is looking about like June in Michigan. The trees are laden with oranges, and the young shoots are coming out. I feel that I want a home here more than any place I was ever in. I liked Illinois, but it is no comparison in landscape and the climate is delightful. Everything grows that can be thought of with the ocean to float."

Esther humorously penned, "If the Pilgrims had landed here instead of Plymouth Rock, they would not have went farther."

It is a testament to Esther's resolution and courage that she was a success in life with so little formal education. She continued, "I am in hopes that Archie will come here and publish a paper. I expect Robert will come. I have written to the boys and Mr. Morris. I do not know what they will do or how soon they will come. In Robert's last letter [from South Pass City] he said that they were expecting good times as there would be plenty of water for gulch mining. But we could never make a home there for we wanted to live where we could raise something. Still I like it there and if we could make it pay, I should have been contented for it doesn't make much difference where we are if all our family is with us and we are getting our living."

Revealing her mindfulness, she wrote, "I have strung out my letter, but sometimes write much and do not say anything, just as I talk and when I got here, I wanted to talk with you.

"I feel very much at home with Libbie and hope it will supply a place she much needs. I hope Robert will come to us soon. Libbie had a letter from Aunt Charlotte Browne and one from Libbie Browne Chatfield. I had a very pleasant reception appearance and made many pleasant acquaintances."[7]

Esther's hope for her family to move to Los Angeles was not realized. Archie decided to make Wyoming Territory his home. John and Ed remained in the South Pass City area and owned a partial interest in a pool table at the Metropolitan Saloon in Miner's Delight. Robert went to Laramie. Esther reluctantly left Los Angeles and joined Archie and Robert in Laramie.

She reported to Frankie in the fall or winter of 1872 from Laramie, "Mr. Morris cannot live with either of his boys for he treats them just as [if] they were nobody while he would [treat] a young man of their age with consideration and still he expects them to take care of themselves and him if he needs it. Mr. Morris is at South Pass. We left considerable property there and he is trying to make the most of it, but the place is deserted or nearly so. Ed is on the railroad [Green River]. Robert is here, Archie's wife is visiting in Illinois so that I am keeping house for Robert and Archie."

Esther admitted her feelings about the reality of her situation as she continued, "Well now about myself. I am selfish so felt bad about what caused me to go to California and did not want to come back to this cold country, but Archie had settled in Laramie. I thought to stay in California but was disappointed in my relations. I did not think less for Robert to come, for your mother would make us all the trouble she could if we had a good time with Libbie and Charlie. They will fight whenever they like and with whoever don't like them. Libbie and Eliza can't get along as well as strangers."

Esther continued with sad news, "Archie and Sarah lost their little boy. [Charles died on August 23, 1872.] He was a fine child and it was a great loss. Sarah is in Illinois and will be here in a month or so.

"I have gotten used to being unsettled and moved about so don't feel frightened to think of what will come next. I try to be ready for my fate, for I begin to feel that I have but little to do but alter all my life to control and keep a home for old age. I feel myself adrift, not knowing what will befall me next but still I find those that stay put are not satisfied any better than those that change."

She shared a dismal outlook on a woman's lot in life. "Grant fought to free the negroes now the South is fighting to free their masters. I guess we all have to fight our own way for freedom, but we women must complain and grumble and maybe that's all we are good for. Now Frank, tell me of your troubles and babies and your husband and yourself."[8]

Esther's life story repeated itself. She always made some money sewing and making hats, but it never amounted to enough to allow her to live on her own or to make her own life choices. Now she was facing old age with complete dependence on her husband or sons. Once again, she tried to make the best of a difficult situation.

W. E. Chaplin, a long-time employee, friend, and competitor of Archie in the newspaper business, later wrote a detailed tribute to Esther. He said, in part, "They were living in Laramie during the period in the early 70's when Mrs. Morris made long visits to the home of her son, Editor E. A. Slack of the Daily Independent and the Daily Sun. My first acquaintance with Mrs. Morris was when the Slacks lived in the Wanless club house. There were three apartments in that one-story building; one was occupied at that time by A. G. Swain, cashier of the Wyoming National Bank. One by Editor Slack and one by the Wanless family. In 1874 Colonel Slack built a home on North Second Street, a small brick structure which still stands just to the south of the electric light plant."[9]

Mary Elizabeth (Libbie) McQuigg Hall and Captain William Moore were married in early 1874. *(Libbie Hall Moore photograph, courtesy of Cliff Hall Collection. Moore photograph, Los Angeles Bureau of Engineering, Department of Public Works.)*

On August 14, 1873, an organizational meeting was held to nominate a candidate for the territorial legislature. Esther was elected president of the new Woman's Party and Mrs. Eliza Boyd, secretary. Both were drafted as candidates of the Woman's Party. But Esther had second thoughts, and on August 30, 1873, she wrote, "To the women of Albany County, Laramie City. While I fully appreciate the honor conferred upon me by the women of Albany County in selecting me as their candidate for the office of representative, I respectfully tender my resignation. In withdrawing from the political contest, I do not withdraw from the women's cause but hope that their influence will be actively exerted for the right. Respectfully yours, Esther Morris."[10]

In early 1874, a cheerful piece of family news arrived from California. Frankie's sister Libbie Hall, thirty-one, married forty-six-year-old Captain William Moore.

The Los Angeles Department of Public Works reported on Libbie and her new husband, "Captain Moore held the office of city surveyor from 1857 to 1875. He was a man of wit and humor with quaint expressions. He was both a scholar and linguist who could converse with the old timers of the city in Spanish or in many other tongues. His wife . . . was also an early Los Angeles pioneer. As a girl of sixteen years Mrs. Moore had come to California with her mother via the Isthmus of Panama to San Francisco thence to Los Angeles by Stagecoach. Mother and daughter homesteaded government land in 1865, a parcel of which at Western and Adams is still in possession of the latter's children. Both Captain and Mrs. Moore were prominent factors in the early social life of Los Angeles."[11]

Progressive Men of Wyoming reported that Archie was active in political issues in Laramie and outspoken in his editorial columns. He officially joined his mother's lifelong political party and became a liberal Republican. Joseph Carey, who had arrived in Cheyenne in 1869 as the U.S. Attorney for Wyoming Territory, encouraged Archie to move to Cheyenne. As a fellow Republican, Carey realized having Archie own and edit a newspaper in Cheyenne would likely be a boon to both men, as well as to the Republican party.

Larson added, "J. M. Carey wrote to M. C. Brown in February 1876, asking the Laramie attorney to talk to Slack about moving his *Laramie Sun* to Cheyenne and making it Republican. Slack moved to Cheyenne in March 1876, and no doubt added strength to the Republican party."

W. E. Chaplin wrote, "In 1876 Colonel Slack sold his business to Hayford & Gates of the Daily Sentinel and moved to Cheyenne. From 1873 to 1876 and thereafter for two years in Cheyenne I saw Mrs. Morris on many occasions and became quite well acquainted with her. She liked boys and gave me some notice."[12]

With the move, Archie was on his way to becoming the most colorful and powerful editor in Wyoming Territory and ultimately, the state of Wyoming.

Also, in 1876, Robert accepted a highly desirable job in Albany,

New York. He and his mother had always been extremely close and as he provided Esther with a home, she moved back east with him. For Esther, this was the completion of a full circle of the United States. After spending her early days in New York, she moved to Illinois, and then to Wyoming Territory. Following that, she enjoyed a long stay in California, returned to Wyoming Territory, and then arrived again in New York.

CHAPTER SIXTEEN

"TIMES WE SHOULD LEAN"

ESTHER'S BROTHER Daniel and their sister Charlotte Susan each lived less than two hundred miles from Albany, New York, a circumstance that allowed Esther to both keep house for Robert part-time in Albany and to stay with family part-time in Weedsport, Owego, and Spencer.

Like most women of her time, Esther was financially dependent on the men in her family, and she did not have control over that part of her life, which restricted her choices. Voluntary reliance on men for financial support was one thing, but it was quite another when dependence was forced.

Esther attended the fiery July 4, 1876, National Woman Suffrage Convention in Philadelphia, which was designed to celebrate the centennial of the Declaration of Independence of the United States. The *History of Woman Suffrage* states, "Elizabeth Cady Stanton spoke upon the aristocracy of sex, and the evils arising from manhood suffrage. Judge Esther Morris, of Wyoming said a few words in regard to suffrage in that territory."[1]

Susan B. Anthony gave a "Declaration of Rights of the Women of the United States." She said, in part, "While the nation is buoyant with patriotism, and all hearts are attuned to praise, it is with sorrow we come to strike the one discordant note on this 100th anniversary of our country's birth. We deny the dogma of the centuries, incorporated in the codes of nations—that woman was made for man, her best interests, in all cases, to be sacrificed to his will. We ask of our rulers, at this hour, no special favors, no special privileges, no special legislation. We ask justice, we ask equality, we ask that all civil and political rights that belong to citizens of the United States, be guaranteed to us and our daughters forever."[2]

The suffrage movement played a large part in Esther's life after she returned to New York. Lib's friend, Anna Dickinson, the suffragist leader who had spoken in Cheyenne in the autumn of 1869, prior to the passage of the equality legislation, now sometimes lived with Libbie Browne Chatfield and her husband, Levi. Even though Esther and Robert lived in Albany, both saw Lib and Anna often.

Robert became infatuated with the charming Anna Dickinson. He gave an update on Anna and wrote also of the living arrangements he shared with his mother in a letter to Frankie in February 1877. He explained, "It is three years this month since I came east and until very recently, I have cherished the hope of returning. . . .There is something in Western life that has always seemed to lure me back. It must be the freedom of the country, the independence that every man feels when out of the influence of old communities, where everything moves in settled grooves. But I find myself so well provided for here, that I have little desire to return now.

"Anna Dickinson played an engagement here a short time since and I had the pleasure of seeing her several times. I have taken great interest in her success from the fact that she is a personal friend, and an intimate friend of our cousin, Libbie [Browne] Chatfield. It was at her house Anna stayed most of last winter and wrote her play."

He continues with family updates, "Mother has been boarding with Cousin Mary [Mary Davie, daughter of Esther's brother Daniel] at Auburn through winter, having spent the summer and half of the Fall with me. . . . Archie thinks of coming east in the spring and mother will probably return with him. Ed, who is now with father at South Pass, writes for mother to come there and I think it's probable that she will spend the summer with them. As your affectionate cousin, Robert C. Morris, Office of Secretary of State, New York."[3]

John Morris spent his last years in South Pass City and Miner's Delight in failing health, with Ed at his side. Historian Huseas chronicled John Morris's final years and the decline of South Pass City: "John Morris continued to get into trouble with the law. In 1874, he sold most of his billiard equipment, except for one table on which he continued to pay the license until his death. The only businesses left in South Pass City were one hotel, a billiard saloon, the post office and stage station, supported by the twenty-four voters still in residence."

Jon Lane, Curator at South Pass Historic Site, shared a document showing John Morris's purchase of a Brunswick pool table in May 1875. The four-page document states: "Purchase price, one hundred seventy-five dollars with an interest rate of eight percent per annum from 4 May 1875 until paid."[4]

John Morris died on September 29, 1877. The *Laramie Daily Sentinel* reported his death, "The Cheyenne *Sun* [Archie's newspaper] chronicles the death at South Pass City, of John Morris. Deceased was the father of Robert C. and Edward J. Morris, and stepfather of Mr. Slack of the *Sun*. He was sixty-three years old at the time of his death and had been in South Pass nine or ten years." John was buried in South Pass City.[5]

A short note Esther wrote to Frankie in October 1877 showed her wishes to visit Flint without having to see E.H. and his wife. Esther explained, "I shall accept your kind invitation to visit you on my way to Illinois, as I wish to see you and your family. It may be as well not to mention my coming and let my visit be a quiet one and as I would not like to disturb the others."[6]

Later, on December 20, 1877, Esther described her feelings about John's death in a letter to Frankie. Esther had been married to him for thirty-one tumultuous years. Some of that time was good, but there were many times throughout the years when Esther felt lonely and angry. After alternating between happiness and sadness, her final year with him in South Pass City left her feeling humiliated and shamed. She wrote, "I have felt sad at the death of Mr. Morris. Although sudden, it was not unexpected. I was sorry to be away from him, but he was keeping saloon in the place where he lived, and I would have been in the way, for men doing wrong do not want those to look, that see it in this light. He was able to see to this himself as long as he lived. His disease was dropsy, and when it reached the heart he was drowned in a moment. Edward was talking to him and in an instant, he was gone. Edward had been with him since I couldn't. He left some fifteen hundred or two thousand in stock, which he gave to Edward who writes, as soon as he can sell will come east. I should be leery to have him [Edward] stay in the house of any aunt."

One interesting implication of this letter, although she did not state it directly, shows that during their younger years, John hid his drinking from Esther and the boys. That behavior may have been one reason for his many absences. When at home, he apparently did not imbibe in their presence. It is clear Esther felt embarrassed by Ed, as he followed his father in drinking heavily.

Esther continued her letter of December 20 with her feelings following yet another McQuigg family quarrel. She had obviously freely shared her thoughts, putting herself in the middle of another family squabble.

She told Frankie, "I thank you for the remembrance of me at this time, for I do indeed have my trials and need sympathy. . . . I may not be always in the right but am willing to learn redress from those of my own blood for whatever we do does affect each other. We cannot escape the reputation of our own family, so be it good or bad, and when I hear my brothers or sisters accuse each other unjustly, I have told them so. . . . I don't remember to ever have reproved any of them, only for complaining and quarrelling with each other. . . . If any of them will tell me where I have done wrong, I will either make restitution or humbly beg their pardon. My motto has been, better make the best of a bad job than to spoil a good one and there is no use of crying for spilt milk."

Then she moves on to the family report, "My greatest treasures have been my children and if they are not perfect, they're as good as I could expect considering the investment in them, and who their mother is. There is some of Cain and Abel in us all.

Esther sat for a portrait in middle age. The photograph is imprinted in the right corner "Frank Reistle, Denver." *(Wyoming State Archives)*

"Archibald, in Cheyenne, is doing well in his business. He has no living children. [In 1873, Archie and Sarah had a daughter named Esther, who lived for just a few weeks.] I hear that [Frankie's sister] Libbie and [husband] Mr. Moore get along nicely but have no children. I was glad they came to see you and that your father was so well pleased with him. He [Mr. Moore] is a very clever man."[7]

In January 1878, Esther wrote again to Frankie, this time with more introspection. "It being the first of the year, I have been looking over the past and trying to see what I have left undone that I ought to have done, and what I did that I ought not to have done, for I believe in penitence as well as confession. I read your letter again and there was an implied reproof in it. You spoke of stirring people up and qualified it saying you did believe I did not approve of it myself. Now, Frankie, you need not be sensitive or think I judge on that subject. I have never done it, only where a sense of justice compelled me to do it and was the oppressed complained of that selfishness from the oppressor. When the south held four million in bondage, they wanted to be let alone and fought to their deaths. Now in time they whine and cry for help, which is the real character of a tyrant."

Esther continues with an evaluation of the McQuigg family, "Well I learned one thing going west and that was, a great deal of the quarrelling comes from hunger as well as much from drinking. [Esther's sister] Charlotte's capital for help was to make out that someone had abused her for years. It was her father for keeping money for her cows and [her husband] Fred for beating her, and her children [Libbie and Julia Browne] thought she did not know anything. Well the girls went from home and married men of more intelligence than her husband. They wanted a Delmonicos [an up-scale restaurant], so she was of no great asset amongst them. About like your mother to you or me to my daughter-in-law. Of course, it is not agreeable to be laid aside like a last year's almanac, but such is fate and Charlotte must abide as well as I."[8]

In the spring of 1878, Esther visited Frankie's mother, Eliza Jane, and Frankie's sister and brother, Libbie (and William Moore) and Charles Hall, in Los Angeles. This trip was not as glorious as Esther's earlier visit.

An undated letter with a missing front page, apparently written to Frankie after Esther returned to Owego, explains the trouble she found during this visit to California. "Charlie [Hall] made you a visit and I thought him a smart young man. He was very good to his mother and I think Mrs. Moore [Frankie's sister Libbie] will be good to him and she often said he was the best man in the world, and as they have the best land in the best country, I could not see a reason for them to complain as they did.

"Libbie said her and her mother was not harmonious. Still, they were inseparable and could not live without each other. While it looked sometimes as though they could not live with each other. I could see how much [Esther's sister] Charlotte and your mother [Eliza Jane] were alike; could not live with others and would not live so as others could live with them. I was glad to get away alive. I let them have all of California. I did housekeeping so that Libbie could get away from her mother and Mr. Moore got her away from me, and if he had not, someone else would. I lost about $500 by it, but I have not gone cold or hungry yet for it."

This lengthy letter continues with Esther's opinions and feelings regarding a forty-year-old issue between the remaining McQuigg siblings. When Esther and her brother Daniel visited their brother John in Ohio in 1838 after the death of their sibling Charles in Cincinnati, they were responsible for transporting Charles's legacy to New York. They were instructed to deliver it to brother E.H. who was entrusted to disperse the money to his siblings when necessary. E.H. made promises but failed to follow through on them.

Esther ended this letter with a brief bit of information about health matters, explaining, "I had a letter from Mary Davie the other day and she said [Esther's brother] Daniel was complaining a good deal of his back and I suppose it is kidneys. He is a good old man and is likely to go to sleep with fathers at any time. I sometimes feel there is more reason to mourn because we are left here, because others go, for I do believe that I have more friends in heaven than here." She closed by writing, "My health is quite good, and I am comfortably situated. Robert will write you in a few days and send my photograph. Love to Damon and the children from your Anty Morris."[9]

Apparently, Esther felt that being a McQuigg was exhausting work. Even though she had endured troubles with John, Esther's life must have seemed more peaceful when she lived across the country from most of her siblings.

In August 1878 Esther wrote to Frankie, "I know that I wrote you last, but I have heard that Libbie [Moore] now has a little daughter which was really more than I expected and we all expect to congratulate her on the occasion. There is nothing that changes a home like a baby. Your friends [California relatives] had everything else to make themselves comfortable. Charlie is married by this time, as he is a practical young man. Your mother [Eliza Jane] now that the rest are provided for will have enough so that poverty need not trouble her, and that was her greatest trouble. Still, she lives on as little as anyone I ever saw. As far as I know there now seems to be a general peace going through the family.

"We are still living in Albany and are very comfortable. We have a fresh flat on the first floor and hall parlor, dining room, kitchen, three bedrooms. Robert and I went to Saratoga, but we live in the biggest part of the city, so we are very comfortable at home, and I have been about so much that I am glad to stay there. Aunt Esther."[10]

Esther wrote to Frankie again in September. She explained, "I am pleased to learn that your father has not only fitted up his own house, but that he put yours in good order. I always think of Flint as a pleasant place even if all are not happy that are there."

Esther and Frankie had discussed Eliza Jane's general well-being and her lack of money, along with her new plans to do some mining in northern California. Esther added her thoughts about her own difficulties, stating, "While I have not one dollar that I can call my own, I am living as well and comfortable as I ever did in my life. Still at times I feel that I ought to be more useful, but so long as I cannot see my way to do anything different, I shall try and be positive and not stir up or irritate others. There are times we should lean as well as times we should stand."[11]

Robert also sent an update for Frankie in September 1878, giving their address as 203 Elm Street. He told his cousin, "Ed talks of coming to see us the next winter, but he disappointed us last year, so that we have not much faith he will come.

"We like to live in Albany very much, though the uncertainties

This is the only known photo of Sarah "Sallie" Slack, Archie Slack's wife. It was taken in front of their home on Carey Street in Cheyenne, probably with her daughter Hattie. *(Wyoming State Archives)*

of a political situation could not admit of our regarding it as a permanent home, I am at present under the direction of the State Comptroller in an examination of the financial condition of the charitable institutions of the state. I expect in a few days to accompany Mr. Algar with whom I am associated in this work, on a tour of inspection of the various institutions of this state, including asylums for the insane, blind, deaf and dumb, and the reformatories. The work is interesting and very agreeable to me."[12]

The political situation in Albany prevented Robert's continued employment, and he found a new position in Springfield, Illinois.

As she had in 1844, Esther once again moved from New York to Illinois.

As much as she loved New York and living in Albany, putting some distance between herself and her siblings gave Esther relief from the family squabbles. Strong personalities did not always result in harmonious relationships.

However, joyous news Esther received from Cheyenne told of the birth of a daughter, Harriett Louise Slack, to Archie and Sarah. The baby, who had been born on June 15, 1878, was called Hattie.[13]

CHAPTER SEVENTEEN

"Life Is Like a Dream"

ROBERT TRAVELED AHEAD to Springfield and quickly became acquainted with Frankie's longtime friend, Josephine Cleveland. Frankie and Josie probably met during the Civil War when they both worked for the United States Sanitary Commission providing aid to soldiers.[1]

Robert wrote to Frankie in October 1879, "Miss Cleveland [Josie] is in the office of Public Health on the same floor so that we can be quite neighborly. She received my introduction in a friendly manner and expresses the greatest regard and friendship for you and Damon.

"Miss Cleveland lost an adopted girl of 12 years several months ago. It seems to have been a great affliction to her, as the little girl had been with her since she was quite small. I am sure Mother and I will both find a very valuable friend in Josie Cleveland. She seems to be known by everybody and is always spoken of in the kindest way."

Robert wrote of Esther's intention to "leave Albany on Tuesday next" and travel to Flint to visit Frankie and her family. He had decided to rent a house so he and Esther could share a little home of their own. "We will take much more comfort and it will furnish employment for mother's surplus activity. Your affectionate cousin, Robert C. Morris. F. H. Wines, Secretary Public Charities, Springfield, Illinois."[2]

Robert found a house at 5523 South Fifth Street, six blocks from the old Illinois State Capitol building where he worked.

His descriptive letters to Frankie provide a deeper look into the domestic realities of Esther's life. His letters clearly show their interdependence. She was financially dependent on him, while providing the bachelor a comfortable home. It is possible that Robert remained single, in part because of his responsibility and her care.

The mention of "mother's surplus activity" suggests her intention to design hats again or that she had some other sewing projects. Perhaps, once again she could earn some money of her own.

Esther's visit to Frankie's family in Flint included not only Damon, but their five children: Hobart, age ten; Mabel, nine; Lucy, five; William three; and Bertha, just months old. Frankie's daughter Bertha later told her own daughter, "As children we dreaded Aunt Esther's visits because she was so bossy. Visits in those days lasted weeks or even months."[3]

Esther stayed in Flint for at least three months. She did not enjoy her stay, due in large part to discord between her brother E.H. and Frankie. They had different personalities and contrasting views of life. He was a skinflint and emotionally miserly, while Frankie was generous in all ways. On this visit, Esther might have created some of the tension herself because she likely shared her opinions with Frankie's entire household, including the five young children.

Contributing her thoughts in her February 1880 letter, Esther wrote to Frankie, "As I expected, I have been busy getting settled in our new home.

"I have thought of you so much since I was at your house and it always makes me feel so tired, just as it did when I was in California. I felt the same towards [Frankie's sister] Libbie. I do not feel there's any lack of affection in our family. It's a sense of injustice that makes me despise a lack of it and we may see it in each other and not recognize it in ourselves. It is quite possible the Hobart [side of the family] were miserly and the McQuigg [side] spend thrifts and each in turn despised the other."

Esther summarized, "I have been almost sorry I went to Flint, because I look back to it with only the saddest of feelings because all hope died out for any of my family. We shall all die as we lived.

Death will settle it with us and that can't be far off for any of us, and it won't amount to much."

She continued with a humorous warning to Frankie, "I told Miss [Josie] Cleveland not to grieve for her adopted child for if you kept on you would die from worry and she would get Damon with all his family and she would make a great stepmother. Much love to all, your Aunt Esther."[4]

Esther's letters often reveal that she held strong opinions and did not hesitate in sharing them. However, she also had a compassionate side, and she sometimes felt hurt by the actions and opinions of others. Although life experiences and societal restrictions held her back from achieving more, sometimes her own personality also stood in the way.

Julia Browne Bemis, Lib Browne Chatfield's sister, lost her last child. Julia's first child had died at six months of age, the second child at the age of five, and this, the last child, died in March at age six. Esther shared her grief with Frankie in April 1880, 'Poor Julia knows how hard it is to be so bereft. She loved her children so voraciously. She will suffer terribly. She will not be likely to have another and even if she does, she will have no confidence that she can keep it."[5]

Two days later Robert added his feelings regarding Julia, "My heart aches when I think that she is now deprived of all her jewels." Later in his letter he spoke of a visit from Archie's family. "We are expecting to see Archie's wife and little girl [Hattie] very soon. They leave Cheyenne sometime next week and Archie will come for them about the first of June. We have been looking forward to their visit with a great deal of pleasure since we came to Springfield. We are gradually finding ourselves more at home and I do not feel we shall ever have any reason to regret coming here."[6]

Esther's oldest brother Daniel passed away in Auburn, New York, at age seventy-eight. She shared, "I did feel a sense of relief when I heard of the death of brother Daniel. He was a good old man and did not wish to be a burden to anyone." She followed that with an update on failing relatives, reporting that an elderly aunt "is old enough to six foot it at any time."

She ended her letter to Frankie with, "We have had such a nice visit from Archie and Sarah. She came first and was here for a week. Archie came after her. I wish you could come to Springfield and get rid of the shadows of the past, still you may not feel as do I."[7]

Frankie's stepmother, Elizabeth "Libbie" Forman McQuigg died on June 28, 1880 at the age of seventy-eight. Esther wrote to Frankie soon afterward expressing her admiration of "Mrs. Mac" and encouraging Frankie to take care of her father and be patient with her sister Libbie in California.[8]

Now, Esther's brother E.H. faced life on his own. Esther referred to his changed domestic situation in an undated letter that was likely written between election day in 1880 and January 12, 1881. She wrote, "Frank, you stayed the nearest to your father and you understood him and his surroundings. You know how he has been petted and amused. He will now have to be pitied and amused, and if you do not give him your attention, I shall be sorry even if you have to give some of your responsibilities to others. Tell me of your mother. My heart always aches for her."

Ever interested in politics, Esther ended with her views on James A. Garfield's election on November 2, 1880: "I felt a load lifted off from me like we got by great. We have had a fill of the silent soldier [Rutherford B. Hayes] with his boon companion. I prefer a citizen to a soldier of the regular army, but neither of them can ruin the country while God and the people stay at the helm."[9]

That year the population of the United States had grown to 50,189,209 with thirty-eight states, plus eight organized and two unorganized territories.

In a November update to Frankie, Robert told of his thirty-day vacation. He spent two weeks in Cheyenne, then he and Archie spent two weeks in Colorado. The brothers visited Leadville, Pikes Peak, and "other noted points within a hundred miles of Denver." On his return to Illinois he traveled through the state visiting various state institutions with the State Board of Charities Chairman, Mr. Grimshaw.

"I fear that I shall have to give up all writing, at least for a time. My eyes have given me considerable trouble for more than a year, and I am assured by the best oculist in Chicago that they will not re-cover until I give them a rest. I am seriously thinking of going into a business of some kind." He stated his preference for a nice book and stationery store in Chicago. "I have about completed the family ge-nealogy of the McQuigg family, and I hope soon to send you a copy. Your father could no doubt add some material facts to it. Your affec-tionate cousin, Robert C. Morris. Have you read Howell's [William Dean Howell 1880] new novel: "The Undiscovered Country?"[10]

On January 12, 1881, Esther sent the following to Frankie: "I had a nice New Year's Day. Robert is looking to go to Chicago to reside. Suffrage is active in Springfield and [suffragist] Mrs. [Frances] Willard is here. I shall write the President of the State Alliance and will attend the convention. The legislature is in session and our town is quite lively. I think I'll visit Archie next summer."[11]

A whimsical snippet from Esther's letter to Frankie in February 1881, reads, "I need not tell you that I have found this place [Spring-field] very peaceful. I hope I may be permitted to glide down or up to the next world quietly, and as smoothly as I have lived." She ap-pears more upbeat about her life and writes she is busy with her sewing and perhaps adding to the household income and has had plenty of visitors.

"Life is so much like a dream. I can hardly think of many things that have occurred as real. I do feel that I have so much to be thankful for that I ought not complain about anybody or anything but do all the good I can. Robert will be there [in Flint] on the 4th of March and the President will be inaugurated and the papers will be full of it. The world moves on while wonders never cease." Pres-ident Garfield was inaugurated on the extremely snowy day of March 4, 1881.[12]

Robert found a business opportunity in Chicago in the office of W.T. Keener, dealer in American and foreign medical books and a writer of medical books and articles. His books were sold by sub-scription at 96 Washington Street, Chicago.[13]

He wrote of this success to Frankie in June, explaining, "I have found a situation in Chicago, with a view of entering into partnership on the first of September. Mother left for Dubuque [to visit her sister Eliza and brother-in-law Joshua Wyatt Parker and their family] and spent two weeks in Chicago. She thought Chicago had never appeared as bright and cheerful before. I do not expect her to return here until September as Archie is anxious that she should visit Wyoming during the summer and will send her a railroad pass to go and return. Your affectionate cousin, Robert C. Morris, Address Care of W. T. Keener, 96 Washington Street, Chicago, Ills. Lock Box 144."[14]

Esther had no need to worry about Frankie caring for her widowed father, E.H., for long. Just a little more than a year after Frankie's stepmother died, E.H. married again. He and his new wife, Adeline Cole, took a wedding trip to San Francisco.[15]

Esther and Robert moved into their rental on 388 Webster Avenue in Chicago, and Robert provided details in October. He told Frankie, "Mother returned about the fifth of the month [from visiting Archie in Wyoming] and we are now comfortably fixed for the winter in our own home. The house is more convenient and satisfactory in every way than any we have ever occupied. It's about 1½ miles from the Court House and business center. It is on the north side several blocks west of Lincoln Park and is where we have plenty of light and air. It is on the corner and there are no other houses within seventy-five feet of us. We will be glad to have you visit us at any time when you can make it convenient to come."[16]

Robert did not stay with W.T. Keener for long. In early 1882, in Chicago, he partnered with C.T. Wilkinson, although what type of business they engaged in is not known. Due to financial problems, they lost the business in less than a year. By November, the strain showed on both Esther and her son.

Robert told Frankie, "My business had caused me a great deal of anxiety. I am working with Mr. Wines again at the State of Illinois Board of Charities. You will be glad to know that my system of bookkeeping has found a success and is now generally adopted throughout the state.

Ed Morris married near South Pass City in 1881. Soon after, he and his new wife, Bertie, relocated to Green River in 1882. South Pass City was nearly abandoned by 1880, yet many of the buildings remained standing when this photograph was taken in 1927. *(Photograph by author's great aunt Ivadell A. Swindler, Author's Collection)*

"Mother says she would like to congratulate Damon and to tell him that it gave her as much pleasure to hear of his success as it did to have [Robert's twin brother] Ed elected county clerk in Wyoming on the same day. Archie is anxious that mother should come stay with him and if my affairs do not interfere, she will probably go there before long. I have no doubt she would be more contented there than in Chicago. Her health is very good, but she is inclined to worry considerably about my affairs. That does not help matters any; it certainly does no good. Always your affectionate cousin, Robert C. Morris, 307 West Monroe Street."[17]

In the years since John's death, Esther, Archie, and Robert had been estranged from Ed, apparently on his own in Wyoming Territory. The family received word of his marriage to Elizabeth [Bertie] Chambers at Miner's Delight, near South Pass City, on August 31, 1881. Following Ed's election as Clerk of Sweetwater County he and Bertie moved to Green River, the new county seat, in 1882. Ed now held the same position as Archie had fifteen years earlier when South Pass City was the county seat.[18]

What a relief it must have been for Esther to know Ed was out of the faded mining district. Although she continued to be concerned about Robert and the failure of his business, once again Esther retraced her steps. She left Illinois and moved back to Wyoming Territory, to Cheyenne to stay with Archie, Sarah, and granddaughter Hattie.

CHAPTER EIGHTEEN

"Ready to Maintain Prerogatives"

In Cheyenne, Esther spent several months with Archie, Sarah, and granddaughter Hattie in their new home on Carey Avenue.

Robert secured employment as the stenographer for the Territory and joined the family in Cheyenne. He purchased a house at 2114 Warren Avenue where Esther could join him and finally grow her dream garden. Because Esther's life centered on her family, she likely felt overjoyed to be living in the same territory with all three of her sons, even though Ed lived many miles away in Green River.

In July 1883, Archie's wife, Sarah, gave birth to a daughter they named Esther. Once again, they suffered the loss of a child, when the tiny infant died just a month and one day later.

Esther's arrival in town stirred up at least one detractor, possibly upset by Archie's newspaper editorials or the topic of woman suffrage in general. A letter to the editor in the *Cheyenne Weekly Leader,* a competitor to Archie's newspaper, was printed on September 20, 1883. In the letter, entitled "Woman Suffrage in Wyoming," the unidentified author shared the opinion that women did not make good jurors:

> As to holding office, I believe there have been but two women honored with that trust, Mrs. M.A. Arnold was superintendent of public instruction, which she filled with signal ability; Mrs. Esther Morris, mother of our townsman, Mr. E.A. Slack, was police justice. I believe it is not contempt of court to say that the best energies of Judge Morris' mind, together with all the machinery of her court, were expended in efforts at maintaining family discipline,

On her return to Cheyenne, Esther first spent several months at the new home of her son Archie and family, located at 19th and Carey. (*Wyoming State Archives*)

and to so great a degree was the judex [*sic*] sunk in the mater familias [*sic*] that that court left no 'modern instances' as guides to the courts of this day.

Mrs. Morris, a well-preserved old lady, is now living in this city. . . .

I think it but just that our next court should see present as jurors the best minds and character to be found among the ladies of our county. They should fulfill the duties [as jurors] or give up the privileges of suffrage.[1]

Esther settled into her new city and her new home. As usual, though, Robert provided the details of daily life to Frankie. In December 1883 he shared recent events with Frankie beginning with his arrival in the spring as the official stenographer of the territory. He wrote, "At present I am reading law, which I trust may be of some advantage to me. In the words of Dickens' Mrs. Gamp, 'Much good may it do you, for harm it can't.'"

Esther's bungalow at 2114 Warren in Cheyenne, shown in a 2016 photograph, provided a place of her own for the flower gardens she'd always wanted. *(Author's Collection)*

"Cheyenne is in many respects a very pleasant place to live in and I think it can be truthfully said to be the most enterprising and wealthy city of its size, 6,000, in the United States. Society is very gay here and I go out more than I have for years.

"He continues with a report on Esther, "Mother's health is very good, and she is cheerful and contented. Just now she is busy crocheting tidies out of macramé cord. But she reads a great deal, and only the other day finished "Ben Hur" [*Ben-Hur: A Tale of the Christ* by Lew Wallace, 1880], the novel you recommended to me. It is a very interesting book.

"Several railroads will be built the coming season, and a large influx of capital immigration is expected. I attend six courts at the various county seats throughout the territory, so that I am only here about half of the time.

"My position as private secretary to the governor [William Hale] is not one of much profit, but has some advantages. The territorial stenographer's office is worth a little over twenty-five hundred dollars a year and is out of politics."[2]

In May 1884, Robert wrote a follow-up, "Archie expects to go to the Republican Cultural Convention which occurs at Chicago on the third of June. At present Mrs. Slack is visiting her relatives at Springfield, Ill, and will return with Archie sometime in June.

"Mother is in excellent health and at present is absorbed in getting her garden started. I expect to start for Green River, 300 miles west of here in two hours. I go up to spend Sunday with Ed. Everything is booming here at present, and we are all quite prosperous."

Esther, at seventy-one, still spry and with undimmed spirit, found her gardening doubly rewarding as she shared her bounty with others. Archie later wrote, "People stopped by to admire her oasis and left with the flowers she shared to brighten their own homes."[3]

While Esther enjoyed her home and garden, Archie's forceful and energetic editorial style elevated him to his place as a leading newspaperman in Wyoming. His longtime friend and competitor, W.E. Chaplin, later said of Archie: "When aroused to action he never hesitated to call things by their proper names. Any subject seemed to grow in his mind from day to day until his competitor was overwhelmed. In financial matters he was generous, caring little for money except for the use he could put it to in carrying on his business and supporting his family. He was a philosopher and his advice to others was always the very best. He was a practical printer and, on many occasions did a great deal of his own mechanical work."[4]

While Archie wielded press power in the decisions made in the territorial capital, Cheyenne, and Robert traveled throughout the territory as its stenographer, Ed made a name for himself in the town of Green River, located on the Union Pacific with a population of 327 in 1880.

In July 1884, Robert brought Frankie up-to-date on his recent travels. He wrote, "In my recent journey, I travelled six hundred miles by stage, and have to travel about three times that number of miles by stage during the year and five thousand miles by rail.

Esther's son Archie, known as E.A. Slack in his professional life, became a leading newspaperman in Wyoming. (*Wyoming State Archives*)

I attend court twice a year at six county seats which compels me to move about considerably. Our little city [Cheyenne] is making much progress this season, and the outlook is most encouraging. Mother is in good health and often converses about you."[5]

Larson's *History of Wyoming* presents a different view of life in the territory. The Wyoming cattle boom and other resources did not bring as large a rise in population as was expected. After pointing to larger population growth in the states and territories around Wyoming, Larson summed up the problem this way: "It was indubitably a hard life in Wyoming—'Hell on women and horses' and death on cattle. Governor John W. Hoyt asserted in his 1878 report that 'Wyoming scenery is a subject for poet and painter' and wrote about the 'indescribable charms of a frontier life under sunny skies and in the midst of sublime surroundings,' but these charms were not edible."[6]

Even so, during the 1880s, Cheyenne grew from a rough-and-tumble town into a cultured city. Local historian William Robert Dubois III, Archie's great-grandson, recalled the numerous developments of those years in a recent article written as part of the city's 150th anniversary celebration. Among others he listed: "The first telephone exchange in Cheyenne was established in 1881. The new opera house seated one thousand people and was graced with an appearance by Lily Langtry who was driven around town in an elegant Tally-ho drawn by six matching white horses. The Cheyenne Club, organized in the early 1880s, gained international fame with membership consisting of the cattle barons who spent summers in Cheyenne and winters in Europe. The club was sumptuously furnished in the manner of an English club. Rules were very strict—no profanity, no cheating at cards, no smoking of pipes and no games on Sunday."[7]

In 1884, Robert used his brother's business letterhead, "*Daily and Weekly Sun* with E.A. Slack, Proprietor," when he wrote a letter to Frankie reporting the death of Levi Starr Chatfield, the seventy-six-year-old husband of Lib Browne Chatfield. In the biography of Anna Dickinson, J. Matthew Gallman reports, "For several years she [Anna] had stayed with Betty [Lib] Chatfield, but although she remained close to Betty, Dickinson eventually tired of Mr. Chatfield's drinking."[8]

Robert continued, "Mother is preparing to visit Ed and his wife for a few weeks and will go to Green River next week. I spend about six months in Cheyenne. The remaining part of the year is divided between five county seats, each of which I visit twice a year.

"I think of going to New Orleans sometime next winter to attend the Exhibition [1884 World's Fair]. Archie will probably go.

"I sent you a fair picture of Archie's home. His little girl's name is Hattie, a family name on Mrs. Slack's side of the house."[9]

Archie's family grew. Sarah gave birth to another daughter, Dora Frances Slack, on August 15, 1885.

The women connected to Esther's family were strong leaders and early women's rights role models. Susan Emily Hall, the sister of Eliza Jane Hall, was named a "Woman of Distinction" by the New York State Senate in 2012 for her work as a Civil War nurse. (*Cliff Hall Collection*)

By 1887, Esther and her McQuigg siblings were embroiled in a dispute over E.H.'s handling of the money left by their brother Charles back in 1838. E.H. made various promises over the years to his siblings, which were not fulfilled. Frankie obviously solicited advice or sympathy from Robert, who showed little sensitivity in his dismissive reply.

Robert's April 1887 letter stated: "The matter about which you write is something in which I have never taken any interest, other than it has always been a source of deep sadness to me that there should have existed a sense of wrong between Mother and any of her family. However, I have not taken sides in the matter and do not propose to at this time. In the absence of that affectionate regard which ought to exist between brothers and sisters, it was not strange your father did not care to leave any legacy to his sisters or brothers' children, especially as he did not recognize any legal or moral value to their claims. The qualities of a martyr are one of the chief glories of woman, and it is perhaps as natural for her to bear the trouble and disappointments of life as it is up to man to overcome them."[10]

Even though he and Frankie corresponded for another twenty years, there is no evidence she brought up the subject again.

After experiencing forty years of rancor, Frankie's parents, Eliza Jane Hall and E.H. McQuigg, died within five months of each other. Eliza Jane died at age seventy in March 1887. E.H. died in August 1887 at age eighty.

Robert wrote to his cousin, expressing his sympathy at her mother's death, without acknowledging nor apparently understanding Frankie's lifetime of pain from her mother's desertion and her lifelong struggle in her relationship with her father.

He wrote, "Cousins Julia Browne Bemis and Jean Browne spent several weeks with us on their return from California last summer. Cheyenne is now a city of about 10,000 and is quite attractive in many ways. Just now everything is prosperous, and we look forward to having a thriving city. Railroads are coming from several directions and the prospects are that the territory will enjoy great prosperity for some years to come."

He updated Frankie on his brothers' successes, "Ed is living at Green River, where he has been County Clerk for four years, but for several years has been engaged in general merchandise. He is also cashier at the bank there and postmaster. The firm Hunter & Morris do the largest business there and have a very bright future. Ed has a good wife but has not been blest with any children.

"Archie has been doing remarkably well for several years and is now employing between thirty-five to forty men in his printing establishment. He has two little girls who are a great comfort to us all. I continue to be the bachelor of the family with no immediate prospect of having my condition changed, although I am trying to better my condition all the time and hope to surprise my friends someday."[11]

When Esther's brother E.H. died, on August 24, 1887, Frankie was left in charge of his affairs. She wrote to Esther for advice. Esther in turn wrote, "It seems he changed his will as it is dated 1886 and left [all siblings] out of his last will. You have nothing to do with it as it is not legal. But as a family affair, it may be a bone of contention in the next generation.

"There are two distinct types in our family. Our grandfather Hobart was stingy to meanness and McQuigg grandfather practical so there has ever been a feud in the family. Had your father divided up a few thousand and scattered it as he said he would, it would have been more just and would have been thought liberal by those that did not know it was a trust. But he has passed away and the work to be done remains for us to finish."

She wrote at length about the division of the estate and the distribution of the earlier inheritance which E.H. had agreed to distribute among his siblings. He had apparently never given an accounting of that money and now Frankie was left to deal with crushed expectations and hard feeling.

Esther closed by sharing details of family news and then concluded her letter in an upbeat mood about her garden, her health, and her immediate family.

This photograph of Esther is undated but is traditionally thought to have been taken near the date that Wyoming became a state in July 1890. (*Wyoming State Archives*)

CHAPTER NINETEEN

"EMBLEM OF OUR LIBERTIES"

IN APRIL 1888, Esther wrote what proved to be her last letter to Frankie. She discussed family matters from fifty years past and provided information on the deaths of two family members.

Esther apparently felt guilt at not having kept a better eye on family concerns. She explained, "My husband [Artemas] sickened and died [in 1843]. I was obliged to go west and was too full of trouble to think much about others for at least two years.

"But after thirty years I have lived in Illinois, Wyoming, had been to California, sometimes to Brother Daniel's in Auburn, New York. I was poor and had to fall back on my children for support and could do nothing for others."

Esther continued with matters closer to home in Wyoming, "My children know but little about it [the family quarrels] as they are into other associations and while my health is good, I do not expect to live always. I think every letter will be the last letter I write. I do not need glasses but of course, do not see very well. I am out of doors most of the time in summer. We had a very pleasant winter and today is delightful."

When Lib Browne Chatfield's husband died she moved back to Owego, where she and her sister Julia then shared a home. Lib continued her long relationship with Susan B. Anthony and kept Esther informed on suffrage. Esther penned, "We shall hear from Owego and Libbie [Browne Chatfield]. Most likely she will pass by Flint never to be content in Owego.

She concluded, "We have all been well within a few weeks. Archie's little girl had the scarlet fever but is getting well. Archie will go to the [Republican] Convention in Chicago, so we move on. Ed is doing well in Green River. He and his wife made us a visit this winter. So, on the whole I have nothing to complain of. This ever your affectionate, Aunt Esther Morris." She included a P.S. "If God does not give us money, may he give us wisdom."[1]

By this time, Archie had made quite a name for himself as a newspaper editor, but the job carried hazards.

Historian Larson wrote, "Editors sometimes wrote scurrilous attacks on one another and the public. The courts could not be depended upon to give redress and were rarely appealed to by persons who were libeled."

Sometimes, the disagreements resulted not only in snide comments, but also escalated to violence. Larson recounted the 1889 fight that former territorial governor George W. Baxter started with Archie. Baxter hit Archie with a cane. Archie struck back and began choking him, but others separated the men.

"Slack was six foot one and weighed 230 pounds in the 1870's, and apparently did not lose any weight thereafter. He was known by his editorial contemporaries as 'The Cheyenne Avoirdupois,' 'adipose Archie,' and 'the obese and oily Col. Slack.' In his footnote Larson added, "Slack became the most influential editor in territory and state. . . ."[2]

W. E. Chaplin, who worked with Archie for more than thirty years in various ways, described him years later in a recollection for the *Annals of Wyoming*:

> I had an excellent opportunity to learn his true character. He was a man of indomitable energy, tremendous will power, and high personal character. To his help he was kind, sympathetic and agreeable, or exacting, domineering and exasperating, as the man or mood moved him. He was a philosopher.[3]

On the home front, Archie was as passionate regarding his family as he was with public issues. He always behaved in a caring fashion to his mother, wife Sarah, and daughters Hattie and Dora.

It was later written of him, "As a husband and father, Colonel Slack may be cited as a model. His devotion to his family, and his love of home, have long been recognized and commented upon."[4]

In 1889, the issue of Wyoming statehood provoked Archie's passion. Discussion of possible statehood had begun as early as 1868 and had heated up in October 1869 when the first territorial legislature met. Now, throughout the territory, and particularly in Cheyenne, the issue came to the forefront. Newspapers frequently carried reports of the discussions about the topic. But, Wyoming's road to statehood proved to be a rocky one.

The Constitution of the United States allowed Congress to set criteria for statehood. One of the guidelines set by Congress was a population of 60,000.[5]

Joseph M. Carey had been serving in the U. S. House of Representatives as "Territorial Delegate" from Wyoming Territory's at-large district since 1885. He sent a request to the United States Congress requesting statehood. Congress did not act on Carey's 1888 request. Despite that, Territorial Governor Francis E. Warren proceeded as if Congress had already passed the bill, and he set the date for election of delegates to the state convention in Cheyenne for July 8, 1889.[6]

Historian Phil Roberts pointed out, "Though women had full voting rights and opportunities to seek and hold office, not one woman ran for a delegate slot. The future state which had prided itself for being the first government to grant women equal political rights was to have a state constitution drafted, debated, and passed entirely by men."[7]

As Esther had said nearly twenty years earlier in her letter to Isabella Beecher Hooker, apparently women needed to be "educated up to" their new rights.

The statehood issue was argued in the legislature by lawmakers, on the streets by the general public, and in the newspapers by editors and others. Larson wrote that two newspaper editors took opposite positions. "John F. Carroll of the *Cheyenne Leader* was a member of the Democratic platform committee, and Edward A. Slack of the

Cheyenne Sun served on the Republican platform committee. The *Leader* wanted delay for as much as five years; the *Sun* advocated immediate statehood."[8]

The battle lines were drawn, and the arguments began. Lewis J. Palmer, Sarah Slack's beloved nephew from Springfield, Illinois, was the only convention delegate who flatly stated opposition to woman suffrage. He was outvoted, and female suffrage was included in the Wyoming State Constitution.

At the conclusion of the convention, voters in the special election held on November 5, 1889, approved the Wyoming State Constitution by an overwhelming majority. On March 26, 1890, Territorial Representative Joseph M. Carey introduced a Wyoming statehood bill in the United States House of Representatives. The bill for Wyoming statehood passed in the House on March 26 and in the Senate three months later—on June 27. On July 10, 1890, President Benjamin Harrison signed the bill, which made Wyoming the forty-fourth state.[9]

In Cheyenne, Archie continued coverage of the entire process in the *Cheyenne Daily Sun.* Beginning with the Constitutional Convention, through arguments in the United States Congress, to the achievement of Wyoming statehood, he printed enthusiastic daily headlines and updates.

On July 10, 1890, in a small front-page item, the newspaper reported that the president had referred the bill to the attorney general for legal review. On July 11, 1890, the *Sun* front page stated, "The new star has arisen," explaining that the bill had become law the day before and carried Joseph M. Carey's pronouncement of victory: "Proclaim to the people that Wyoming is a member of the indestructible union of American states. To them extend hearty congratulations. The president signed the bill at 5:30, Washington time."[10]

Just a couple of weeks shy of age seventy-eight, Esther likely felt the proud realization of her family's contributions to Wyoming statehood. The people of the territory had celebrated each step of the process, with the newspapers carrying information about each

Theresa A. Jenkins was the first speaker at the official Wyoming Statehood celebration on July 23, 1890. She was praised by newspapers as the most eloquent and forceful speaker of the day. (*Wyoming State Archives*)

event between March and July 1890; however, the grand "official" festivities to recognize the passage of the bill took place in Cheyenne on Wednesday, July 23, 1890.

Archie's *Cheyenne Daily Sun*, in a special illustrated edition that cost ten cents, reported:

> The statehood celebration yesterday was a magnificent success. . . .The day was bright with sunshine, tempered with a light breeze and softened by the shadows of occasional clouds. At an early hour people began decorating their dwellings as well as mercantile houses, offices, and banks in the business portion of the city.[11]

Mrs. Theresa Jenkins was chosen to speak on behalf of the women, although Esther and Amalia Post, who in 1870 in Cheyenne became one of the first women to serve on a jury in the United States, would also take part in the day's activities. Historian T.A. Larson later reported:

> Mrs. Theresa Jenkins offered the first speech, a review of the struggle for woman suffrage. The *Cheyenne Leader* avowed the next day that her address was the most forceful and eloquent of the day, although it conceded at one point she was carried away by a 'fairest and rarest flight of oratory.'
>
> Fifty years later, Mrs. Jenkins' daughter recalled for the *Wyoming State Tribune* that her mother had been heard by everyone in the audience, which extended to a point four blocks away, because she had practiced on the open prairie with her husband riding off in a buggy to greater and greater distances and shouting back, at intervals, 'Louder.'[12]

The *Cheyenne Daily Sun* quoted Jenkins's speech, including this section that honored Esther and Amalia Post:

> Esther Morris, like Queen Esther of old, has dared to brave the anger of man rather than her own people should perish.
>
> We ask no trophies at our feet, no laurel on our brows, but we do ask for these two, Mrs. Morris and Mrs. Post, a wreath of immortelles fashioned in the motto of 'Faithfulness,' and hung on the walls of 'Endurance."[13]

Following Jenkins, Esther gave a 44-star silk flag that the women of the state had purchased to Territorial Governor Francis E. Warren. Archie's newspaper reported this as, "The great incident of the celebration, the presentation of the flag." He expounded:

> In the days of the past there came to this region a woman who had been reared among the hardy minds of the east. She brought with her, her family, her garden seeds, her doctrine of woman's equality before the law. Her sons live to do her honor, her garden seeds have been planted and

Amalia Post joined Esther Morris in representing women at the official Statehood Celebration. (*Wyoming State Archives*)

she has proven to the world that this desolate plain can be made to blossom as the rose, and to-day she sits with us at the age of 77 a free citizen equal with her sons.

Mrs. Esther Morris, one of Wyoming's historical characters, who is regarded as the 'mother' of the woman suffrage movement in this state, and who is otherwise honored and respected for her great ability and heroic womanhood, was by general consent accorded the post of honor, and made the presentation to Governor Warren on behalf of the women of Wyoming.

Her "oration" was quite brief. Archie shared:

Gathering the folds of the beautiful flag around her, she said: "On behalf of the women of Wyoming, and in

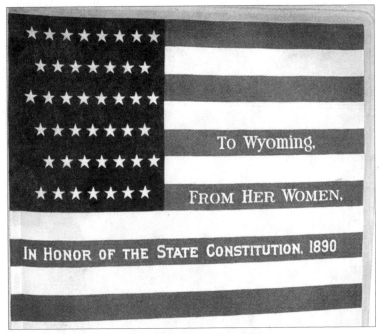

Esther presented this 44-star flag to Territorial Governor Francis E. Warren from the "women of Wyoming" during the official Statehood Celebration. (*Wyoming State Museum*)

> grateful recognition of the high privilege of citizenship which has been conferred upon us, I have the honor to present to the state of Wyoming this beautiful flag. May it always remain the emblem of our liberties, and 'the flag of the Union forever.'"[14]

The words used by Archie in this newspaper article set the groundwork for the mythic title, "Mother of Woman Suffrage," which defined Esther and the history of Wyoming for the next eighty years.

CHAPTER TWENTY

"MORE CANDID THAN DIPLOMATIC"

I N THE YEARS following the impressive statehood celebration, Esther continued her interest in politics, especially the suffrage issue. She watched as her sons each became successful.

Archie increased his notoriety and political power with his editorials, and Robert continued his important work as the territorial stenographer. But Ed, though successful in Green River, like his father struggled with rheumatism, a term the family apparently used to refer to drunkenness

Ed and W.P. Hunter had formed the Hunter Morris General Merchandise in 1887. He was "doing well," as Esther informed Frankie in a letter and was making more money than Archie or Robert. Ed built a house at 6 West Second North Street where he and Bertie made their home, and later, as Robert became more involved in the businesses, he acquired the house next door where he lived part-time. In 1888, Ed and Hunter formed the Hunter Morris National Bank of Green River.[1]

Ed, who had served as the Sweetwater County Clerk, also became involved in the organization of the Green River city government. At the first election of city officials on July 15, 1891, Green River elected Ed to serve as its mayor. He assumed the office on August 3, 1891, was re-elected in 1892 and for a third term in 1897.[2]

Robert, in his working travels around the state, visited Green River many times, and the former close relationship between Esther's twins rebounded.

In 1891, Robert joined Ed in the general store. They purchased the business from Hunter and built the Morris Mercantile Building.

The Morris Mercantile Building in Green River housed the merchandise store, their bank, and the post office. (*Wyoming State Archives*)

Recalling their father's retail experience during their childhood, and incorporating Robert's experiences in New York and Chicago, the brothers chose a good business for the growing town. Robert's attention to detail and Ed's natural sales ability became a successful combination.

The brothers placed a large ad in the *Green River Advertiser* on August 28, 1891, displaying a beautiful drawing of the new brick building and touting their products.

The two-story Morris Mercantile building housed the store, the Morris Bank, and the Green River Post Office. The first elevator in Green River carried people to the offices on the second floor.[3]

By 1891, Robert worked part of the year in Washington, D.C., for United States Senator Joseph M. Carey. Senator Carey chaired the Committee on Education and Labor in the Fifty-second Congress, and Robert served as committee clerk.

He wrote a brief note to Frankie on May 4, 1892, wherein he expressed concern about Ed's illness: "This is the second year that I have spent in Washington, D.C. as the clerk of one of our Senators.

I find it very pleasant to spend a part of the year here and have contact with the most agreeable people.

"I have just returned from Wyoming where I left our folks unusually well. Archie and his wife leave for California May 15th and expect to attend a convention in San Francisco, then spend several weeks traveling about the state. When I'm not here I devote my time to the courts and relieving Ed in the store at Green River. Last summer Ed came very near dying from acute rheumatism and had to go away for several months and still has occasional binges of it and has talked of spending several weeks at Mt. Clemens, Michigan. [Mt. Clemens was famous for its mineral baths.] My health has been never better."[4]

A few months later, Robert used the letterhead, "The Morris Mercantile Company, Green River Wyoming," on September 18, 1892, and explained to Frankie that Ed had sought relief from his condition by traveling to the spa. "Ed left here a few days ago and has arrived in Mt. Clemens. His rheumatism has troubled him more or less since his [illegible word] severe illness a year ago, and we are in hopes he will benefit by this trip. He will stay there a month, and as it is only a little way from Flint, I urged him to go over and see you. I am looking after the mercantile establishment during Ed's absence and have my hands full and will return to Washington in December.

"Archie had a delightful visit to the Pacific Coast but did not visit Southern California. They went to Portland and as far as British Columbia, returning by the way of San Francisco.

"Mother is quite well at present, though she has to harbor her strength more than several years ago. Last month I took her to Salt Lake, where we spent a couple of weeks very pleasantly. She often goes to Denver which is only 100 miles south of Cheyenne. I presume you realize it is a city of 150,000 and much larger than Detroit was twenty years ago.

"It is probable that I will be able to visit you sometime next summer. Of course, we are all going to the [1893 Chicago] World's Fair."[5]

After leaving Mt. Clemens Ed visited Frankie. On his return

Ed Morris developed a successful business life in Green River and was involved in politics there. (*Sweetwater County Museum*)

home, he wrote a letter on May 25, 1893, on "Morris Mercantile Company" letterhead. He explained, "My trip to Michigan was of great benefit to me as far as my health was concerned and it was a great pleasure to me to meet yourself and family.

"I am going down to Cheyenne to see my mother tomorrow. I have not seen her since last fall. Robert writes me that she is not as strong as she was. As Aunt Charlotte and Uncle Parker [Esther's sister Charlotte Susan and Esther's sister Eliza's husband Joshua Wyatt Parker] have both died this winter, I think it has its effect upon mother. These things affect elderly people and they worry as they think their time is getting short in the world. Remember me kindly to Damon and the children. Your cousin, Ed Morris."[6]

A couple of years later, in 1895, Archie acquired the *Cheyenne Daily Leader* and consolidated his newspapers under that name. A later biography of Archie in *Progressive Men of the State of Wyoming* states that the newspaper was said to be "one of the ablest edited and most influential newspapers in the far west. We can only say in conclusion, that which we have already said before, that Col. Edward A. Slack is one of the powers behind the throne."[7]

Esther, ever interested in suffrage and public affairs, was still involved, now at age eighty-two. Robert wrote on "Executive Office, Cheyenne Wyoming" letterhead in June 1895 to share exciting news with Frankie: "Mother has been selected as a delegate to the National Convention of the Republican Leagues which convenes at Cleveland, Ohio on June 19th. We felt somewhat reluctant to have her make this long journey, but she seems so anxious to go, and at the same time see some of her old friends in Illinois, that we have not overruled her wishes in the matter. She will be accompanied by Mr. and Mrs. Burke, neighbors of ours who will take care of her until her return about June 22nd. If your daughters should happen to be in Chicago, she would be delighted to see them. She will be at the Great Northern Hotel opposite the Chicago Post Office."[8]

On June 17, 1895, the *Chicago Tribune* featured Esther in a long article headlined, "Pioneer of Woman's Suffrage in Wyoming." The article contained some information known only to the family, pointing to the likelihood that Archie was the main author. It stated, in part: "Any history of the [suffrage] movement would be incomplete without a brief sketch of Mrs. Esther Morris, who is justly regarded as the mother of woman suffrage in Wyoming, having inaugurated the movement there, and was the first woman who ever administered the office of justice of the peace. To her also belongs the honor of enlisting in the cause the co-operation of Colonel William H. Bright, a Democrat, and president of the first Legislative Council of Wyoming."

Archie used the title of Mother of Woman Suffrage for Esther in 1890 in his newspaper, but this statement was the first time

Esther was given credit in national print for woman suffrage in Wyoming. Thus, Archie created the root of the long-lived myth.

The article continued, "In the long conflict with slavery she was an early earnest worker. An incident during her young womanhood illustrates in a striking manner the moral courage which is a part of her character. An abolitionist meeting was held in the Baptist Church of her native village, and so incensed were the proslavery element of the community that a prominent citizen declared that if the ladies would leave the church they would tear it down. Esther who was not twenty years of age, stood up in her pew and addressing the meeting said, 'This church belongs to the Baptist people, and no one has the right to destroy it. If it is proposed to burn it down, I will stay here and see who does it.'"

However, although she did attend church there, no other written record exists of this particular event. The article left many gaps and inconsistencies in the story of Esther's life. As Esther said, she did not share much about her siblings' issues and early life with her sons.

The article continued to sing her praises with ornate prose, also pointing to Archie as the author, stating: "Few women in any period have been endowed with greater gifts than Esther Morris. Her originality, wit and rare powers of conversation would have given her a conspicuous position in any society. But the charm of her personality lies in her cheerful disposition under all conditions. It is as natural for her to look on the bright side of things as it is for a flower to turn to the sun that gives it warmth and life, a faith in the eternal goodness of god, that makes her old age one of joy and cheerfulness. Those in trouble have always found in her a kind friend and counselor."

The *Chicago Tribune* article ended with the statement: "Her declining years may be said to have fallen in pleasant places, for she has that of which the poet sings is most desirable in old age— honor, love, obedience and troops of friends."[9]

Back in Cheyenne, Robert was involved in the formation of the Wyoming State Historical Society. In 1897, he served as secretary of the group and was a member of the board of trustees.

One of the lasting legacies of Esther and her three sons is Frontier Days, the annual week-long rodeo and celebration of the West held in Cheyenne. Many stories circulated through the years about the origin of the annual celebration. One was printed in the *Cheyenne Daily Sun-Leader* by Archie in August 1897. The article states the origin was a letter from Frederick W. Angier, a traveling passenger agent for the Union Pacific. Angier envisioned a celebration to be held in Cheyenne, thus creating the concept of a Frontier Day.[10]

As reported in his *Cheyenne Daily Sun-Leader,* at the organizational meeting on August 30, 1897, Archie outlined the benefits of an annual Frontier Day to promote Cheyenne. He stated, "Thus, Denver has the Plain and Festival Day, Greeley has an annual potato day and other towns have peach and melon days. The celebration proposed for 'Frontier Day' is unusual and novel in every aspect. It will be something before unheard of and will be worth travelling many miles to see." After Archie's exuberant presentation, Cheyenne's mayor, William R. Schnigter, appointed a committee of local businessmen to obtain funds and organize the event.

Warren Richardson chaired the committee, and he later called Archie "the father of Frontier Days, the man who originated the idea, who developed the sentiment that resulted in its complete success."

Through September, daily updates in Archie's *Cheyenne Daily Sun-Leader* kept enthusiasm high. On September 23, Archie published the "Frontier Day" edition, commemorating the first such event, with sections on cowboys, pioneers, Indians, and naming the numerous contributors who had helped fund the festivities.[11]

The Frontier Day celebration was an example of the growth and changes since Esther's arrival in the rugged Wyoming Territory twenty-eight years earlier. Many Indians were on reservations, and the buffalo were all but gone. Eastern Shoshone Chief Washakie, who recognized the inevitability of westward expansion and helped smooth the path, died February 20, 1900. Two days later, his funeral, conducted by the Rev. John Roberts, included full United States military honors. A U.S. military installation on Wind River Reservation was renamed Fort Washakie in his honor. The Wind River

::FRONTIER::DAY::EDITION::
The Cheyenne Daily Sun-Leader.
XXX.--NO 299   CHEYENNE, WYOMING THURSDAY EVENING; SEPTEMBER 23, 1897.   PRICE FIVE

The *Cheyenne Daily Sun-Leader* and the Morris family were avid promoters of Frontier Days from the beginning. (*WyomingNewspapers.com*)

Reservation today is home to over 3,900 Eastern Shoshone and 8.600 Northern Arapahoe enrolled tribal members. The reservation contains about 2,268,000 acres of land.[12]

Esther witnessed the changes and growth in the East and the West throughout the settlement of the vast continent. During her lifetime, the United States had gone from a new country with more than seven million people and to an industrialized world power of more than seventy-six million by 1900. Population in New York City was 3.4 million, Los Angeles was 102,479, and Cheyenne had grown to more than 14,000.

On August 8, 1900, Esther celebrated her eighty-eighth birthday. Later that year, the first major modern automobile show at Madison Square Garden was held in New York City and the Hershey bar was produced for sale in Pennsylvania.

In December 1900, Robert wrote to Frankie from Washington D.C., reporting on Esther's inexhaustible spirit. First he spoke of his brothers: "Ed returns [from the hot springs] very much benefitted in health and I am in hopes he will have no further serious trouble with the rheumatism. His general health was never better. He enjoyed his visit with you tremendously. Our business at Green River is very good just now and the outlook encouraging. My greatest anxiety has been Ed's health. He seemed very glad to get himself squared away and writes cheerful letters.

"Archie talks of coming down to Washington with his wife sometime this winter. They are getting to be great travelers, having visited California and Illinois last summer."

Then his thoughts turned to politics, "Congress adjourns next

Thursday, and I expect to spend a week in New York. It is always pleasant to be there at Christmas time.

"Mother votes the Republican ticket [she likely voted for President William McKinley in 1900]. Ed is somewhat changeable. He was loyal to his friends. I voted for [Democrat] William Jennings Bryan. Of course, I was terribly beaten, but trust I have sufficient philosophy to take defeat gracefully."[13]

Robert corresponded again with Frankie in March 1901: "Mother has passed a comfortable winter without doing much around the house. She is quite active, however, and frequently walks two or three miles in a day. She reads but is growing deaf. Mr. and Mrs. Slack are very well, and their daughter [Hattie who had married Wallace Bond in 1899] seems very happy in her new home. The land office in Cheyenne, with Archie in charge, is prospering under the McKinley Administration. Ed has all he can do looking after the business at Green River and is in excellent health. Fortunately, he has been relieved from rheumatism since his stay at Mt. Clemens.

"Just now I'm quite taken up with architects for the new library building. We have $50,000 for it. [Robert was involved in raising money for the Carnegie Library in Cheyenne.]

"Mother continues to be in good health and is quite active, but she is quite old and requires much rest and comfort. She has an excellent housekeeper, keeping up her home, though she hates giving it up on her own."[14]

In her lifetime Esther witnessed life and death, war, and the settlement of a vast country. She argued for change in the status of blacks and women. Her coast-to-coast travels provided perspective that most women of her time never had.

Esther outlived her ten siblings. Mindwell McQuigg died in 1836; Charles in 1838; George in 1850; John in 1854; Jane McQuigg Archibald in 1856; Daniel in 1880; Jesse in 1884; E.H. in 1887; Charlotte McQuigg Browne in 1893; and Eliza McQuigg Parker in 1901.

Esther experienced the end of her own adventurous life when she passed away at ten o'clock on the night of April 2, 1902, with

Robert, Archie, Sarah, and their girls by her side. Edward and Bertie were in Denver, but left immediately when they received word of her death. They arrived in Cheyenne in time for her funeral.[15]

Esther's lengthy death notice appeared, along with her favorite poem, Addison's "I Will Fear No Evil,"—quoted in its entirety— in the *Cheyenne Daily Leader* the day after her death and on April 24 in the *Owego Gazette*. Archie, who most likely wrote the piece, filled the obituary with flowery prose and called her "a born reformer, a true descendent of her liberty loving ancestors who came across the ocean to gain their religious freedom" and stated that she liked to see the "bright side of life, and she seemed to thoroughly enjoy the newness of things." He referred to her straightforward manner, writing. ". . . she never flattered people to put them in good humor. Her remedy was different. It might be caustic instead of an anodyne. A few pertinent suggestions for removal of the cause, accompanied by some keen, witty, comment, carried the remedy home to the complainant or sufferer."

He continued, explaining that his mother was ". . .a true pioneer, in the domain of thought, as well as in material things. She welcomed innovation and anyone with a new idea was well received at her home." And he remarked that she was ". . .one who was always frank, in fact, at times more candid than diplomatic. Perhaps the most marked trait of character in the deceased was her fearless independence. It did not always make her friends, but in the end, she won the respect of those who could not agree with her opinion."[16]

CHAPTER TWENTY-ONE

"NEEDING A HEROINE"

Esther became a heroine almost by accident. Her legend was largely built by others.

Historian Larson reports, "The first public suggestion that Mrs. Morris had any other claim to fame than that of having been first woman justice of the peace occurred in 1889 when M.C. Brown [a friend of Esther and family], while discussing woman suffrage in the constitutional convention, declared that Mrs. Morris had presented a bill and asked favorable action of the legislature. No one previously had said that she had presented a bill, and there is no evidence to support Brown's statement."[1]

Myth-building about Esther continued with Archie's statement in his *Cheyenne Daily Sun* comment on July 24, 1890: "Mrs. Esther Morris, one of Wyoming's historical Characters, who is regarded as the 'mother' of the woman suffrage movement in this state. . . ."[2]

The story went nationwide in the 1895 article in the *Chicago Tribune*, likely written by Archie, which referred to her as the "mother of woman suffrage in Wyoming."

Archie loved words, and he loved his mother and he definitely wrote her obituary. In her 1902 "In Memoriam" (*see Appendix C*), he further engraved the myth for posterity, writing, "Her mission in life has been fulfilled. The work she did for the elevation of womankind will be told in years to come when its purpose will be better understood."[3]

Following Esther's death, the subject faded for a few years until another myth-builder, Wyoming historian Grace Raymond Hebard, became enamored with the story and enhanced it. In an October

1913 three column newspaper article on Wyoming giving women the vote, she wrote, "The guarantee of civic equality between the sexes was incorporated in the Wyoming statute book, December 10, 1869. It owed its existence to Colonel William H. Bright and Mrs. Esther Morris, who thus became respectively the father and the mother of equal suffrage. Later in the article she stated, "These two minds acting upon each other were the flint and the steel that lighted the torch of real democracy."[4]

By the time Hebard published her 1913 conclusions, ten states and one territory had granted suffrage for women. Wyoming, Utah, Idaho, Colorado, Washington, California, Arizona, Kansas, Oregon, Illinois, and the Territory of Alaska moved the issue forward by allowing women to vote, sit on juries, hold public office, and, as Esther said, become citizens. The citizens of the West proved once again how strongly they cherished freedom.

Esther had known William Bright and his wife Julia for only a short time in South Pass City in 1870. However, they did have a large impact on Esther's life. Bright created and proposed the 1869 Wyoming suffrage bill, which gave Esther and the other women in the territory the right to vote and to hold public office including that of justice of the peace. Passage of the bill allowed them to help design the world they occupied.

By June 1871, William and Julia Bright had left South Pass City for Denver in the Colorado Territory. A few years later in 1877 while living in Denver, Bright enthusiastically supported an unsuccessful attempt to pass a woman suffrage law in Colorado. Colorado eventually passed suffrage legislation in 1893.[5]

According to U.S. Census records, the Brights lived in Leadville in 1880. They appear again in 1885, but this time in Pitkin County, Colorado. Their mining days behind them, the Brights returned to Washington, D.C. The 1900 census records show William Bright worked as an elevator conditioner. Later, in the 1910 census, he is shown at age eighty-three working as an electrician. William died on April 29, 1912, and Julia on November 20, 1915. Both are buried in the Congressional Cemetery in Washington D.C.[6]

Julia Bright, who, in her own way, fought for woman suffrage by influencing her husband about the suffrage bill, probably voted once in 1870 in South Pass City. After they left Wyoming, she never again lived in a place where she was allowed to vote.

⚬

The mythology about Esther gained strength as suffrage once again became a topic of national interest after World War I. At this time, the uproar on both sides escalated. Demonstrations for and against the issue expanded throughout the country with progress in favor of the idea slowly moving forward. Heroes and heroines often provide spark for such movements. Because Esther was deceased and had received publicity during her life, she was, in a sense, available for the role, and conclusions could be drawn largely without interference.

Herman G. Nickerson, who ran against William H. Bright for the position of representative to the first Wyoming Legislature in 1869, came to the public's attention again just months prior to the congressional vote approving the Nineteenth Amendment that finally granted woman suffrage in the entire United States. In February 1919, Nickerson sent the following letter to the editor, headlined "Historical Correction," which was published in the *Wyoming State Journal* in Lander. The letter states:

> To Mrs. Esther Morris is due the credit and honor of advocating and originating woman's suffrage in the United States. At the first election held at South Pass on the 2d day of September 1869, Col. Wm. H. Bright, democrat and myself republican, were candidates for the first territorial legislature. A few days before election Mrs. Morris gave a tea party at her residence at which there were about forty ladies and gentlemen present. Col. Bright and myself being invited, for a purpose, for while sitting at the table Mrs. Morris arose and stated the object of the meeting. She said: "There are present two opposing candidates for the first legislature of our new territory, one of which is sure to be elected and we desire here and now to receive from them a public pledge that whichever one is elected will introduce and work for the passage of

an act conferring upon the women of our new territory the right of suffrage."

Of course, we both pledged ourselves as requested and received the applause of all present. There were no Republicans elected at the first election, the legislature was solidly democratic. Colonel Bright, true to his promise introduced the bill and it became law, passed in a jocular manner as an experiment, as Col. Bright informed me on his return home.[7]

Prior to Nickerson's letter of 1919 no one had ever mentioned this "tea party" or a meeting at Esther Morris's residence before the 1869 election. Even Hebard's 1913 article giving both Esther and Bright the credit for the Wyoming suffrage vote did not mention a tea party. Historian Larson points out Nickerson had written a letter in 1914 in which he said the Democrats had adopted woman suffrage in 1869 because they believed it would aid their party. "In that letter he did not mention Esther Morris."[8]

Soon after the August 18, 1920, ratification of the Nineteenth Amendment, Grace Raymond Hebard followed up on Nickerson's tea party story in her article "How Suffrage Came to Wyoming," printed in the Wyoming State Historian's report in 1920 and reprinted as a pamphlet. Hebard's article contained a variety of accounts in the overstated language of the times, such as:

. . . the Bright family in their small log cabin had many friends, no one more choice and intimate than Mrs. Esther Hobart Morris, who with her husband and three sons had also come to the great undeveloped West.

The article continued with Hebard paraphrasing a letter received "a few years ago" from Julia Bright at her "widowed home in the east" telling about their relationship with Esther prior to the 1869 Legislature. Hebard wrote:

In this remote mining camp of South Pass City, hundreds of miles removed from a railroad, surrounded by the crafty red man, the highway robber, and the howling wolves and crying coyotes, these two congenial families discoursed and discussed the limited rights of women in civil affairs,

> Mrs. Morris usually being the brilliant leader of the con-
> versation. The inspiration derived from these fireplace con-
> ferences with the master mind of Mrs. Morris gave Mr.
> Bright the final courage to carry into action his convic-
> tions born of after-war [Civil War] observations.

An interesting story, but unverifiable. A letter in the Hebard file at the University of Wyoming shows Hebard wrote to Mrs. Bright asking for details on the suffrage incidents in October 15, 1919, but it was returned unopened to Hebard because Mrs. Bright had passed away on November 18, 1915. There is no letter from Mrs. Bright to Hebard before her death in the file, and none has been found elsewhere.

Further in the article, Hebard correctly quotes part of Robert Morris's letter to *The Revolution* in 1869 which clearly showed Esther and Robert had never met William Bright before their visit to his home. Hebard also wrote, "I asked Mr. Morris if he had ever heard his mother make any statement that had influenced Mr. Bright to work for suffrage, Mr. Morris made this exact statement, 'Oh yes, indeed my mother used to talk about it, and I remember plainly when Mr. Bright came to our house he said to my mother that he was going to introduce the Woman Suffrage bill for her.'"

Finally, Hebard quoted a good portion of H.G. Nickerson's 1919 newspaper article about the tea party word for word. [9]

Conveniently Hebard's article in the State Historian's report was published after Julia Bright was dead and Robert Morris was incapacitated. Robert Morris suffered a paralytic stroke in 1915 and died a few months after Hebard's article in January 1921 in a private nursing home in Cheyenne. The Esther myth was confirmed once again in Robert's 1921 obituary in the *Cheyenne State Leader*.

The newspaper called him "the son of Mrs. Esther Morris, the 'mother' of woman's suffrage in Wyoming." [10]

Furthermore, with all Robert and Esther's news-filled letters written to Frankie throughout the years, a collegial friendship with Julia Bright was only mentioned once, after the 1869 vote, and William Bright was not mentioned at all. Had such a "tea party" or lobbying meeting taken place, it is inconceivable that neither she nor Robert wrote about it in their letters to Frankie nor did they write that Bright intended to "introduce the bill for her."

In 1921, H.G. Nickerson carved a monument to honor Esther, which he and Grace Raymond Hebard erected in the dying town of South Pass City. A few families like the Sherlocks, close friends of the Morris family, remained in South Pass City well into the twentieth century. But the town where Esther had lived was essentially a ghost town. Nickerson's inscription read, "Site of office and home of Esther Morris. First woman justice of peace. Author of female suffrage in Wyoming." The myth was now literally cut in stone.

Suffragist Carrie Chapman Catt also wrote of Esther's tea party in *Scribner's* magazine in 1923, stating, "At this point twenty of the most influential men in the community, including all the candidates of both parties, were invited to dinner at the shack of Mrs. Esther Morris. In her ears were still ringing the words of Susan B. Anthony, one of whose lectures she had heard just before setting out upon her western journey." She explained that each man gave Esther his solemn pledge to support the effort.[11]

Esther Morris became an official heroine—the symbol of woman suffrage in Wyoming—and as such she benefitted the suffrage movement and eventually all women in the United States and possibly the world. Heroes and heroines are historically well-loved in American society, and Esther Morris was no exception.

The myth endured. For a couple of generations, students in Wyoming learned this romantic story of her efforts, and Esther and her tea party grew in importance. Unfortunately, books about Esther and her fictitious tea party are still being written.

In 1939, the Wyoming Historical Landmark Commission organized a well-publicized tour to recognize its appreciation of Wyoming's outstanding pioneers. They dedicated six monuments in Wyoming in the space of five days. On July 2, 1939, the caravan departed from Cheyenne, led by Commission Chairman Warren Richardson, accompanied by some twenty others, including Governor Nels Smith.

HOME & OFFICE SITE OF
ESTHER HOBART MORRIS
FIRST WOMAN JUSTICE
OF THE PEACE
IN THE WORLD
FEB. 14, 1870

AUTHOR WITH W. H. BRIGHT
OF THE FIRST
EQUAL SUFFRAGE LAW
DEC. 10, 1869

A stone memorial was placed at the site of Esther's home and office in South Pass City in 1939 and strengthened the myth that Esther had helped author the Wyoming Woman Suffrage bill. (*Author's Collection*)

The Owen Wister Monument at Medicine Bow was the first stop, followed by the Joy Monument on the Lincoln Highway (now Interstate 80) at the Continental Divide between Rawlins and Wamsutter. After spending the night in Rock Springs, the caravan headed to Star Valley for a celebration of the Lander Cut-Off Monument on July 3. On July 4, the group began with the dedication of the Snake River Canyon Road Monument, then they traveled to Jackson to dedicate the John Colter Monument in the city park. The illustrious group traveled to Fort Washakie on the Wind River Reservation on July 5 to dedicate the graves of Sacajawea and Chief Washakie. Ninety-year-old Dick Washakie laid a wreath at his father's grave.

The final stop on the unprecedented trek was South Pass City on July 6 with a tour of the ghost town and a dedication of the

Esther Morris Monument held at noon. Following remarks by some old-timers who may have known Esther, her great-grandson, William Robert Dubois Jr. of Cheyenne placed a wreath at the base of the monument. The group then returned to Lander to enjoy a picnic lunch and entertainment in Pioneer Park.[12]

This public dedication strengthened Esther's legacy, but momentum to make her one of the most revered women in Wyoming and one of the leaders of United States suffrage was still gaining speed.

On November 13, 1953, Senator Lester C. Hunt wrote to Frank Bowron of Casper, president of the Wyoming State Historical Society. Hunt was impressed by the Statuary Hall in the U.S. Capitol in Washington, D.C., and the recent dedication of the Marcus Whitman statue that commemorated the Oregon Trail pioneer who first crossed South Pass in 1835 on his way west. The state of Washington had chosen Whitman for the honor. Forty-two of the forty-eight states had representative statues honoring their distinguished citizens, Hunt explained, but Colorado, Montana, Nevada, New Mexico, North Dakota, and Wyoming had none. Hunt wrote in part:

> . . . since Wyoming Territory was the first organized unit of government in the world to give the right of suffrage to women, and since Wyoming gave to the nation the first woman Governor, a statue from this state should honor women. I do think of Esther Morris, the first woman Justice of the Peace in the United States, and the lady who requested at a tea party at her home that Colonel Bright, the Democratic candidate for the first territorial legislature, and Captain Nickerson, the Republican candidate for the territorial legislature in 1869, introduce a bill giving these rights to women.
>
> I will, of course, take no part in the deliberations on the selection of the person to be honored.

Hunt's letter sparked interest in the project and the official Esther Morris Memorial Commission was created by Governor Milward Simpson in 1955. The Wyoming State Historical Society queried citizens, asking for the names of "interested parties throughout the state who should be memorialized." Esther Morris "was by far the most popular, with Jim Bridger coming in a weak second."[13]

The official Esther Morris statue was created by Avard Fairbanks, the Utah artist who had sculpted the Marcus Whitman statue. On April 6, 1960, it was unveiled in the United States Capitol in the Rotunda, as Statuary Hall was already full. Former Wyoming Governor Nellie Tayloe Ross, the first woman governor in the United States and the first woman director of the United States Mint, gave the dedication address. Ross referred to Esther's famous "dinner party." But she also said, "I do not glean from what I read of Esther Morris that she was an unpleasantly aggressive, high-powered, demanding sort of woman. On the contrary, she seems to have been very clever and tactful in adopting methods by which to achieve an objective." Ross also called Esther, "a lady in the best sense of the word," and concluded, "It is plain though that she had iron in her blood aplenty." All three of Wyoming's congressmen, Senator Joseph C. O'Mahoney, Senator Gale W. McGee, and Representative Keith Thomson attended.

Thomson said, "Esther Morris' tea party might well be as honored in American history as the Boston Tea Party. The Boston Tea Party set off a chain of events which freed the colonies from England. Esther Morris' tea party set off a chain of events which freed American women from the status of inferior citizenship."

Vice President Richard Nixon and House Speaker Sam Rayburn received the statue on behalf of the United States.[14]

The nation now recognized Esther's fame.

On Dec. 8, 1963, a bronze replica of the statue was placed in front of the Wyoming State Capitol. Esther was officially a heroine, albeit accidental.

Appropriate to 1960 social norms, Esther's outstanding statue was a depiction of attractive womanhood, but some thought it did not display the stern determination and strength of character that appear in photographs of her.

South Pass City was added to the National Register of Historic Places on February 26, 1970. Today it is operated as a Wyoming State Historic Site.

Esther Hobart Morris and Chief Washakie, who lived in the same area and the same era, represent Wyoming in Statuary Hall in Washington, D.C. Both are minorities there among the many white men. (*Author's Collection*)

In addition to the statues, Esther was honored by coins and other memorabilia, and in 1976 was recognized by the U.S. Postal Service with a bicentennial first day of issue cover.

Meanwhile, in the 1950s myth-buster historian Dr. T.A. Larson launched his decades-long campaign to topple Esther from the pedestal where she had been placed as the "Mother of Woman Suffrage."

He thoroughly researched the documents, then used old-fashioned logic and concluded the tea party story was false. Larson's research included statements made by Esther's old friend, Judge John Kingman. In *History of Woman Suffrage,* printed in 1888, Kingman wrote at length on the process of the Wyoming suffrage law and its aftermath. He said that William H. Bright "whose character was not above reproach, had an excellent, well-informed wife." She was strongly in favor of suffrage and he often deferred to her. Kingman gave Bright full credit for the bill, with some assistance from urgings for passage from others.[15]

As early as 1954, Larson, head of the History Department at the University of Wyoming, mounted a newspaper campaign reporting in the *Laramie Boomerang*, "My study indicates that the men in the 1869 legislature, for reasons of their own, handed the women the right to vote on a platter with virtually no agitation on their part."[16]

Although the public was reluctant to let Esther's myth go, Larson continued his campaign by teaching classes at the University of Wyoming, and giving speeches and lectures, and writing more newspaper articles. Progress was slow, he said in a 1997 interview with the author, but finally nearly two generations after he began his crusade, general acceptance of the facts won out.

In his *History of Wyoming*, Larson summed up his research and conclusions. "Hubert Howe Bancroft [an early day historian] sent agents into Wyoming who interviewed more than one hundred leading citizens in 1885," Larson wrote. "With the aid of these interviews and other material gathered from various sources, Bancroft in 1890 published 148 pages of Wyoming history. He did not mention Esther Morris."

Larson expounded further, regarding the need suffragists had for heroines. "With good reason," he explained, "they resented the fact that women had been neglected in history books." Then he continued, "Needing a heroine for Wyoming, they turned to Esther Morris. She was the inevitable choice for glorification because hers was the best public record ('first woman judge') of any woman in Wyoming before Esther [Estelle] Reel was elected state superintendent of public instruction in 1894." Yet Esther Morris's judicial work was not enough. It was essential that she be identified as the one who had brought woman suffrage to Wyoming, had made Wyoming "the first true republic," the first state with woman suffrage. She looked the part – "heroic in size, masculine in mind," as Grace Raymond Hebard said.[17]

Replica statues of Esther Morris and Chief Washakie were installed outside the Wyoming State Capitol until the 2019 restoration when they were moved inside out of the weather. *(Starley Talbott Thompson photograph)*

Larson attributed to William H. Bright and other legislators who supported woman suffrage in 1869 and 1871, and to Governor John A. Campbell, and Edward M. Lee, "major credit" for the Wyoming suffrage bill. "Moreover," he explained, "many men and women in the East had set the stage, without which there would have been no woman's rights drama in Wyoming in 1869."

Larson also credits Esther Morris and a long list of others with contributions to the cause. Included in the list are Julia Bright; Amalia Post; Almeria Paine who was the wife of Seth Paine whom Esther had known in Illinois and South Pass City; M.B. Arnold's wife Melvina Arnold; Judge J.W. Kingman; Anna Dickinson; Redelia Bates; and James Hayford.[18]

Other historians followed Larson. Michael A. Massie, in his excellent analysis of events, "Reform Is Where You Find It: Roots of Woman Suffrage in Wyoming," wrote: "If one continues to believe that forty supporters of woman suffrage squeezed into the Morris house or that Esther moved the tea party outside, then explaining how Esther could command enough respect to generate such enthusiasm for a controversial issue in an unstable, tumultuous gold mining town is difficult, especially since she had moved to South Pass City less than three [four] months before the September election. The town's leaders, many of whom had resided in the town for more than a year, would find difficulty in locating forty citizens during the peak of the mining season to endorse any issue not related to mining, Indians, or anti-Republican sentiment."[19]

Historian Dr. Phil Roberts, quoted in a book by Wyoming historian Mike Mackey, added emphasis with this humorous yet true statement: "You couldn't fit forty people in what has been designated as the Morris home if you greased them up before trying to shove them through the door, much less hold a tea party there."[20]

As Mark Twain is credited with saying, "Never let the truth get in the way of a good story." Unfortunately, the tea party fable is still in circulation, even though the truth is a much more compelling story.

In 2000, Wyoming presented another statue to the United States. In the U.S. Capitol in Washington D.C., the Esther Morris statue was joined by one of Eastern Shoshone Chief Washakie. The statue of Washakie stands in Emancipation Hall.

Replicas of the statues of Esther Hobart Morris and Chief Washakie stood on either side of the entrance to the Wyoming State Capitol as sentinel representatives of the history of the Equality State for many years. In 2019, during a massive restoration and updating of the Capitol building, the statues were moved inside to protect them from the elements. They will eventually be placed in the Student Learning and Visitor's Center.

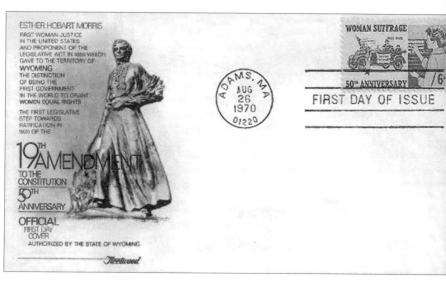

On the Fiftieth Anniversary of the Nineteenth Amendment, Fleetwood issued a first day cover featuring Esther Hobart Morris. The envelope and postmark saluted woman suffrage. *(Author's Collection)*

"Far in Advance of What We Were"

Esther Morris lived a purposeful life. She was the sterling representation of a woman who though "not educated up to it" rose each morning taking on enormous responsibilities. She was never a long-term financial provider for herself and children because that possibility had been denied to her. Through her daily life and interactions with others she exemplified the values she inspired in her sons: the pursuit of education and cultural training, as well as aspiring to work well-done. With her unfailing encouragement, Esther's boys undertook three very different paths and succeeded.

This woman was outspoken on behalf of those issues she believed in strongly. Her support of the anti-slavery movement, suffrage, and equal rights for women never waned.

Looking back from a distance, one of the unintended consequences of Esther's life was fame. She never sought acclaim but found it thrust upon her. While she did not plan to openly campaign for suffrage, the choices she made in the face of adversity brought her to the belief that women were as intelligent and capable as men and should be allowed to profit from employment, to act as full citizens, to create laws, and even to govern a nation.

T.A. Larson, in a truthful oversimplification, summed up Esther's life by saying, "Esther represented lots of unhappy women at that time with no education and no rights."[1]

Some have said that the driving factor of history is the daily life of ordinary people. While living her ordinary life in an extraordinary way, Esther propelled herself into the history books by seizing an unusual opportunity in an unusual place at the right time. With the world watching, she fulfilled her position as South Pass City's justice of the peace with dignity and competence. Her judicial work proved women capable of holding public office, while she demonstrated thoughtful intelligence in her decision-making.

She made significant contributions to suffrage and the promotion of Wyoming. Even though much of her fame was not of her doing, it could not have happened without her.

Esther Morris not only assisted the suffrage movement, but she was also the first woman to hold judicial office in the nation. Esther became the most famous female office holder prior to the passage of the Nineteenth Amendment.

Born in 1812, Esther was the oldest of the women in her family, and the only one of her generation to cast a ballot. She voted before any of the younger women in the family, but only because she lived in Wyoming. She had voted in many state elections before her death in 1902. If she was present in Wyoming during national elections, she may have voted for eight presidents.

The long battle for woman suffrage in the United States gained a strong foothold on June 4, 1919, when the United States Senate voted to pass the Nineteenth Amendment. Ratification of the amendment by the states finally came on August 18, 1920, giving most women the responsibility and privilege to vote in all elections. The Senate's approval of the amendment, which had originally been introduced in the U.S. Congress in 1878, came fifty years after Governor John A. Campbell signed the historic Wyoming suffrage bill.

In October 1919, Isabella W. Campbell, the widow of Governor John Campbell, wrote from Washington, D.C. to the women of Wyoming:

> The spirit of justice to women and their intelligence influenced Governor Campbell to sign the bill. It was that exactly and nothing more. I am glad to say this to the women of Wyoming in their heyday of victory for the cause, a result which to me clearly vindicates Governor Campbell's action in the matter. So, I clasp hands with

you across the distance which separates us, and, joined
by my daughter, thank you for the opportunity which has
been given me for greetings and good wishes.[2]

On November 2, 1920, most women across the United States
were eligible to vote for the first time. Voting created the opportunity
for women to think for themselves, act on their decision, and take
responsibility. The mark on the ballot provides a voice, and history
has proved that women can make a difference in the larger issues of
the day.

The timeline for woman suffrage was dependent upon citizenship, race, ethnicity, literacy, state of residency, and other barriers.
Since some groups were not allowed to become citizens, the women
(and men) in those groups could not vote. Finally, the passage of
the Federal Voting Rights Act of 1965 removed most of the road-
blocks, with the exception of those for criminal records, mental in-
competence, and other statewide exemptions.[3]

<hr/>

For more than half of the twentieth century, South Pass City was a
ghost town. In 1966, the Wyoming Seventy-fifth Anniversary Commission purchased the town as a birthday present for the citizens of
Wyoming. South Pass City was added to the National Register of
Historic Places on February 26, 1970, and is currently a state historic
site, administered by the Wyoming State Parks and Cultural Resources Department.

Historian Todd Guenther, a former curator for the South Pass
City site, explained the wealth of historic information discovered
there more recently. He said, "During the archaeological dig and
reconstruction of 1993, there were around fifteen-hundred features
uncovered including homes, businesses, and restaurants."[4]

A visit to the present-day South Pass City is an entertaining and
educational entrance into a bygone era. The historic site can provide
additional educational opportunities with a telling of the full story
of Esther Morris, including the myth. South Pass City's place in
suffrage can be expanded with the story from the mining days
through the period when the myth grew to the present, explaining

Esther Morris's true contributions to the history of Wyoming and national suffrage.

—◦—

In their series "Overlooked," about people whose contributions have not been acknowledged, The *New York Times* gave Esther long overdue credit on April 18, 2018. While the article contained many of the same erroneous facts that are often repeated of her birth and life, the piece also credited her as the nation's first female judge.

Despite the factual events of her life and the appropriation of the myth that surrounded her as a symbol to promote suffrage, Esther Morris does not yet have a place in the Women's Rights National Historic Park in Seneca Falls, New York. As another link in the chain from Abigail Adams to the 1920 Suffrage Amendment, Esther Morris deserves official recognition alongside the other women.

The complete and accurate story allows Esther Morris to be placed in her appropriate position in history.

The Rest of the Story

O N July 25, 1902, Esther's sons—Archie, Robert, and Ed—
moved the remains of their father, John, from South Pass City
to Cheyenne City Cemetery, now Lakeview Cemetery. John had
died on September 27, 1877. The *Cheyenne Daily Leader* carried a
brief notice, including the headline, "Beside Loving Wife."[1]

━━◆━━

E.A. "Archie" Slack (Archibald Artemas)

Archie was active in Republican politics most of his adult life. As
such, President McKinley appointed him as receiver of the United
States Land Office in 1898 and reappointed him in 1902. Diagnosed
with kidney disease, Archie retired from the newspaper business in
1904, devoting time to his family and health. Archie's son-in-law
Wallace C. Bond and Capt. Harry A. Clarke took over daily opera-
tions of the *Daily Leader*.

Robert reported to Frankie on January 12, 1906:

> Archie's health was seriously affected about six months ago
> and the doctors pronounced him afflicted with Bright's
> disease a very serious malady. His health has much im-
> proved since then, but kidney troubles are treacherous,
> and it may be only a temporary relief. I have grave fears
> of his recovery, but he may live for several years longer.[2]

Archie succumbed on March 23, 1907, at the age of sixty-
four. His funeral was held on March 26, 1907, at the Cheyenne
Masonic Temple, with the Knights Templar, the Masons, the Elks,
and the Grand Army of the Republic conducting the services. He

was buried in the family plot in Lakeview Cemetery. W.E. Chaplin, Archie's long-time friend and newspaper competitor, wrote Archie's obituary, which was published in Archie's newspaper, the *Cheyenne Daily Leader*.

Chaplin wrote, in part:

> Colonel Slack was one of the strong men of Wyoming. For three decades he was a power in the state, and his trenchant editorials were observed in every corner of the state. He was ever prominent in public affairs and his influence in the making of the history of Cheyenne and of Wyoming will never be forgotten. He was always at the fore in the promotion of matters of public improvement and enterprise. To him, in part Cheyenne is indebted for its splendid municipal water and sewer systems, for the successful Railway Employees Building and Loan Association, for the Frontier Days celebration, and for many other things that are monuments to his public spirit and energy.

Of Archie's journalism career and other matters, Chaplin wrote:

> In the broader field of public affairs, it may be said that scarcely a measure can be named which has been originated for the benefit of Wyoming and carried to successful consummation within the last quarter of a century, where he was not among the first and foremost, and sometimes the only leader in the fight. His paper was the first to advocate statehood for Wyoming. He took the lead in the organization of the State Editorial Association [now the Wyoming Press Association]; he was instrumental in the establishment of adequate Wyoming exhibits at all national expositions [St. Louis and Chicago] . . . He was prominent in Grand Army circles and was at one-time commander of J.F. Reynolds Post.
>
> Several years ago, Colonel Slack purchased the lots on Capitol Avenue running from the Inter Ocean Hotel to Seventeenth street, and erected a number of small stores and office buildings, as well as the fine building which became the home of the Cheyenne Leader, and which he had built according to his own plans, specially adapted for a newspaper plant.[3]

Money was never the focus of Archie's life or work, but his later efforts left an ample estate for Sarah and the family. His will, dated June 13, 1905, left their home and all its contents to Sarah, along with a legacy of $1,200 per year. His esteemed sons-in-law, William R. Dubois and Wallace C. Bond, were executors of his estate. Archie requested, upon Sarah's death, any residue of the estate be divided between daughters Hattie and Dora.

The death of E.A. "Archie" Slack created a void both in the community, the state, and, of course, in his family. His obituary again thrust Esther into history as "the mother of woman suffrage in Wyoming."

Edward "Ed" John Morris

Fifty-year-old Ed Morris passed away on September 7, 1902, in Green River. Ed's obituary appeared in the weekly *Rock Springs Miner*, and stated, "These words strike all, especially old timers, very forcibly. For some time he had been ill and the worst was expected, but when the end came, it brought a shock with it. Rock Springs mourns with Green River over the great loss Sweetwater county, in fact the entire state, has sustained."

On September 8, 1902, private services were held at his residence in Green River. Ed had been a Mason and, at the time of his death, was the Grand Treasurer of the Grand Commandery of the Knights Templar. That organization conducted his public funeral, which was held in Cheyenne on September 9, 1902.

A Democrat, Ed had in later years been more "identified with the Republican Party." The obituary states that in 1889 Ed "was elected and served as a member of the constitutional convention prior to the admission of Wyoming to statehood."

Ed served as the first mayor of Green River, keeping that position for three terms. He was president and manager of the mercantile and cashier of the Morris State Bank. He had been trustee and treasurer of the Green River school district for a number of years. He was also a longtime Elks member and first recorder of Sweetwater Lodge No. 2, Ancient Order of United Workmen.

The newspaper explained, "In every capacity, he was honest, faithful and fearless," and later stated, "As a man of generous impulses, Ed will ever be remembered, for in his saddest hour he had a joke for his friends. Buoyant and hopeful, he always looked beyond the present, encouraging others to higher things. His heart beat for humanity. . . . The state loses one of its most valuable, progressive and worthy citizens. . . ."[4]

Robert Charles Morris

With the family's lifelong devotion to reading, it was natural for Robert to write the proposal to the Carnegie Foundation for a donation to build a Carnegie Library in Cheyenne.

According to a 1902 article published in *Library Journal*, he requested ". . . an up-to-date library building with separate apartments for the comfort of all persons who visit there; reading rooms for adults as well as for children; room for periodicals and newspapers; quiet places for reading, as well as a place for holding meetings. Unfortunately, some persons seem to think that any old place is good enough for a library; that all that is needed . . . are a few cheap pine shelves for books, a rickety old table, and a half dozen or more wooden chairs."[5]

Andrew Carnegie provided a $50,000 grant, along with a yearly maintenance fund of not less than $3,000. Robert served as secretary of the building committee. The Laramie County commissioners levied an annual one-half mill property tax for library maintenance; citizens offered public subscriptions for the building site and the Laramie County Auxiliary Association raised funds for library equipment. The library, completed in 1902, held 50,000 books.

A total of 2,509 Carnegie libraries were built in the United States between 1883 and 1929. Sixteen were built in Wyoming. Cheyenne was the first in the state to receive a grant in December 1899. Robert also helped raise the money for four others, including the beautiful Carnegie Library in Green River.

Robert suffered a paralytic stroke in 1915. He then lived in a private hospital for six years until his death, at age sixty-nine. He died on January 21, 1921. The early edition of the *Cheyenne State Leader* first carried a notice that Robert, "Son of Mother of Woman's Suffrage," was comatose and "approaching death." The newspaper also commented on his career, explaining:

> For many years Mr. Morris was official reporter for the Wyoming state supreme court and it has been said he was the most expert reporter the state ever had, certainly excelled by none. From court reporting he went to Green River to participate actively in the general mercantile business conducted by his brother, Edward Morris. Mr. Morris took over the business after his brother's death.[6]

The later edition of the same day reported his death and noted his work in helping to obtain Cheyenne's Carnegie Library. Once again he was referred to as the son of Esther Morris, calling her "the 'mother' of woman's suffrage in Wyoming."[7]

Robert's remains joined those of Esther, John, Ed, and Archie at Lakeview Cemetery.

Sarah Frances Neely Slack

Sarah died six weeks after her brother-in-law Robert. Both Robert Morris and Sarah Slack for several years were cared for at a private hospital for two patients at 2020 Carey Avenue, previously Ferguson Avenue. Census records indicate a head nurse and six additional nurses probably worked rotating shifts to care for them, along with two servants. Sarah passed away on March 2, 1921. The *Cheyenne State Leader* carried her obituary the following day, stating in part, "A long and useful life of a beloved woman comes to an end. . . ."

She had been unable to walk for many years prior to her death, according to the report, which also told of her wedding to Archie at the governor's mansion in Springfield, Illinois, and referred to their time in South Pass City, Laramie, and Cheyenne."[8]

Archie and Sarah's daughter, Hattie Slack Bond, wrote a short biography of her mother's life. She wrote, in part:

> . . . The last six years of my mother's life were a time of pain and helplessness, but her fine mind was never clouded. Her bible and the beautiful poetry with which

her mind was stored were her consolations, and she kept
her interest in people and events until the last. . . .

In her final tribute to Sarah, Hattie also wrote:

> . . . My mother was a quiet, reserved woman and one had
> to know her intimately to appreciate the sense of humor
> which was one of her most endearing qualities.
>
> She was devoted to her church and her family and
> while her retiring disposition prevented her from taking
> an active part in politics, she was keenly interested in civic
> affairs and regarded casting her ballot as a serious duty.[9]

Esther, along with both husbands and all her children and their
spouses, were gone. All but Artemas Slack are buried in Cheyenne.

Frances "Frankie" McQuigg Stewart

Esther's family corresponded with Frankie for more than fifty years.
Frankie passed away on February 6, 1918, at age seventy-seven.
Frankie's husband, Damon, had passed away in 1905. Frankie lived
to see her beloved first-born child, Hobart, die at forty-six near his
home in Clio, Michigan, from injuries incurred when he was struck
by an electric trolley car. She predeceased her remaining five children.

Frankie was praised in her obituary for lifelong social conscious-
ness stating: "She had been active in the social and religious life of
Flint for the past sixty-two years. In spite of her advanced years she
devoted four and five hours each day to Red Cross work for several
months, and through extensive reading, kept herself well informed
on world events. She was a member of the First Congregational
church and the Woman's Relief Corps."[10]

As was true for so many of the strong women in Esther's life,
Frankie—with a lifelong interest in suffrage and public affairs—
never had the privilege to vote.

Eliza Jane Hall and Her Family

Esther's ever independent sister-in-law, friend, and mother of con-
fidant Frankie—who fought for suffrage her entire life, never had
the privilege of voting. She passed away on March 22, 1887, and is
buried at Angelus Rosedale Cemetery in Los Angeles, California.

Frankie's sister **Mary Elizabeth Hall Moore** [Libbie] died on January 14, 1915 in Los Angeles, age seventy-two. Her two children, Florence Gardiner Moore and William Hanson Moore, survived her.

Charles Victor Hall, the third child of Eliza Jane, made millions in oil and real estate in the early days of Los Angeles. He married Josephine Dalton. Their two children, Frank Dalton Hall and Rowena May Hall, outlived them. Charles and Josephine divorced, and he was remarried to Maria Suetans. He died at age seventy-nine on July 21, 1933.

Susan Emily Hall, sister of Eliza Jane and aunt of Frankie, who served for the duration of the Civil War as a nurse, died in 1912, just four days before her eighty-sixth birthday, in Pasadena, California. Despite Hall's acclaimed service to her country, she died before passage of the Nineteenth Amendment, which would have allowed her to vote.

Hall was honored by the state of New York on March 21, 2012, one hundred years following her death, as part of the celebration of Women's History Month. The New York State Senate unveiled its annual tribute to "Women of Distinction" from New York State's history, and Susan E. Hall joined New York honorees, including Susan B. Anthony, Sojourner Truth, Eleanor Roosevelt, and astronaut Eileen M. Collins.[11]

The Browne Family

Charlotte Elizabeth "Lib" Browne Chatfield died on April 29, 1917, at seventy-three. Despite a lifetime working for suffrage, Lib was never entitled to vote.

Lib was in touch with Susan B. Anthony throughout life, including during Anthony's stay at Libbie's home in Owego in 1894. In a letter written to Lib Browne Chatfield in 1904, Anthony reminisces about their experiences together. In referring to Anna Howard Shaw's proposed campaign visit to Tioga County, Anthony wrote:

> You will see that Harriet Stanton speaks two weeks from
> tomorrow, and Miss Shaw closes the campaign. When
> you see Miss Shaw advertised again at Binghamton, go
> and see her and tell her who you are. That you were my

private secretary and trusted friend during the publication of the Revolution. I am sure she will give you a welcome, but if she does not, it will be the worse for herself and not you. Sincerely yours, Susan B. Anthony.[12]

Julia Frances Browne Bemis passed June 17, 1920 in Owego at seventy-four, missing by only two months the ratification of suffrage for women.

Jean McQuigg Browne finished her family history of Hobarts and McQuiggs in 1912 and lived until she was seventy-nine. She died June 12, 1939, and lived long enough to enjoy the privilege of voting.[13]

The Dubois Family
William Robert Dubois arrived in Cheyenne as the twenty-two-year-old supervising architect of the Carnegie Library which Robert Morris had been so instrumental in promoting. Born in Chicago in 1879, he trained as an architect and first worked at his craft in New Mexico. After coming to Cheyenne, he courted Archie and Sarah's daughter Dora Frances Slack. They married on November 5, 1904. His distinctive architectural style can be seen in several public buildings in Cheyenne, including the Wyoming Supreme Court Building, east and west wings of the state Capitol Building, and the Plains Hotel.

William and Dora Slack Dubois had five children: William Robert Dubois, Jr.; Berthe Frances; George Allen; Dora I.; and Edward Neely. Sadly, fifty-two-year old Dora Slack Dubois was killed in a train/car accident in Cheyenne in 1938. Their daughter Dora I. Dubois then kept house for her father until he passed away in 1953 at age seventy-four. William Robert Dubois, Jr., married Elinor Noh. Their children were Josephine, William Robert Dubois, III, and Thomas.

William "Bill" Robert Dubois, III, a great-grandson of E.A. "Archie" Slack, was born on September 8, 1936. Bill, a retired high school history teacher, continues to be active in Cheyenne celebrations

Architect William Robert Dubois married Archie Slack's daughter Dora.
William Robert Dubois III still lives in Cheyenne. *(Wyoming State Archives)*

and activities. He remembers his grandfather, architect William
Dubois. Bill Dubois recalls, "Grandfather Dubois lived on the same
block as us, with cousins and maiden Aunt Dora. Grandfather was
a fine pianist and organist as well as an avid gardener. He was gruff,
but my aunt said he got that way after my grandmother was killed
in a train/car accident in 1938. Grandfather just never recovered
from the loss."[14]

≈━●━≈

FAMILY TREE:
ESTHER, HER SIBLINGS, AND THEIR OFFSPRING

Abbreviations:

B – Birth	M – Marriage
C – Children	D – Death

Daniel McQuigg, Jr.
B: 27 Sep 1801. Spencer, Tioga County, NY
M: About 1823. Eleanor Cummings (1801-1868)
C: 1. Cordelia (1824-1848)
   2. Horace (1829-1834)
   3. Adeline (1831-1847)
   4. Mary Jane (1834-1908)
      M: 29 Jan 1853. John Thomas Marshall Davie
      C: John Eldridge (1854-1920)
         Robert Graham (1857-1860)
         Kathleen Schuyler (1859-1948)
            M: 15 Feb 1882. Frederick Elliott Storke
         William Campbell (1861-1870)
         James S. (1867-1869)
         Margaret S. (1868-1868)
         Archibald McQuigg (1873-1881)
   5. Charles (1837-1855)
D: 21 Apr 1880. Weedsport, Cayuga County, NY

Charles McQuigg
B: 28 Feb 1803. Spencer, Tioga County, NY
D: Spring 1838. Cincinnati, Hamilton County, OH

John McQuigg
B: 8 Feb 1805. Spencer, Tioga County, NY
M: 3 Feb 1830. Electa Miles (1812-1905)
C: 1. George (1830-1892)
      M1: 28 Oct 1852. Caroline Smith (1831-1856)
      C: Lucy B. (1844-1857)
         John (1856-1924)
      M2: 3 Feb 1858. Catherine (Kate) Mann Edwards (1834-1911)
      C: Emme (1858-1943)
         Charles (1869-1921)
         Anna (Annie) E. (1862-1944)
  2. Frances Electa (1853-1933)
D: 7 Aug 1854. Middle Port, Meigs County, OH

Edmund Hobart McQuigg (E.H.)
B: 10 April 1807. Spencer, Tioga County, NY
M1: 16 May 1839. Eliza Jane Hall (1816-1887) (Div. 1854)
C: 1. Frances McQuigg (Frankie) (1842-1918)
      M: 23 Oct 1867. Damon Stewart (1834-1905)
      C: Hobart Addison (1868-1915)
         M: 18 May 1904. Mary Charlotte Dewey (1865-1939)
         Mabel (1870-1940)
         Lucy Tilden (1873-1940)
         William Charles (1876-1928)
         Bertha (1879-1962)
         Frances Elizabeth (1882-1965)
      D: 6 Feb 1918. Flint, Genesee, MI
  2. Mary Elizabeth (Libbie) (1842-1915)
      M: 3 Jan 1874. William Moore, Jr. (1827-1897)
      C: Florence Gardner (1878-1963)
         William Hansen (1880-1946)
      D: 14 Jan 1915. Los Angeles, Los Angeles County, CA
M2: 20 Oct 1856. Elizabeth Forman (Libbie) (1801-1880)
M3: 28 Sep 1881. Adaline Cole (1813-1895)
D: 24 Aug 1887. Flint, Genesee County, MI

Jane McQuigg
B: 31 Dec 1808. Spencer, Tioga County, NY
M: About 1831. Alvah Bosworth Archibald (1805-1862)
C: 1. Frederick Archibald (1833-1863)
    2. Mary Jane Archibald (1835-1836)
D: 23 July 1856. Owego, Tioga County, NY

Jesse McQuigg
B: 30 Oct 1811. Spencer, Tioga County, NY
M: About 1843. Mary Freeland (1819-1882)
C: 1. Mary (1846-1911)
        M: Frank M. Baker (1846-1916)
        C: George Hobart (1871-1913)
        D: 6 Jan 1911. Owego, Tioga County, NY
    2. Charles F. (1849-1870)
    3. George L. (1851-1919)
        M: 13 Feb 1873. Mary B. Freeman (1854-1926)
        C: Edmund Hobart (1873-1914)
            Nina (1875-1943)
D: 18 Jan 1884. Flint, Genesee County, MI

Esther Hobart McQuigg
B: 8 Aug 1812. Spencer, Tioga County, NY
M 1: 15 Dec 1841. Artemas Slack (5 Mar 1811 – May 1843)
    C: 1. Archibald Artemas (Edward Archibald, E.A.) (2 Oct
            1842 –23 Mar 1907)
            M: 22 Sep 1870. Sarah Frances Neely (1841-1921)
            C: Charles Henry Slack (1871-1872)
                Esther (1873-1873)
                Harriett Louise Slack (1878-1940)
                    M: 1899. Wallace Cooper Bond (1875-1950)
                Dora Frances Slack (1885-1938)
                    M: 15 Nov 1904. William Robert Dubois
                        (1879-1953)
                    C: William Robert Dubois, Jr. (1905-1982)

M: Elinor Noh (1907-1979)
C: Berthe Frances Dubois (1907-2004)
George Allen Dubois (1909-1999)
Dora Isabel Dubois (1917-1983)
Edward Neely Dubois (1925-2002)
William Robert Dubois III 1936-)
M2: 17 Feb 1846. John Morris (1812-1877)
C: 2. John Morris, Jr. (1849-1852)
3. Robert Charles (8 Nov 1851–22 Jan 1921)
4. Edward John (8 Nov 1851–7 Sep 1902)
M: 31 Aug 1881. Elizabeth (Bertie) Chambers (1862-1948)
D: 2 Apr 1902. Cheyenne, Laramie County, Wyoming

Mindwell McQuigg
B: 22 Nov 1814. Spencer, Tioga County, NY
D: 7 Aug 1836. Owego, Tioga County, NY

Eliza McQuigg
B: 22 Feb 1817. Spencer, Tioga County, NY
M: 19 Feb 1832. Joshua Wyatt Parker (1812-1893)
C:1. Charlotte Jane (Jennie) (1834-1924)
M1: 9 Aug 1855. William B. Hale (1821-1924)
M2: 5 May 1869. Robert Sessions West (1833-1889)
2. Eliza Frances (Fannie) (1837-1913)
M: 2 Oct 1861. Henry Curtiss (1831-1867)
C: Charles Parker Curtiss (1862-1917)
Florence May Curtiss (1865-1935)
3. Charles Valcaleau (1843-1930)
M: 15 June 1868. Maria T. Deaver (1844-1904)
4. William Wyatt (1847-1891)
5. Franklin Augustus (1850-1918)
M: 25 Sep 1872 Mary Ellen Ratcliff (1850-1932)
C: Frank Ratcliff (1873-1935)
Delmar Haynes (1883-1973)
Bessie Louise Parker (1886-??)

6. Carrie Belle (1859-1935)
>   M: 29 Apr 1891. Eugene Anderson (1858-1932)
D: 31 Jul 1901. Dubuque, Dubuque County, IA

Charlotte Susan McQuigg
B: 17 Jun 1820. Spencer, Tioga County, NY
M: 18 Oct 1842. Frederick Browne (1816-1873)
C: 1. Charlotte Elizabeth (Libbie or Lib) (1843-1917)
>   M: 1 Jun 1871. Levi Starr Chatfield (1808-1884)
2. Mary Jane (1845-1846)
3. Julia Frances (1846-1920)
>   M: 8 Jun 1870. George Pickering Bemis (1838-1916)
>   (Div. 1910
>   C: Frederick (Freddie) Browne (1872-1872)
>   George (Georgie) Pickering (1873-1878)
>   Robert (Robbie) Emery (1874-1880)
4. Jean McQuigg (1859-1939) (Author of the Hobart and
>   McQuigg family histories)
D: 26 Jan 1893. Owego, Tioga, NY

George McQuigg
B: 4 Oct 1822. Spencer, Tioga County, NY
D: 16 Nov 1850. At sea, on board *Masconomo*, off Mazatlán,
Sinaloa, Mexico

APPENDIX C

In Memoriam

The text of a pamphlet titled "In Memoriam," which is believed to have been a funeral handout, is included here. It is a lightly edited version of the obituary from the Cheyenne Leader *and was probably written by Archie Slack.*

ESTHER MORRIS PASSED peacefully away last night, April 2, 1902. Had she lived until the month of August next, she would have attained her ninetieth year. Truly a ripe old age. She was a woman of wonderful vitality and will power; but her indomitable energy was not more remarkable than her mental activity. She was a born reformer, a true descendent of her liberty loving ancestors who came across the ocean to gain their religious freedom.

When little more than a girl she was urged to become a missionary and to accept the preparatory education, but Esther McQuigg declined because she wanted to be herself. This tendency to individual freedom early manifested itself and on account of her original manner of looking at things she was a great favorite and welcome visitor among the best and most intelligent families of the village of Owego, New York, where she lived until she was married. Artemas Slack, her first husband, who died a few months after their marriage, was a civil engineer on the New York and Erie railroad and afterwards in the service of the Illinois Central.

Removing to Illinois in 1842 she married John Morris, a prosperous merchant at Peru, where they resided until 1868 when they removed to Wyoming, experiencing many of the vicissitudes common to pioneer life in the West. It was in Wyoming that Mrs.

Morris was instrumental in securing the passage of the law giving equal suffrage to women, and at a later period administered the office of Justice of the Peace.

Mrs. Morris was optimistic. She was always cheerful and happy, looking on the bright side of life, and she seemed to thoroughly enjoy the newness of things. The freshness and freedom captivated her. Having a brave spirit she never needed encouragement, but was always cheering up those around her and driving away the clouds about them. Her resourceful nature enabled her to get good out of evil and keep the bright side uppermost. But she never flattered people to put them in good humor. Her remedy was different. It might be caustic instead of an anodyne. A few pertinent suggestions for removal of the cause, accompanied by some keen, witty, comment, carried the remedy home to the complainant or sufferer.

She had the courage that went well with her masculine mind and made her an advocate difficult to cope with. It is needless to say that she was always ready to maintain her prerogatives and to champion her convictions, no matter how great and powerful might be her antagonist.

Her womanly traits were shown in her love of the beautiful. Our pioneer citizens will remember her garden of flowers from which she was ever ready to pluck her choicest varieties for the passer by who stopped to admire the little oasis. This was before the city park near her home was made so beautiful.

Mrs. Morris was intensely practical. While she was gratified by the evidences of civilization and refinement that were making their appearances around her, she had probably enjoyed the anticipation of these changes full as much. Therefore, the idea or origin of things gave her most delight. The breaking of ground, the new lumber, the transplanting of trees, the lawn making, were to her a source of pleasure.

Mrs. Morris was a true pioneer, in the domain of thought, as well as in material things. She welcomed innovation and anyone with a new idea was well received at her home. Not that she did not hold to fundamental truth, but she had an abiding faith that all truth had not yet been revealed to mankind, and her soul longed for a new revelation. She believed that it would surely come, some day. It was light, more light that she craved. Her early faith she cherished as something precious, but her mature mind seemed to be on the alert for something more than this. We say this in explanation for one who was always frank, in fact, at times more candid than diplomatic.

Perhaps the most marked trait of character in the deceased was her fearless independence. It did not always make her friends, but in the end she won the respect of those who could not agree with her opinions.

She loved the beautiful, the true, and the good. Nature's changes were pleasing to her, and even to the very last she was in sympathy with the lines of Tennyson: "Ring out the old, ring in the new, ring out the false, ring in the true."

A brave, cheerful soul has gone to rest. Her quest of truth in this world is ended. Her mission in life has been fulfilled. The work she did for the elevation of womankind, not only in securing equal suffrage for women in Wyoming, but in many ways, will be told in years to come, when her work will be better understood.

But let us here say that it was not the mere privilege of putting a piece of paper in the ballot box that she was striving for. It was something more and something better than this. It has been well said that all reforms are crude and bungling at the outset. They are little more than a protest against existing conditions. Yet people then begin to think, and the work broadens out and assumes a different phase. Observe it in the South, where efforts have been made by T. Booker Washington [*sic*] to raise the manhood of his colored brethren. The capacity of the negro to think intelligently and maintain himself is worth more to him than the contested ballot. The time will come, however, when he can use his political privilege to good advantage, both for himself and his country. Then they will vote their honest convictions and not merely to carry out the wishes of those upon whom they are dependent.

It is often remarked that certain persons lived before their time; but we have always questioned the truth of this well worn saying, so far as the usefulness of a man or woman is concerned. There is something providential about these matters that we do not fully understand. Every man who comes into the world finds his place, and if he is loyal to his best convictions he will exert an influence for good no matter in what era he may live. Mrs. Morris often quoted from Addison's beautiful poem, "I Will Fear No Evil."

I WILL FEAR NO EVIL

The Lord my pasture shall prepare,
and feed me with a shepherd's care;
His presence shall my wants supply
and guard me with a watchful eye;
My noonday walks he shall attend,
and all my midnight hours defend.

When in the sultry glebe I faint,
or on the thirsty mountain pant,
To fertile vales and dewy meads
My weary, wandering steps He leads,
Where peaceful rivers, soft and slow,
Amid the verdant landscape flow.

Though in the paths of death I tread
With gloomy horrors overspread.
My steadfast heart shall bear no ill,
For thou, O Lord art with me still,
Thy friendly crook shall give me aid,
and guide me through the dreadful shade.

Though in a bare and rugged way,
through devious lonely wilds I stray,
Thy bounty shall my wants beguile.
The barren wilderness shall smile,
With sudden greens and herbage crowned,
And streams shall murmur all around.

NOTES

Shortened citations are generally used in the notes. Frequently cited archives and archival material, collections, governmental material, interviews, and letters are identified abridgements, including the following.

SPC	South Pass City, Wyoming
WSA	Wyoming State Archives, Cheyenne, WY
WT	Wyoming Territory

Letters: *Unless otherwise cited all letters are from H95-19, Papers of Frances McQuigg Stewart (Frankie), Wyoming State Archives. This letter file also includes some photographs. Citations are shortened as shown:*

Esther to Frankie	Esther Morris to Frances McQuigg Stewart
Archie to Frankie	E.A. "Archie" Slack to Frances McQuigg Stewart
Robert to Frankie	Robert Morris to Frances McQuigg Stewart
Ed to Frankie	Edward Morris to Frances McQuigg Stewart

Newspapers: All Wyoming newspapers cited can be found digitized at Wyoming Newspapers from the Wyoming State Library at http://newspapers.wyo.gov.

Annals of Wyoming: Copies of *Annals*, 1923–2005, can be found at https://wyshs.org/publications/annals-wyoming-wyoming-history-journal.

1. "She Wanted to Be Herself"

1. Esther Hobart McQuigg was born August 8, 1812, but her birthdate has been variously reported. However, the obituary written by E.A. Slack (her son) in the *Cheyenne Daily Leader*, 3 April 1902, reports "Mrs. Esther Morris passed peacefully away last night. Had she lived until the month of August next, she would have attained her 90th birthday—truly a ripe old age." The headstone placed by her family in Lakeside Cemetery in Cheyenne, Wyoming, reads: Esther Morris, 1812-1902.

2. Abigail Adams to John Adams, Braintree, MA, 31 March 1776. 31 March–5 April 177, 4 pages. Adams Family Papers, Massachusetts Historical Society, Boston, MA.

3. Cokie Roberts, *Ladies of Liberty: The Women Who Shaped Our Nation* (New York: William Morrow, 2008), xxi.

4. Esther Hobart McQuigg Morris to Frances (Frankie) McQuigg Stewart, Cheyenne, Wyoming Territory, 24 August 1887. Papers of Frances McQuigg Stewart, H95-19, Wyoming State Archives, Cheyenne, WY.

5. *Fourth Series,* vol. 5. Massachusetts Historical Society. 236- 237. Such historical societies at that time often had several volumes of biographical information referred to simply by numerical series. Mather and Cotton were father and grandfather of the over-zealous Cotton Mather of the Salem Witch Trial's fame.

6. Hon. L.W. Royse, *A Standard History of Kosciusko County, Indiana*, Vol. 2 (1919), 676.

7. Jean McQuigg Browne, *Edmund Hobart and His Descendants, 1794– 1912* (Privately Published), 2. Accessible at: https://archive.org/details/edmundhobarthisd00brow/page/n6

8. Federal Census, 1810, Tioga County, NY. Federal Census, 1810, Pennsylvania.

9. Jean Alve, *A Record of Land in Spencer New York State to the First Settlers* (Spencer, NY, Privately Published, 1995)18, 25-26, 43, 46, 51-52, 80, 107-108.

10. Pamela Goddard, former Curator of Education at the Tioga County Historical Society, Tioga, New York, interviews with author, November 1998.

11. "Her Work Done," *Cheyenne Daily Leader,* 3 April 1902, 2. Esther's obituary, written by her son, E.A. "Archie" Slack, is one of the few references that show what she was like as a young person.

12. Esther to Frankie, Peru, IL, 18 May 1866.

13. New York State Census, Tioga County, 1825.

14. Rosamund Stricker Day, granddaughter of Esther's niece Frankie McQuigg Stewart, interview with author, 7 November 1998.

15. New York slavery began in New Amsterdam in 1626, when the Dutch West India Company imported eleven slaves, and ended with the New York State law of 1827 making slavery illegal. Emancipation Day was celebrated on July 4, 1827.

16. Esther to Frankie, Peru, IL, 18 May 1866.

17. New York State Census 1830, Tioga County; Federal Census, 1840 Tioga County, NY, 1840.

≫—●— *2. "She Was a Great Favorite"* —●—≪

1. LeRoy Wilson Kingman, *Early Owego* (Owego, NY: The Owego Gazette Office, 1907); Reprint edition (Owego: Owego County

Historical Society, 1987). Wyoming Valley information: Author's great-great grandfather, who participated in the Revolutionary War, lived in that region of Pennsylvania. He and his family survived the attack. Nearly one hundred years later, those who died in Pennsylvania received honor when Wyoming Territory was named.

2. From a newspaper clipping, photocopied and given to the author by Pamela Goddard, former Curator of Education, Tioga County Historical Society. Photocopy in Author's Collection.

3. Esther's optimistic personality illuminated in "Her Work Done," *Cheyenne Daily Leader*, 3 April 1902, 2; Rodger Fritz, historian, Baptist Church, Owego, NY, interview with author, Agusut 2016.

4. *Owego Gazette*, Alvah Archibald obituary, 26 June 1862. Alvah's obituary states: "He had suffeed most of his life with asthma that turned to consumption, resulting in death. He was intelligent anad honest, possessing as kind a heart as was ever concealed within a human breast, and always enjoying the fullest confidence and respect of all who knew him. He was justice of the peace in Owego for a year before his death."

5. Judith Wellman, *The Road to Seneca Falls* (Urbana and Chicago: University of Illinois Press, 2004), 56.

6. Mary Wollstonecraft, *Vindication of the Rights of Woman: with Strictures on Political and Moral Subjects* (Boston: Peter Edes, 1792) First Printing.

7. Today, consumption would likely be called pulmonary tuberculosis.

8. Vermont Vital Records, Vermont State Archives and Records Administration, Montpelier, VT; Arba Ellis and Genville Mellen Dodge, *Norwich University 1819–1911: Her History, Her Graduates, Her Roll of Honor,* vol 1, 1911, 354–371; Reports to the General Assembly of Illinois, Serventh Judicial Circuit. Expeditures on public works in special charge of Ebenezer Peck, 2nd day of December 1939; 1840 Census La Salle County, IL; U.S. Department of the Interior, Bureau of Land Management, General Land Office Records; New York State Legislature, Assembly Select Committee to Investigate the New York and Erie Railroad Company, 1842, 449.

9. Pamela Goddard, interview, November 1998.

10. Old church record book of marriages of the Owego Station of the Methodist Episcopal Church, owned by the Owego United Methodist Church. Transcription Volume 416 compiles Daughters of the American Revolution records at the New York Public Library.

11. Tioga County Will Book E, vol. 0011-0012, 1840-1881, New York Wills and Probate Records, Tioga County, 1659-1999, Tioga County Historical Society, Tioga, New York.

12. *Owego Advertiser*, Owego, NY, 18 May 1843.

13. Rosamond Stricker Day, granddaughter of Esther's niece Frankie Mc-Quigg Stewart, interview with author, 7 November 1998.

14. Esther to Frankie, Cheyenne, WT, 11 April 1888. The Married Woman's Property Act, giving women some control over their property and finances, was not passed in New York until 1848, five years too late to help Esther.

✒ 3. *"Our Life is Made Up of Labor and Rest"* ✒

1. Esther's father's youngest sister, Diademia McQuigg, and her husband, William Watson, lived two hundred miles south down the Mississippi River in Pittsfield, Illinois.

2. Illinois Statewide Marriage Index, Illinois State Archives, Springfield, IL. Volume A, License #891.

3. James D. Lodesky, *Polish Pioneers in Illinois 1818-1850* (Xlibris Corporation. 2010). 202-205.

4. Margaret Fuller, *Woman in the Nineteenth Century* (New York: Greeley and McElrath, 1845).

5. Ann E. Gordon, *The Selected Papers of Elizabeth Cady Stanton and Susan B. Anthony, Vol. 1* (New Brunswick: Rutgers University Press, 2001), 78-82.

6. Gordon, *The Selected Papers, Vol. 1*, 78-82.

7. Gordon, *The Selected Papers, Vol. 1*, 78-82. Only one of the original signers of the Declaration of Sentiments in 1848—Charlotte Woodward Pierce—would live to see the Nineteenth Amendment passed into law seventy years later. Even so, at ninety-two, she was too ill on Election Day to get out and vote. Elizabeth Cady Stanton met fellow activist Susan B. Anthony in 1851, and they spent the next fifty-one years working for woman suffrage.

8. 1850 Federal Census, La Salle County, Illinois, Peru.

9. Rosamund Stricker Day, interview, 7 November 1998.

10. McQuigg v. McQuigg; Tanner, Gordon, *Reports of Cases Argued and Determined in the Supreme Court of Judicature of the State of Indiana,* Vol. XIII (Indianapolis: The Merrill & Company. 1860) 294-317. The record includes 32 depositions and 180 pages of testimony. Depositions courtesy of Hall Collection created by Cliff Hall, a descendent of Eliza Jane Hall and family historian.

11. *Daily Alta* [San Francisco] California, General Notices, 25 February 1853; McQuigg v. McQuigg, divorce depositions provide comments

about Eliza Jane's activities during this time, including her obtaining a medical degree "from Syracuse."

12. *Edwards' Directory of the Inhabitants, Institutions, Incorporated Companies and Manufacturing Establishments of the City of Chicago...for 1870* (Newberry Library reel #5). This census for this 13th edition was done in May and the directory was published in July 1870 (*Chicago Tribune*, May 1, 1870 and *Chicago Tribune,* July 17, 1870); *Ladies' Own Magazine*, vol. 4, issues 1-6, 1872.

13. 1860 Federal Census Illinois, La Salle County, Peru and Cook County, Chicago.

14. Esther to Frankie, Peru, IL, 18 May 1866.

15. Indiana Supreme Court Case #1439, filed 19 July 1859. 1859 depositions from the Indiana State Archives, Indianapolis, IN. Courtesy of the private collection of Cliff Hall, a descendant of Eliza Jane Hall.

16. Indiana Supreme Court Case #1439, filed 19 July 1859. 1859 depositions. Courtesy of the private collection of Cliff Hall.

17. Esther to Frankie, Cheyenne, WT, April 1888. Many of the letters have no day listed, only month and year.

18. Esther to Frankie, Cheyenne, WT, April 1888.

⇒ 4. *"I Had No Voice in the Matter"* ⇐

1. Esther to Frankie, Chicago, IL, 17 September 1862.

2. Nineteenth Illinois Infantry Veteran Club, *The Nineteenth Illinois: A Memoir of a Regiment of Volunteer Infantry Famous in the Civil War of Fifty Years Ago for Its Drill, Bravery, and Distinguished Services.* 70, 74, 76, 113-18, 148-49, 191, 208, 346-47, 374, 392.

3. Nineteenth Illinois Infantry Veteran Club, *The Nineteenth Illinois,* 70, 74, 76, 113-18, 148-49, 191, 208, 346-47, 374, 392.

4. Frances E. Willard and Mary A. Livermore, *American Women: 1500 Biographies with over 1400 Portraits, vol. 1* (New York, Chicago and Springfield, Ohio: Mast Crowell and Kirkpatrick, 1897), 12-13, 58-59, 245-246; "Tribute to Tompkins County, Civil War Era Nurse," New York Senator Thomas F. O'Mara, 21 March 2012; Susan Cheever, *American Bloomsbury* (New York: Simon and Schuster, 2006).

5. "Robert Barry," records from U.S. National Asylum for Disabled Volunteer Soldiers 1866-1938, Sawtelle, Los Angeles County, CA,; Mrs. John A. Logan, *The Part Taken by Women in American History* (Wilmington: The Perry-Nalle Publishing Company, 1912), 374; Rosamond Stricker Day, interview with author, 7 November 1998.

6. Esther to Frankie, Chicago, IL, 17 September 1862; Rosamond Stricker Day, interview, 7 November 1998.

7. Esther to Frankie, Peru, IL, 30 October 1862.

8. Esther to Frankie, Peru, IL, 10 March 1863.

9. Esther to Frankie, Peru, IL, 4 August 1863. This letter has the implication that either John does not write to Esther or possibly that he is illiterate.

10. Esther to Frankie, Peru, IL, October 1863.

11 Nineteenth Illinois Infantry Veteran Club, *The Nineteenth Illinois*, 70, 74, 76, 113-18, 148-49, 191, 208, 346-47, 374, 392.

12. Archie to Frankie, Chattanooga, TN, 12 May 1864.

13. Esther to Frankie, Peru, IL, 26 April 1864. Charlotte was Esther's sister and Frankie's aunt.

14. Esther to Frankie, Peru, IL, 3 July 1864.

15. Nineteenth Illinois Infantry Veteran Club, *The Nineteenth Illinois*; 70, 74, 76, 113-18, 148-49, 191, 208, 346-47, 374, 392.

16. Archie to Frankie, Chicago, IL, 18 September 1864.

17. Walter Benjamin Palmer, *The History of the Phi Delta Theta Fraternity* (Chicago: Phi Delta Theta Fraternity, University of Chicago, 1906).

18. Archie to Frankie, Chicago, IL, 11 November 1864

19. "Thanksgiving Proclamation," The Alfred Whital Stern Collection of Lincolniana, Rare Book and Special Collections Division, American Memory, Library of Congress.

20. Esther to Frankie, Peru, IL, 24 November 1864.

21. Esther to Frankie, Peru, IL, 6 December 1864, continuation of 24 November 1864 letter.

22. "Lincoln Inaugural Address," March 4, 1865. The Alfred Whital Stern Collection of Lincolniana, Rare Book and Special Collections Division, American Memory, Library of Congress.

23. Robert to Frankie, Peru, IL, 26 March 1865.

⟩⟩⟩ 5. *"Difficult the First Time Trying"* ⟨⟨⟨

1. Archie to Frankie, Chicago University, 15 May 1865. Both Esther and Archie occasionally referred to Frankie as Frank.

2. Archie to Frankie, Chicago, IL, 18 July 1865.

3. Archie to Frankie, 31 Division Street, Chicago, IL, 26 July 1865.

4. Esther to Frankie, Peru, IL, August 22. Although no year is listed, based on context and content, the date was probably 1865.

5. Esther to Frankie, Peru, La Salle, IL, 8 January 1866.

6. Robert Morris to Frankie, included in Esther's letter, Peru, La Salle, IL, 8 January 1866.

7. Esther to Frankie, Peru, IL, 12 March 1866.

8. Esther to Frankie, Peru, IL, 18 May 1866.

9. Esther to Frankie, Peru, IL, 18 May 1866.

10. Esther to Frankie, Peru, IL, 18 May 1866.

11. Abigail Scott Duniway, *Path Breaking: An Autobiographical History of the Equal Suffrage Movement in the Pacific Coast States* (Portland, OR: James, Kerns & Abbott, 1914), 39.

12. Esther to Frankie, Peru, IL, 23 May 1866.

13. Archie to Frankie, Soldier's College, Fulton, Illinois, n.d., presumed to be late winter 1866 or spring 1867.

14. John M. Palmer, *Personal Recollections of John M. Palmer; The Story of an Earnest Life* (Cincinnati, OH: R. Clarke Co., 1901), 39.

15. Mrs. Wallace C. (Harriet Slack) Bond, "Sarah Frances Slack: A Biographical Sketch by Her Daughter," *Annals of Wyoming* 4, no. 3 (January 1927): 354-356. Harriett Slack Bond was known as Hattie.

16. Franklin Ellis, *History of Genesee County, Michigan* (Philadelphia. Everts & Abbott) 1879. 99, 150.

17. Rosamond Stricker Day, interview with author, 7 November 1998.

6. "More Light She Craved"

1. *Chicago Tribune,* 29 January 1868, 2.

2. Gordon, *The Selected Papers of Elizabeth Cady Stanton and Susan B. Anthony, Vol. 2,* 167.

3. Robert to Frankie, New York, NY, 28 May 1868.

4. Robert to Frankie, New York, NY, 27 July 1868.

5. *The Revolution*, Accessible Archives, accessed July 19, 2018, at http://www.accessible-archives.com/collections/the-revolution/. Woman Suffrage Collection.

7. "Land of Unbelievable Horizons"

1. T.A. Larson, *History of Wyoming* (Second Edition, Revised (paperback). Lincoln, NE: University of Nebraska Press, 1990), 12.

2. Henry E. Stamm IV, *People of the Wind River: The Eastern Shoshones 1825-1900* (Norman, OK: University of Oklahoma Press, 1999), 26; Will Bagley, *Fort Bridger*, www.WyoHistory.org.

3. Stamm, *People of the Wind River*, 19-21; David J. Wishart. *The Fur Trade of the American West 1807-1840* (Lincoln, NE and London: University of Nebraska Press, 1979), 145, 179, 189, 202.

4. Stamm, *People of the Wind River*, 19-21.

5. Stephen E. Ambrose, *Nothing Like it in the World: The Men Who Built the Transcontinental Railroad 1863-1869* (New York: Simon and Schuster, 2000), 217-219.

6. James Chisholm, *South Pass, 1868: James Chisholm's Journal of the Wyoming Gold Rush*, Lola M. Homsher, ed. (Lincoln, NE: University of Nebraska Press, 1960), 30, 36.

7. *Frontier Index*, 1868.

8. 1869 Census, Carter County, Wyoming Territory. This census, which was taken in June 1869, shows both John Morris and Archie Slack arrived in South Pass City thirteen months previously. Michael A. Massie, "Reform Is Where You Find It: Roots of Woman Suffrage in Wyoming," *Annals of Wyoming*, 62, no. 1 (Spring 1990), 4.

9. Janet was sometimes referred to as Jeanette. Grace Hebard, interview with Jeanette Smith on 6 July 1920, at South Pass City. Fremont County Pioneer Museum, Lander, WY.

10. Marion McMillan Huseas, *Sweetwater Gold: Wyoming's Gold Rush 1867-1871* (Cheyenne, WY, Cheyenne Corral of Westerners International Publishers, 1991), 31.

11. *Progressive Men of Wyoming*, (Chicago. A.W. Bowen & Co. 1908) 221.

12. Huseas, *Sweetwater Gold*, 96, 97.

13. Michael A. Massie, "Reform Is Where You Find It," 4.

⮕ 8. *"Pleased with This Country"* ⬅

1. Marion McMillan Huseas, *Sweetwater Gold*, 54; Todd Guenther, Central Wyoming College anthropology and history professor, interviews with author, 1994. Guenther also supervised archaeological digs in South Pass City in the 1990s and has worked with the Wyoming State Archaeologist's Office.

2. Guenther, interview, 1994. Guenther shared this comment, "It is an archeological fact of human behavior, the longer people plan to stay in a place, the farther away they move their garbage."

3. *The Weekly Rocky Mountain Star,* 26 May 1869 (Cheyenne, WY), 1; *Cheyenne Weekly Leader,* 8 May 1869, 1; 12 June 1869, 7.

4. T.A. Larson, *History of Wyoming,* 70-71; John Robertson, Adjutant General's Department, *Michigan in the War* (Lansing: W.S. George & Co. State Printers, 1882), 567.

5. Larson, *History of Wyoming,* 70-71; Huseas, *Sweetwater Gold,* 23.

6. Michael A. Massie, "Reform is Where You Find It" 2-22; Susan Layman, "A History of Wyoming's Carissa Gold Mine," *Mining History News,* accessible at http://www.mininghistoryassociation.org. Layman explains, "The name of the lode and mine can be somewhat confusing. 'Cariso' became the 'Carisa,' 'Creasser,' and finally the 'Carissa,' as it has been spelled now for a number of years. All of these changes appear to be simply variant spellings by different people on various documents": Guenther interview, January 9, 1995.

7. Guenther, interview, 1994. Guenther explained more about Esther's cabin, stating, "The archaeological reconstruction of the early 1990s showed evidence the Morris cabin settled so badly on one side the family piled stones two- to three-feet high to prop it up."

8. Esther to Damon Stewart (per Ed Morris), SPC, WT, 13 June 1869.

9. Esther to Libbie Hall (Mary Elizabeth McQuigg), SPC, WT, 22 June 1869.

10. Esther to Frankie, SPC, WT, 13 October 1869.

11. Esther to Frankie, SPC, WT, 13 October 1869.

12. Robert to Frankie, SPC, WT, 17 November 1869.

13. Robert to Frankie, SPC, WT, 17 November 1869.

9. *"Like All the Liberal Papers"*

1. Massie, "Reform Is Where You Find It, 7."

2. Massie, "Reform is Where You Find It," 7.

3. Tom Rea, "Right Choice, Wrong Reasons: Wyoming Women Win the Right to Vote," WyoHistory.org, 8 November 2014, accessible at https://www.wyohistory.org/encyclopedia.

4. Larson, *History of Wyoming,* 80, 82.

5. Mark Twain, letter to San Francisco's *Alta California* newspaper, 5 April 1867. Mark Twain saw Anna Dickinson speak in New York City and wrote a letter to the *Alta California* newspaper, 23 February 1867, which was subsequently printed in the paper on 5 April 1867.

6. Larson, *History of Wyoming,* 236; U.S. Congress, Northwest Ordinance, 13 July 1787.

7. Grace Hebard interview with Janet/Jeanette Sherlock Smith, SPC, 6 July 1920. Grace Raymond Hebard Collection. American Heritage Center, University of Wyoming, Laramie, WY. Collection No. 400008, Box 45, Folder 13.

8. Esther to Frankie, SPC, WT, 13 October 1869.

9. Esther to Frankie, SPC, WT, 13 October 1869. Alfred Theodore Andreas on page 544 of his *1884 History of Chicago,* vol. 1, states, "Seth Paine organized a Woman's Home with the object being to better the class of women, who having no homes are forced to take such accommodation. The Woman's Home gave them comfort and protection of a home at a moderate price. It was located at the corner of Jackson and Halsted streets where the Farwell House now is."

10. Esther to Frankie, SPC, WT, 13 October 1869; C.G. Coutant, *The History of Wyoming from the Earliest Known Discoveries,* vol. 1 (Laramie, WY: Chaplin, Spafford & Mathison, Printers, 1899), 665.

11. Author's analysis of the 1870 census of South Pass City shows population as 76 percent male and 24 percent women.

12. Huseas, *Sweetwater Gold,* 97.

13. *South Pass News,* 27 October 1869, 1.

14. Robert to Frankie, SPC, WT, 17 November 1869.

15. Huseas, *Sweetwater Gold,* 26, 27. The Sweetwater County jail in South Pass City was not completed until April 1, 1870.

16. Coutant, *History of Wyoming from Earliest Known Discoveries,* 665.

17. Guenther, interview, 1994.

18. Robert to Frankie, SPC, WT, 17 November 1869. Even at the age of eighteen, Robert's sense of history is demonstrated in his correspondence. Not surprisingly he later became one of the founders of the Wyoming Historical Society.

⋙●⋘ *10. "Suffrage Is No Child's Play"* ⋙●⋘

1. Larson, *History of Wyoming,* 73, 75.

2. 1850 Federal Census, Washington City, District of Columbia, 27 June 1850; 1860 Federal Census, Washington City, District of Columbia, 17 July 1860; Marriage Records District of Columbia, 1810-1953; A letter Esther wrote to Frankie in early 1870 mentions William Bright's mother's remarriage and contains information about Amos

Kendall. Esther to Frankie, Fragment B and another page, determined to be January 1870, SPC, WT.

3. Huseas, *Sweetwater Gold,* 147.

4. Civil War Draft Registrations Records, 1863-1865, Vol. 4, District of Columbia; Larson, *History of Wyoming,* 89; Huseas, *Sweetwater Gold,* 147.

5. Tom Rea, "Right Choice, Wrong Reasons," WyoHistory.org.

6. Larson, *History of Wyoming,* 79.

7. Massie, "Reform is Where You Find it," 10.

8 "Diary, John A. Campbell," *Annals of Wyoming,* 10, no. 2 (April 1938): 59-78, 70.

9. Larson, *History of Wyoming,* 8

10. Guenther Interviews, 1994-2019; Larson, *History of Wyoming,* 28.

11. Massie, "Reform is Where You Find It," 7.

12. Larson. *History of Wyoming,* 78.

13. Robert to Lib Browne, SPC, WT, 27 December 1869, published 13 January 1870 in *The Revolution.*

14. Esther to Frankie, SPC, WT, Fragment B and another page, probably written January 1870.

11. "I Feel Like I Am a Citizen"

1. T. B. H. Stenhouse, *The Rocky Mountain Saints: a full and complete history of the Mormons, from the first vision of Joseph Smith* (New York: D. Appleton and Company, 1878), 716; The Little Cottonwood District contained such mines as the Flagstaff, Emma, North Star, Savage, and Magnet Monitor.

2. Guenther, interview, 1994

3. Esther to Frankie, 30 January 1870, SPC, WT.

4. Massie, "Reform Is Where You Find It," 13.

5. Esther to Isabella Beecher Hooker, *Chicago Tribune,* 31 January 1871.

6. Guenther, interviews, 1994.

7. W.E. Chaplin, "Woman Suffrage Pioneer Recalled Here," (*Laramie Boomerang,* Sunday, 25 July 1937). William Edward Chaplin apprenticed to E.A. Slack in Laramie. When Slack moved to Cheyenne, Chaplin went with him. He was later editor of the *Laramie Republican* and served as Secretary of State of Wyoming 1919–1923.

8. Eunice G. Anderson, State Historian, *First Biennial Report of the State Historian of the State of Wyoming for the Period Ending September 30, 1920 with Wyoming Historical Collections* (The Laramie Printing Company, 1920), 142.

9. Nathaniel Daniels, letter to Robert and Ed Morris written from National Military Home, Delaware Township, Leavenworth County, Kansas 14 April 1914. Written at age 89. Two pages of the much-photocopied letter are in possession of author. Huseas, *Sweetwater Gold*, 173, shows the letter as housed in the Lander Pioneer Museum, though it can no longer be located there.

10. Massie, "Reform Is Where You Find It,"14. Massie names Archie and Dixson as underwriting the bond. Huseas, in *Sweetwater Gold*, 149, lists different sureties: "John McGlinchey, N. L. Turner and E. D. Strunk, listed themselves as sureties for the $500 bond." Her citation is "*Records of the Board of County Commissioners*, February 14, 1870, p. 12.; March 5, 1870, p. 14."

11. Edward M. Lee, *Letterpress Book of the Secretary of State*, Wyoming Territory, May 25, 1869 to October 1872, Wyoming State Archives. 363.

12. Larson, *History of Wyoming*, 84. A docket has never been found for the second woman commissioned, and no records show that the other served.

⟫═◦═ *12. "Let Alone a Justice of the Peace"* ═◦═⟪

1. Territory of Wyoming v. James Stillman, record of arrest, n.d., Esther Hobart Morris docket, South Pass City Justice of the Peace combined civil and criminal docket, RG 1014, Sweetwater County Justices of the Peace and County Court Records, Wyoming State Archives, 2.

2. Massie, "Reform is Where You Find it," 14.

3. *Wyoming Tribune,* 26 April 1870, 4.

4. Robert to E.H. & Libbie McQuigg, 3 March 1870, SPC, WT.

5. Esther to Frankie, 7 March 1870, SPC, WT.

6. *Milwaukee Daily Sentinel,* 24 March 1870.

7. Robert to Charlotte Esther Giles Converse, SPC, WT, 30 March 1870.

8. *Frank Leslie's Illustrated Newspaper*, 2 April 1870; *Milwaukee Daily Sentinel,* 24 March 1870.

9. *Frank Leslie's Illustrated Newspaper,* 11 June 1870.

10. Esther to Frankie, SPC, WT, n.d., but likely early April 1870.

11. William Yates, " Reminiscences," Green River, Wyoming, 1935, Sweetwater County Museum, Green River, WY. Part of William Yates

twenty-seven- page reminiscence of early Green River was an inter-view of eighty-six-year-old Emma Wilson Stillman Philbrick.

12. 1870 Federal Census, South Pass City, Sweetwater County, Wyoming Territory, 2 June 1870; 1870 Federal Census, Scipio, Millard County, Utah Territory. 17 June 1870; Huseas, *Sweetwater Gold,* 150.

13. Esther to Frankie, SPC, WT, 10 April 1870. John was still a staunch Democrat and not in favor of woman suffrage. Democrat George Wardman lived in Atlantic City and was elected to the first territorial legislature.

14. Anderson, *First Biennial Report,* 144. The proceedings say only that he was credited with the quotation, not by whom; Huseas, *Sweetwater Gold,* 152.

15. Huseas, *Sweetwater Gold,* 152. For Sheeks, who had been twenty-seven when he lived in South Pass City, greater maturity and wisdom came with age. The Wyoming State Historical Society collections contain a letter from Sheeks who at this time was seventy-seven and served as a judge of the Montesano, Washington, Superior Court. He wrote, "Wise as I thought myself fifty years ago, I am willing to admit that I have learned some things since. I have advocated and voted for woman's suffrage and have no doubt of the wisdom and justice of my later ac-tion, whatever the good women of Wyoming may think of my former conduct." Eunice G. Anderson, *First Biennial Report,* 144.

16. Susan B. Anthony, Elizabeth Cady Stanton, and Matilda Joslyn Gage, *History of Woman Suffrage, Vol. III, 1876- 1885* (New York: Susan B. Anthony, 1887) 731-732.

17. Frank G. Irwin obituary, *South Pass News*, 9 April 1870, 4.

18. *South Pass News,* 9 April 1870.

19. Huseas, *Sweetwater Gold*, 77-79.

20. Henry E. Stamm IV, Ph.D., "Chief Washakie of the Shoshone: A Pho-tographic Essay," Jackson Hole Historical Society Online, accessible at https://jacksonholehistory.org.

※═ *13. "Only Lady at the Democratic Meeting"* ═※

1. The Gilded Age was the time of enormous growth and prosperity in the United States from about 1870–1900, named after the novel, *The Gilded Age*, by Mark Twain and Dudley Warner, published in 1873.

2. Huseas, *Sweetwater Gold,* 152.

3. Robert to Frankie, SPC, WT, 6 September 1870.

4. Robert to Frankie, SPC, WT, 8 September 1870.

5. *Laramie Daily Sentinel*, 7 September 1870, 2.

6. Massie, "Reform Is Where You Find It" 15.

7. J. D. Thomas. Blog Entry September 10, 2013; *The Revolution.* September 8, 1870; Our Special Contributors. Accessible Archives, Inc. accessible-archives.com.

8. *South Pass News,* 13 September 1870, 2.

9. Douglas Waitley, *William Henry Jackson, Framing the Frontier* (Missoula, MT: Mountain Press Publishing Company, 1999), 95-96.

10. *South Pass News*, 27 September 1870, 3; Esther Hobart Morris docket, South Pass City justice of the peace combined civil and criminal docket, RG 1014 Sweetwater County Justices of the Peace and County Court Records,

11. Bond, "Sarah Frances Slack," *Annals*, 354-356.

12. Robert to Frankie, SPC, WT, 1 November 1870.

13. Robert to E.H. McQuigg, SPC, WT, 24 December 1870.

14. Susan Cheever, *Drinking in America: Our Secret History* (New York, Hatchett Book Company 1915): Craig Heron, *Booze: A Distilled History* (Toronto, Between the Lines, 2003),143.

15. Mark W. Sorensen, *Ahead of Their Time, A Brief History of Woman Suffrage in Illinois,* IPO [Illinois Periodicals online] website, a digital imaging project at the Northern Illinois University Libraries.

⬗⬕ *14. "Labored More in Faith and Hope"* ⬕⬗

1. Esther to Frankie SPC, WT, undated fragment C, probably January 1871.

2. National Archives, National Historic Publications & Records Commission. https://www.archives.gov/nhprc/projects/catalog/isabella-beecher-hooker.

3. Letter from Esther to Isabella Beecher Hooker, *Chicago Tribune,* 31 January 1871, 2.

4. Gordon, *The Selected Papers of Elizabeth Cady Stanton and Susan B. Anthony, Vol. 2,* 467.

5. Anthony, Stanton, and Gage, *History of Woman Suffrage, Vol. II, 1861-1876,* 442; T.A. Larson, "Wyoming's Contribution to the Regional and National Women's Rights Movement," *Annals of Wyoming*, 52, 1 (Spring 1980), 9.

6. *The New York Herald,* 13 January 1871, 11.

7. *Chicago Tribune* 31 January 1871, 2

8. H.A. Thompson Docket, South Pass Justice of the Peace combined civil and criminal docket, RG 1014, Sweetwater County Justices of the Peace and County Courts Records, Wyoming State Archives, Cheyenne, WY; Water J. Impey, *Distress and Replevin* (London: Printed for the Associated Law Booksellers. 1823), 72. Impey defines replevin as "a procedure whereby seized goods may be provisionally restored to their owner pending the outcome of an action to determine the rights of the parties concerned."

9. *South Pass News*, 12 April 1871, 3.

10. *Wyoming Tribune,* 20 May 1871, 3; *South Pass News,* 24 May 1871, 1.

11. South Pass City Justice of the Peace combined civil and criminal docket, RG 1014.

12. *Cheyenne Daily Leader*, 3 July 1871, 1.

13. Esther to Frankie, SPC, WT, 10 August 1871.

14. Bond, "Sarah Frances Slack," *Annals*, 354; Esther to Frankie, SPC, WT, 16 Jan 1872; Douglas C. McMurtrie, "Pioneer Printing in Wyoming," *Annals of Wyoming* 9, no.3 (January 1933), 740-41. McMurtrie explains the original Gordon printing press that E.A. Slack used to print the *South Pass News* was not destroyed in the fire. The press is currently displayed in the Esther Morris replica cabin at the South Pass City historic site.

15. *Wyoming Tribune*, 18 Nov 1871, Cheyenne, 1.

16. Massie, "Reform Is Where You Find It," 16-17.

⇒⟊ 15. *"I Am Recognized Wherever I Go"* ⟊⇐

1. Esther to Frankie, SPC, WT, 16 January 1872.

2. "A Wyoming Joke," *The Ottawa Free Trader,* Ottawa, IL, 18 Nov 1871.

3. Esther to Frankie, SPC, WT, 16 January 1872.

4 .W.E. Chaplin, "Development and Evolutions of the Union Pacific Railroad," in Eunice G. Anderson, *First Biennial Report, 129-134*; Union Pacific and Central Pacific Time Table, 1869-1870.

5. T.A. Larson, "Wyoming's Contribution to the Regional and National Women's Rights Movement," *Annals of Wyoming*, 52, 1 (Spring 1980), 9.

6. Esther to Libbie Hall, SPC, WT, 22 June 1869.

7. Esther to Frankie, Los Angeles, CA, 27 March 1872.

8. Esther to Frankie, Laramie, WT, fragment of letter written in the fall or winter 1872.

9. W.E. Chaplin, *Woman Suffrage Pioneer Recalled Here; Chaplin Recounts Career of Esther Morris,* Sunday, July 25, 1937. A.G. Swain who lived in one of the Wanless apartments was the son of Louisa Ann Swain, famous for the first vote by a woman, and her husband Stephen Swain. A.G. lived there with his wife Hattie and two children; 1870 Census of Laramie, Albany County, Wyoming.

10. Lavinia Dobler, *Esther Morris, First Woman Justice of the Peace,* 72.

11. "Captain William Moore," City of Los Angeles Bureau of Engineering, accessible at http://eng.lacity.org/captain-william-moore.

12. *Progressive Men of the State of Wyoming,* 220-221; Larson, *History of Wyoming,* 69, 129; W.E. Chaplin, *Woman Suffrage Pioneer Recalled Here,* Sunday, July 25, 1937.

16. "Times We Should Lean"

1. Anthony, Stanton, and Gage, *History of Woman Suffrage Volume III,* 35.

2. Gordon, *The Selected Papers, Volume 3,* 234.

3. Robert to Frankie, Albany, NY, 6 February 1877; J. Matthew Gallman, *America's Joan of Arc: The Life of Anna Elizabeth Dickinson* (Oxford and New York: Oxford University Press, Inc., 2006), 142, 149, 162. Lib Browne Chatfield, whom Anna called "Betty," and Anna were close friends. "Betty" accompanied Anna on one of her multi-state stage tours. For many years, the Chatfield's home was her home when she was not on tour.

4. Four-page sales document between John Morris and J. Brunswick Co. Courtesy of Jon Lane, curator, South Pass City State Historic Site.

5. John Morris obituary, *Laramie Daily Sentinel,* 4 October 1877, 4.

6. Esther to Frankie, Albany, NY, 5 October 1877.

7. Esther to Frankie, Albany, NY, 20 December 1877.

8. Esther to Frankie, Albany, NY, 1 January 1878.

9. Esther to Frankie, probably written in Owego, NY, undated, likely 1878.

10. Esther to Frankie, Albany, NY, 6 August 1878.

11. Esther to Frankie, Albany, NY, 19 September 1878.

12. Robert to Frankie, Albany, NY, 3 September 1878.

13. William Robert Dubois III, interview, Cheyenne, WY, 2016.

17. "Life Is Like a Dream"

1. *Illinois State Journal,* Springfield, IL, November 10, 1897. Josephine Cleveland never married. She was the first president of the Woman's

Relief Corps which preserved battle flag remnants. She was the first and only librarian of the state historical library until her death in 1897.

2. Robert to Frankie, Springfield, IL. 31 October 1879.

3. Rosamond Stricker Day, Bertha's daughter, interview, 7 November 1998. Frankie and Damon had another child, named Frances, who was born in 1882.

4. Esther to Frankie, Springfield, IL, 6 February 1880.

5. Esther to Frankie, Springfield, IL, 3 April 1880.

6. Robert to Frankie, Springfield, IL, 5 April 1880.

7. Esther to Frankie, Springfield, IL, 27 June 1880. "Anty Watson," Diademia McQuigg Watson lived several more years. She died on April 2, 1884, at the age of 95.

8. Esther to Frankie, Springfield, IL, 7 July 1880.

9. Esther to Frankie, Springfield, IL, undated. Rutherford B. Hayes was probably the "silent soldier' and Vice President Wheeler "his boon companion."Author's research indicates the letter was probably written between election day, November 2, 1880 and January 12, 1881.

10. Robert to Frankie, Springfield, IL, 5 November 1880.

11. Esther to Frankie, Springfield, IL, 12 January 1881.

12. Esther to Frankie, Springfield, IL, 26 February 1881. Candace Miller, *Destiny of the Republic: A Tale of Madness, Medicine, and the Murder of a President* (New York: Anchor Books, 2011). Garfield served as president for only four months before being shot on July 2, 1881, at the Baltimore and Potomac Railroad Station in Washington. He died from complications resulting from this wound on September 9, 1881. Through a morbid twist of fate, Robert Todd Lincoln, son of President Abraham Lincoln, had been appointed Secretary of War by President James Garfield and was at the railroad station when he was shot.

13. Wilson H. David, M.D., *Chicago Medical Times, A Monthly Journal*, vol. 13, April 1881 to March 1882 (Chicago: Culver, Page, Hoyne and Co. Printers,1882).

14. Robert to Frankie, Chicago, IL, 22 June 1881.

15. E.H. McQuigg to Adeline Brownell Cole, 28 September 1881; Marriage Records, Genesee County, Michigan, 1867-1952, 304; Sacramento *Daily Record-Union* 19 January 1882.

16. Robert to Frankie, Chicago, IL, 21 October 1881.

17. Robert to Frankie, Chicago, IL,19 November 1882.

18. Federal Census 1880, Miner's Delight, Sweetwater County, WY, shows Edward Morris, age twenty-eight. His marriage was listed in Sweetwater County Marriage Records, 267186, vol. 1, 56, Green River, WY; "Self-Guided Tour of Green River" brochure produced by the Green River Historic Preservation Commission, 1992.

18. *"Ready to Maintain Her Prerogatives"*

1. "Woman Suffrage in Wyoming," *Cheyenne Weekly Leader,* 20 September 1883, 7. Mrs. M.A. (Melvina Hendry) Arnold served as Superintendent of the Public Schools of Laramie County, WT, in 1871, holding the position for two years, according to her obituary in the June 1, 1882, issue of the *Cheyenne Daily Sun.* She was married to Mowry Aldrich Arnold and died in her early forties.

2. Robert to Frankie, Springfield, IL, 16 December 1883.

3. E.A. Slack, "Her Work Done," *Cheyenne Daily Leader,* 3 April 1902, 2; Rick Ewig, "Did She Do That?" *Annals of Wyoming* (Volume 78, Winter 2006) 30. Ewig references a pamphlet, "In Memoriam," not dated, no publisher, Esther Morris biographic file, American Heritage Center, University of Wyoming. With much the same wording and style, likely both the article and the pamphlet were written by Archie. The pamphlet is thought to be a funeral handout.

4. Agnes Wright Spring, *Wyoming Historical Society, Miscellanies* (Laramie, WY: Laramie Republican Company Printers and Binders, 1919), 23.

5. Robert to Frankie, Cheyenne, WT, 17 July 1884.

6. Larson, *History of Wyoming,* 195-96.

7. William Robert Dubois III, "Historic Cheyenne," *Wyoming Tribune-Eagle,* 25 June 2017.

8. J. Matthew Gallman, *America's Joan of Arc: The Life of Anna Elizabeth Dickinson* (New York, Oxford University Press, 2006), 168.

9. Robert to Frankie, Cheyenne, WT, 19 August 1884.

10. Robert to Frankie, Cheyenne, WT, 6 April 1887.

11. Robert to Frankie, Cheyenne, WT, undated, likely 1887.

19. *"Emblem of Our Liberties"*

1. Esther to Frankie, Cheyenne, WT, 11 April 1888.

2. Larson, *History of Wyoming,* 235.

3. W.E. Chaplin, "Some Wyoming Editors I Have Known," *Annals of Wyoming* 18, no. 1 (January 1946), 79.

4. "Col. E.A. Slack Dies as Sun is Setting," *Cheyenne Daily Leader,* 24 March 1907, 1.

5. United States Constitution, Article 4, Section 3, Clause 1; Northwest Ordinance 1787, Article 5.

6. Larson, *History of Wyoming,* 238.

7. Phil Roberts, "Wyoming Becomes a State: The Constitutional Convention and Statehood Debates of 1889 and 1890—and Their Aftermath," 2014, WyomingHistory.org.

8. Larson, *History of Wyoming,* 240.

9. Roberts, "Wyoming Becomes a State," WyoHistory.org; According to an obituary in the *Decatur Illinois Review,* 30 Dec 1901, 2, Louis Palmer later returned to Springfield, Illinois, and married in 1900. Just one year later, at the age of thirty-six, he died following an illness that began as a cold and worsened into pneumonia and heart failure.

10. *Cheyenne Daily Sun.* July 10, 1890, 1; "Wyoming is a State," *Cheyenne Daily Sun.* 11 July 1890, 1.

11. "A Great Day," *Cheyenne Daily Sun,* Illustrated Edition, Thursday, 24 July 1890.

12. Larson, *History of Wyoming,* 260.

13. "A Great Day," *Cheyenne Daily Sun,* Illustrated Edition, 24 July 1890; "Mrs. Jenkins' Oration," in "Excerpts from the *Cheyenne Daily Sun,* 1890," *Annals of Wyoming* 37, no. 1 (April 1965), 54-55, and Esther's presentation of the flag, 56-57, Judge Brown's speech and presentation of state constitution to Amalia Post, 61-62.

14. "Excerpts from the *Cheyenne Daily Sun,* 24 July 1890, 1; *Annals of Wyoming* 37, no.1 (April 1965) 50, 55, 56, 57. The 44-star flag is housed at the Wyoming State Museum, Cheyenne, WY.

❧ 20. "More Candid than Diplomatic" ❧

1. *Self-Guided Tour of Historic Green River,* Green River Historic Preservation Commission, 1993.

2. Minutes of Green River City Council meeting, 3 August 1891, Sweetwater County Museum, Green River, Wyoming.

3. *Green River Advertiser,* Morris Mercantile advertisement, 28 August 1891.

4. Robert to Frankie, Washington, D.C., 4 May 1892.

5. Robert to Frankie, Green River, WY, WT, 18 September 1892.

6. Ed to Frankie, Mt. Clemons, MI, 13 September 1892; and Green River, WY, 25 May1893.

7. *Progressive Men of the State of Wyoming*, 221.

8. Robert to Frankie, Cheyenne, WY, 10 June 1895.

9. "Pioneer of Woman's Suffrage in Wyoming," in *Collections of the Wyoming Historical Society*, vol. 1, Robert Morris, ed.

10. "Frontier Day," *Cheyenne Daily Sun-Leader*, 30 August 1897, 4.

11. Robert D. Hanesworth, "Early History of Cheyenne 'Frontier Days' Show," *Annals of Wyoming* 12, no. 3 (1940), 199-201; "Will Be a Success: The Meeting on 'Frontier Day' Largely Attended," *Cheyenne Daily Sun-Leader*, 31 August 1897, 4; and "Frontier Day Edition," 23 September 1897.

12. Wind River Agency, Fort Washakie, Wyoming. Bureau of Indian Affairs, United States Department of the Interior, 2019, https://www.bia.gov/regional-offices/rocky-mountain/wind-river-agency.

13. Robert to Frankie, Washington, D.C., 16 December 1900.

14. Robert to Frankie, Green River, WY, and Washington, D.C., 3 March 1901.

15. "Mrs. Morris Dead," *Cheyenne Daily Leader*, 3 April 1902, 4. The article included the names of her pall bearers: "The pall bearers at the funeral tomorrow will be Judge C.N. Potter, W.E. Chaplin, Judge R.H. Scott, G.W. Hoyt, LeRoy Grant and W.J. Creswell." *Cheyenne Daily Leader*, 4 April 1902, 4.

16. "Her Work Done," *Cheyenne Daily Leader*, 3 April 1902, 2.

⊱⊶ 21. *"Needing a Heroine"* ⊷⊰

1. T.A. Larson, *History of Wyoming*, 90.

2. "Excerpts from the *Cheyenne Daily Sun*, 1890." *Annals of Wyoming*, 37, no. 1 (April 1965), 56.

3. "Her Work Done," *Cheyenne Daily Leader*, 3 April 1902, 2; "In Memorium," pamphlet.

4. "The First in Nation," *The Laramie Republican*, 2 October 1913, 3.

5. Massie, "Reform Is Where You Find It," 17,18.

6. Federal Census 1880 Colorado; Federal Census 1900 Washington D.C.; Federal Census 1910 Washington D.C.; Colorado State Census 1885. "William Henry Bright," Findagrave.com, Memorial #122200120; "Julia A. Bright," Findagrave.com, Memorial #122200465. There is no extant record of the U.S. 1890 census, as it was burned in a fire at the Commerce Department in 1921.

7. "Historical Correction," H.G. Nickerson, *Wyoming State Journal*, 14 February 1919, 1. Massie in "Reform is Where you Find It," writes there were actually nine candidates, running for the three Council positions from the county, so neither Bright nor Nickerson were guaranteed to be elected.

8. Larson, *History of Wyoming*, 92.

9. Grace Raymond Hebard, "How Woman Suffrage Came to Wyoming," in Eunice G. Anderson, *First Biennial Report,* 135-146.

10. *Cheyenne State Leader,* 22 January 1921.

11. Carrie Chapman Catt and Nettie Rogers Shuler, "Woman Suffrage and Politics the Inner Story of the Suffrage Movement," *Scribner's,* 1923, 75. In the months before she traveled to South Pass City, Esther lived in New York City with nieces Lib and Julia Brown who worked for *The Revolution.* She probably met Susan B. Anthoy and Elizabeth Cady Stanton and surely attended at least one lecture.

12. "Activities of Wyoming Historical Landmark Commission," *Annals of Wyoming* 11, no. 4 (October 1939), 301-306.

13. "Esther Morris Turns 50," *Wyoming Postscripts*, Wyoming State Archives blog, Dec. 30, 2013, https://wyostatearchives.wordpress. com

14. *Acceptance of the Statue of Esther Morris presented by the State of Wyoming,* Proceedings in the Congress and in the Rotunda, United States Capitol, April 6, 1960 (United States Government Printing Office, Washington, D.C., 1961) 28-35. When Statuary Hall was completed in 1857, planners could not conceive of making room for one hundred statues from fifty states. Of the hundred statues in the National Statuary Hall Collection currently ninety-one are of men and nine of women.

15. Anthony, Stanton, and Gage, *History of Woman Suffrage 1876-1885*, *Vol III*, 729-730.

16. T.A. Larson, Letter to the Editor, *Laramie Daily Boomerang,* 30 November 1954, 12.

17. T.A. Larson, personal interview with author 1997; Larson, *History of Wyoming*, 94.

18. Larson, *History of Wyoming*, 94.

19. Massie, "Reform Is Where You Find It," 19, 20.

20. Mike Mackey, *Inventing History in the American West: The Romance and Myths of Grace Raymond Hebard* (Powell, WY: Western History Publications, 2005), 28.

⊷ *Afterword: "Far in Advance of What We Were"* ⊷

1. Larson, interview, 31 October 1994.

2. Gordon, *The Selected Papers of Elizabeth Cady Stanton and Susan B. Anthony, Vol. 2,* 494-495.

3. History of Voting in America, Washington Office of Secretary of State, 2008. Northern California Citizenship Project Timeline, 2004.

4. Guenther, interview, 9 January 1995.

⊷ *Appendix A: The Rest of the Story* ⊷

1. "Beside Loving Wife," *Cheyenne Daily Leader*, 26 July 1902, 4.

2. Robert to Frankie, Green River, WY, 12 January 1906.

3. "Col. E.A. Slack Dies As Sun Is Setting," *Cheyenne Daily Leader*, 24 March 1907.

4. "Edward J. Morris Dead," *Rock Springs Miner*, 11 September, 1902, 3; *Cheyenne Daily Leader*, 9 Sept 1902, 4. "At the grave, Blue Lodge services were held."

5. "The Carnegie Public Library of Cheyenne, Wyoming," *Library Journal*, vol. 27, June 1902, 327-328. Cheyenne's Carnegie Library, located at 22nd and Capitol streets, was demolished in 1971.

6. "Robert C. Morris, Son of Mother of Woman's Suffrage and Pioneer Court Reporter, Believed Approaching Death," *Cheyenne State Leader*, early edition, 22 January 192.

7. "Robert Morris Dies After a Long Illness," *Cheyenne State Leader*, evening edition, 22 January 1921. Robert's obituary, "Robert C. Morris Passes Away in Cheyenne," mentioned his assistance in acquiring the Green River Carnegie Library and appeared in the *Green River Star*, on Feb. 4, 1921, 1. *Cheyenne State Leader*, 26 Jan 1921, 4. "The Carnegie Library fathered by Robert Morris was closed from 2 to 3 o'clock to honor Mr. Morris."

8. "Mrs. Slack Dies; Widow of Pioneer Cheyenne Editor," *Cheyenne State Leader,* 3 March 1921, 8.

9. Bond, "Sarah Frances Slack," *Annals,* 356.

10. Obituary, Mrs. Frances McQuigg Stewart, February 7, 1918.

11. New York State Senate Women of Distinction Awards. www.nysenate.gov/newsroom/press-releases/thomas-f-omara/senate-unveils-historical-women-distinction-exhibit-including.

12. Gordon, *The Selected Papers of Elizabeth Cady Stanton and Susan B. Anthony, Vol II,* 494-495.

13. Findagrave.com Memorials #11275545; 112755344.

14. William Robert Dubois, III, interviews with author, 1997-2019.

BIBLIOGRAPHY

Acceptance of the Statue of Esther Morris, Presented by the State of Wyoming. Proceedings in the Congress and in the Rotunda, United States Capitol, April 6, 1960. Washington D.C.: Government Printing Office, 1961.

"Activities of the Wyoming Historical Landmark Commission." *Annals of Wyoming* 11, No. 4 (January 1927).

Adams, Jad. *Women and the Vote*. Oxford: Oxford University Press, 2014.

Adler, David A. *Frederick Douglass, a Noble Life*. New York: Holiday House, 1910.

Alve, Jean. *A Record of the Land in Spencer New York State to the First Settlers*. Spencer, NY: Private printing, 1995.

Ambrose, Stephen E. *Nothing Like it in the World, The Men Who Built the Transcontinental Railroad 1863-1869*. New York: Simson & Schuster, 2000.

Anderson, Eunice. *First Biennial Report of the State Historian of the State of Wyoming for the period ending September 30, 1920 with Wyoming Historical Collections*. Laramie, WY: The Laramie Printing Company, 1920.

___. *Second Biennial Report of the State Historian of the State of Wyoming for the period ending September 30, 1922: Proceedings and Collections of the Wyoming State Historical Department 1921-1923*. Cheyenne, WY: Wyoming Historical Department/Mills Company, 1923.

Andreas, Alfred Theodore. *History of Chicago Volume I*. Chicago, IL: Private printing, 1884.

Anthony, Susan B., Elizabeth Cady Stanton, Matilda Joslyn Gage. *History of Woman Suffrage, Volume II, 1861-1876*. Rochester, NY: Susan B. Anthony, 1881.

___. *History of Woman Suffrage, Volume III, 1876-1885*. Rochester, NY: Susan B. Anthony, 1887.

Bagley, Will. "Fort Bridger." https://www.wyohistory.org/encyclopedia/fort-bridger Nov. 8, 2014.

___. *So Rugged and Mountainous*. Norman, OK: University of Oklahoma Press, 2010.

___. *South Pass: Gateway to a Continent*. Norman, OK: University of Oklahoma Press, 2014.

___. "South Pass." https://www.wyohistory.org/encyclopedia/south-pass, 8 Nov 2014.

Baldwin, Elmer. *History of La Salle County Illinois*. Chicago, IL: Rand, McNally & Co, 1877.

Barry, Kathleen. *Susan B. Anthony. A Biography of a Singular Feminist*. New York: Ballantine Books, 1988.

Beach, Cora. *Women of Wyoming*. Privately published, 1927.

Bebel, August. *Woman in the Past, Present and Future*. San Francisco, CA: G. B. Benham, 1897.

Bond, Mrs. Wallace (Harriet) C. "Sarah Frances Slack, A Biographical Sketch by her Daughter." *Annals of Wyoming* 4, No. 2, (January 1927).

Boswell, H. James. *The Blue Book of Portland and Adjacent Cities*. Portland, OR: Private printing, 1921.

Boylan, Anne M. *The Origins of Women's Activism*. Chapel Hill, NC: University of North Carolina Press, 2002.

Brown, John Edwin. *The Scroll of Phi Delta Theta, Volume 15, October 1890-June 1891*. Columbus, OH: Published by the Fraternity, 1891.

Browne, George Waldo. *The History of Hillsborough New Hampshire 1735-1921*. Manchester, NH: John B. Clarke Company, 1922.

Browne, Jean McQuigg. *Edmund Hobart and His Descendants 1794-1912*. Private printing: 1912.

___. *John and Mildred Lawson McQuigg and Their Descendants 1740-1912*. Private printing: 1912.

Buhle, Mary Jo and Paul. *A Concise History of Woman Suffrage*. Urbana and Chicago, IL: University of Illinois Press, 1978.

Cain, William E. *William Lloyd Garrison and the Fight Against Slavery: Selections from the Liberator*. Boston and New York: Bedford Books of St. Martin's Press, 1995.

Cary, John H. and Julius Weinberg, eds. *The Social Fabric: American Life from 1607 to 1877*. New York: Little, Brown and Company, 1984.

Catt, Carrie Chapman and Nettie Rogers Shuler. *Woman Suffrage and Politics the Inner Story of the Suffrage Movement*. New York: Scribner's, 1923.

Chaplin, W.E. "Some Editors I Have Known," *Annals of Wyoming* 18, No. 1 (January 1946).

Chatfield, A.G. *Documents of the Assembly of the State of New-York 1842.* Albany, NY: Thurlow Weed, Printer to the State, 1842.

Cheever, Susan. *American Bloomsbury.* New York: Simon and Schuster, 2006.

___. *Drinking in America: Our Secret History.* New York: Hatchett Book Company, 1913.

Coutant, C.G. "History of Wyoming, written by C.G. Coutant, Pioneer Historian, and heretofore unpublished. Chapter VIII." *Annals of Wyoming* 12, No. 4 (October 1940).

___. *The History of Wyoming, from the earliest known discoveries, Volume I.* Laramie, WY: Chaplin, Spafford & Mathison Printers, 1899.

Curry, Josiah Seymour. *Chicago: Its History and its Builders, a Century of Marvelous Growth.* Chicago, IL: S.J. Clarke Publishing Company, 1912.

Davis, R. Edward. *Early Illinois Paper Money.* Chicago, IL: Hewitt Brothers, n.d.

Demlinger, Sandor. *Stagecoach: Rare Views of the American West 1849-1915.* Atglen, PA: Schiffer, 2004.

Dobler, Lavinia. *Esther Morris, First Woman Justice of the Peace.* Riverton, WY: Big Bend Press, 1993.

Documents of the Assembly of the State of New-York, sixty-fourth session 1842, Volume IV. Albany, NY: Printed by Thurlow Reed Printer of the State, 1842.

Dubois, Carol and Richard Candida Smith. *Elizabeth Cady Stanton Documents and Essays.* New York: New York University Press, 2007.

Dunaway, Abigail. *Path Breaking: An Autobiographical History of the Equal Suffrage Movement in the Pacific Coast States.* Portland, OR: James, Kerns and Abbot Co., 1914.

Ellis, William Arba. *Norwich University 1819-1911 in Three Volumes.* Montpelier, VT: The Capital City Press, 1911.

Etulain, Richard. *The Life and Legend of Calamity Jane.* Norman, OK: University of Oklahoma Press, 2014.

"Excerpts from the *Cheyenne Daily Sun*, 24 July 1890." *Annals of Wyoming* 37, No. 1 (April 1965).

Fleming, Sidney Howell. "Solving the Jigsaw Puzzle One Suffrage Story at a Time." *Annals of Wyoming* 62, No.1 (Spring 1990).

Flexner, Eleanor and Ellen Fitzpatrick. *Century of Struggle: The Woman's Rights Movement in the United States.* Cambridge, MA: The Belknap Press of Harvard University Press, 1959.

Frost-Knappman, Elizabeth and Kathryn Cullen-DuPont. *Women's Suffrage in America*. New York: Facts on File, Inc, 2005.

Fuller, S. Margaret. *Woman in the Nineteenth Century*. New York: Greeley and McElrath, 1845.

Gallman, J. Matthew. *America's Joan of Arc: The Life of Anna Elizabeth Dickinson*. New York: Oxford University Press, 2006.

Gay, H.B., ed. *Historical Gazetteer of Tioga County, New York*. Syracuse, NY: W.B. Gay and Co., 1888.

Golden, James L, Goodwin F. Berquist, William E. Coleman, J. Michael Sproule. *The Rhetoric of Western Thought: From the Mediterranean World to the Global Setting*. Dubuque, IA: Kendall Hunt Publishing Company, 2003.

Gordon, Ann, ed. *The Selected Papers of Elizabeth Cady Stanton and Susan B. Anthony, Volume II*. New Brunswick, NJ: Rutgers University Press, 2000.

___. *The Selected Papers of Elizabeth Cady Stanton and Susan B. Anthony, Volume III*. New Brunswick, NJ: Rutgers University Press, 2003.

Gray, Dorothy. *Women of the West*. Lincoln, NE: University of Nebraska Press, 1976.

Green River Mayors 1891-1995. Green River Historic Preservation Commission. City of Green River, Wyoming, 1995.

Green River Historic Self-guided Tour. Green River Historic Preservation Commission. City of Green River, Wyoming, 1993.

Guenther, Todd, Erin Hammer, and Fred Chaney. "The Women Who Carried the Star of Empire Westward: Eliza Spalding and Narcissa Whitman," *Overland Journal* (Winter 2002).

Gurian, Jan. "Sweetwater Journalism and Western Myth." *Annals of Wyoming* 36, No. 1 (April 1964).

Hafen, LeRoy R, ed. *Mountain Men and Fur Traders of the Far West*. Glendale, CA: Arthur H. Clark Company, 1972.

Hanesworth, Robert D. "Early History of Cheyenne Frontier Days Show." *Annals of Wyoming* 12, No. 3 (July 1940).

Haynie, J. Henry. *The Nineteenth Illinois; a memoir of a regiment of volunteer infantry famous in the Civil War of Fifty years ago for its drill, bravery, and distinguished services*. Whitefish, MT: Kessinger Publishing, 2010.

Hebard, Grace. Interview with Jeanette Smith on July 6, 1920 at South Pass City. Hebard Collection, American Heritage Center, University of Wyoming, Laramie, WY.

Hoffman, Urias. J. *History of La Salle County, Illinois*. Chicago, IL: The S.J. Clarke Publishing Co., 1906.

Homsher, Lola M. *South Pass, 1868, James Chisholm's Journal of the Wyoming Gold Rush*. Lincoln, NE: University of Nebraska Press, 1988.

Hurd, D. Hamilton. *History of Rockingham and Strafford Counties New Hampshire*. Philadelphia, PA: J.W. Lewis and Co., 1882.

___. *History of Hillsborough County New Hampshire*. Philadelphia, PA: J. W. Lewis and Co, 1885.

Huseas, Marion McMillan. *Sweetwater Gold, Wyoming's Gold Rush 1867-1871*. Cheyenne, WY: Cheyenne Corral of Westerners International Publishers, 1991.

Hymowitz, Carol and Michaele Weissman. *A History of Women in America*. New York: Banta, 2011.

Impey, Water J. *Distress and Replevin*. London, England: Printed for the Associated Law Booksellers, 1823.

Irving, Washington. *The Adventures of Captain Bonneville, U.S.A. In the Rocky Mountains and the Far West*. New York: G.P Putnam, 1868.

James, Edward T., Janet Wilson James, Paul S. Boyer, eds. *Notable American Women 1607-1950: A Biographical Dictionary, Vol II G–O*. Cambridge, MA: The Belknap Press of Harvard University Press, 1971.

Kett, H.F. *Past and Present of La Salle County, Illinois*. Chicago, IL: H.F. Kett and Co, 1877.

Kingman, Leroy Wilson. *Early Owego*. Owego, NY: Owego Gazette Office, 1907.

___. *Our County and its People: A Memorial History of Tioga County New York*. Elmira, NY: W.A. Fergusson, 1897.

___. ed. *Owego Sketches by Owego Authors*. Owego, NY: Ladies Aid Society of the Baptist Church, 1904.

Koehler, Lyle. *A Search for Power: The "Weaker Sex" in Seventeenth Century New England*. Urbana, IL: University of Illinois Press, 1980.

Kreck, Dick. *Hell on Wheels: Wicked Towns Along the Union Pacific Railroad*. Golden, CO: Fulcrum Publishing, 2013.

Lane, Jon, and Susan Layman. *Images of America, South Pass City and the Sweetwater Mines*. Charleston, SC: Arcadia Publishing, 2012.

Larson, T.A. *History of Wyoming*. Second Edition, Revised (paperback). Lincoln, NE: University of Nebraska Press, 1990. The 1965 edition, 1978 edition, and 1990 edtion were each revised in turn.

___. *Wyoming: A Bicentennial History*. New York: W.W. Norton, 1984.

___. "Wyoming Statehood." *Annals of Wyoming* 37, No. 1 (April 1965).

___. "Wyoming's Contribution to Regional and National Women's Rights Movement." *Annals of Wyoming* 52, No. 1 (Spring 1980).

Laybourn, Margaret. "Renaissance Man in Cheyenne." *The Senior Voice.* Cheyenne, WY: May 2014.

Leonard, William Andrew. *Stephen Banks Leonard of Owego, Tioga County, New York.* Owego, NY: Printed for Private Circulation, 1909.

Lodesky, James D. *Polish Pioneers in Illinois 1818-1850.* Bloomington, IL: Xlibris Corporation, 2010.

Loewen, James W. *Lies Across America.* New York: The New Press, 1999.

Logan, Mrs. John A. *The Part Taken by Women in American History.* Wilmington, DE: The Perry-Nalle Publishing Company, 1912.

McCullough, David. *John Adams.* New York: Simon and Schuster, 2001.

McMillen, Sally G. *Seneca Falls and the Origins of the Women's Rights Movement.* Oxford, England: Oxford University Press, 2008.

McMurtrie, Douglas C. "Pioneer Printing in Wyoming." *Annals of Wyoming* 9, No. 3 (January 1933).

Mackey, Mike. *Inventing History in the American West: The Romance and Myths of Grace Raymond Hebard.* Powell, WY: Western History Publications, 2005.

Massie, Michael A. "Reform is Where You Find it; Roots of Woman Suffrage in Wyoming." *Annals of Wyoming* 62, No. 1, (Spring 1990).

Mather, Cotton. *Magnalia Christi Americana, or the Ecclesiastical History of New England.* Hartford, CT: Silas Andrus, 1820.

Miller, Richard F. ed. *States at War Volume I.* Lebanon, NH: University Press of New England, 2013.

Millard, Candace. *Destiny of the Republic: A Tale of Madness, Medicine, and the Murder of a President.* New York: Doubleday, 2011.

Morris, Robert C., ed. *Collections of the Wyoming Historical Society, Volume I.* Cheyenne, WY: Sun-Leader Publishing House, 1897.

Moynihan, Ruth Barnes. *Rebel for Rights Abigail Scott Duniway.* New Haven, CT: Yale University Press, 1983.

National Park Service Database of Soldiers and Sailors of the Civil War. https://www.nps.gov/civilwar/soldiers-and-sailors-database.htm

Nickerson, H G. "Early History of Fremont County." *State of Wyoming Historical Department Quarterly Bulletin* 2, No. 1 (Cheyenne, July 15, 1924).

___. "Historical Correction." *Wyoming State Journal*, 14, February 1919.

Palmer, George Thomas. *A Conscientious Turncoat: The Story of John M. Palmer, 1817-1900.* New Haven, CT: Yale University Press, 1941.

Palmer, John M. *Personal Recollections of John M. Palmer: The Story of an Earnest Life.* Cincinnati, OH: R. Clarke Co, 1901.

___. *The Bench and Bar of Illinois, Historical and Reminiscent, Volume I.* Chicago, IL: The Lewis Publishing Company, 1899.

Palmer, Walter Benjamin. *The History of the Phi Delta Theta Fraternity.* Oxford, OH: Published by the Fraternity, 1906.

Peirce, Henry B. and Duane Hamilton Hurd. *History of Tioga, Chemung, Tompkins, and Schuyler Counties, New York.* Philadelphia, PA: Everts & Ensign, 1879.

Peru 1835-1985 Sesquicentennial Book Commemorating 150 Years Peru, Illinois. Peru, IL: 1985.

Progressive Men of the State of Wyoming. Chicago, IL: A.W. Bowen and Co, 1908.

Redford, Robert. *The Outlaw Trail, A journey through time.* New York: Grosset and Dunlap, 1979.

"Reminiscences of a Member of the Wyoming Constitutional Convention." *Annals of Wyoming* 12, No. 4 (October 1940).

Reports Made to the General Assembly of Illinois. Springfield, IL: Illinois Journal Printing Office, 1872.

Revolution, September 8, 1870. Elizabeth Cady Stanton and Parker Pillsbury, editors. New York City: National Woman Suffrage Association, 1868-1872. Accessible Archives, Inc. Accessible-Archives.com.

Rea, Tom: "Right Choice, Wrong Reasons: Wyoming Women Win the Right to Vote." WyoHistory.org.

Roberts, Cokie. *Ladies of Liberty: The Women Who Shaped Our Nation.* New York: William Morrow, 2008.

Roberts, Phil. "Wyoming Becomes a State; The Constitutional Convention and Statehood Debates of 1889 and 1890 and their Aftermath." Wyominghistory.org.

Robertson, John, Adjutant General's Department. *Michigan in the War.* Lansing, MI: W.S. George and Co. State Printers, 1882.

Rodriguez, Cristina M. "Clearing the Smoke-Filled Room: Women Jurors and the Disruption of an Old-Boys Network in Nineteenth-Century America." *Yale Law Journal* (1999).

Romans, H.R. *American Locomotive Engineer—Erie Railway Edition.* Chicago, IL: Crawford-Adsit Co., 1899.

Royse, Hon. L.W. *A Standard History of Kosciusko County, Indiana, Volume II*. Chicago IL: The Lewis Publishing Company, 1919.

Salafia, Matthew. *Slavery's Borderland, Freedom and Bondage Along the Ohio River*. Philadelphia, PA: University of Pennsylvania Press, 2013.

Savage, James W. and John T. Bell. *History of the City of Omaha, Nebraska and South Omaha*. New York and Chicago, IL: Munsell and Company, 1894.

Scharff, Virginia. *Twenty Thousand Roads, Women, Movement, and the West*. Berkeley and Los Angeles, CA: University of California Press, 2003.

Schernone, Laura. *A Thousand Years over a Hot Stove, A History of American Women Told Through Food, Recipes, and Remembrances*. New York: W.W. Norton and Company, Inc., 2003.

Schoenbachler, Matthew. *Murder & Madness the Myth of the Kentucky Tragedy*. Lexington, KY: University Press of Kentucky, 2009.

Shaffer, Duane E. *Granite: New Hampshire's Soldiers in the Civil War*. Columbia, SC: University of South Carolina Press, 2008.

Sherlock, James L. *South Pass and Its Tales*. Basin, WY: Wolverine Gallery, 1978.

Sibley, John Langdon, M.A. *Biographical Sketches of Graduates of Harvard University in Cambridge, Massachusetts, Volume II 1659-1677*. Cambridge, MA: Charles William Server, University Bookstore, 1881.

Siebert, Wilbur H. *Reminiscences of Levi Coffin: 1876 and The Underground Railroad from Slavery to Freedom*. Cincinnati, OH: Western Tract Society, 1876.

Smith, Frances Gurney M.D. *A Compendium of Domestic Medicine, Surgery and Materia*, Second edition. Philadelphia, PA: Lindsay and Blakiston, 1857.

Sorenson, Mark W. *Ahead of their Time; A Brief History of Woman Suffrage in Illinois*. IPO (Illinois Periodicals online) Website, a digital imaging project at the Northern Illinois University Libraries.

Spring, Agnes Wright. *Near the Greats*. Frederick, CO: Platte 'N Press, 1981.

___. *Wyoming Historical Society, Miscellanies*. Laramie, WY: The Laramie Republican Company Printers and Binders, 1919.

Stamm, Henry E. IV. *People of the Wind River, The Eastern Shoshones 1825-1900*. Norman, OK: University of Oklahoma Press, 1999.

___. "Chief Washakie of the Shoshone: A Photographic Essay." Jackson Hole Historical Society and Museum Online. https://jacksonholehistory.org/chief-washakie-of-the-shoshone-a-photographic-essay-by-henry-e-stamm-iv-ph-d/.

Steele, Richard F. *An Illustrated History of Stevens, Ferry, Okanogan and Chelan Counties State of Washington.* New York: Western Historical Publishing Company, 1904.

Stenhouse, T.B.H. *The Rocky Mountain Saints: a full and complete history of the Mormons, from the first vision of Joseph Smith.* New York: D. Appleton and Company, 1878.

Stone, Irving. *Men to Match My Mountains.* New York: Berkeley Books, 1956.

Strahorn, Carrie Adell. *Fifteen Thousand Miles by Stage, Volume I 1877-1880.* New York: Knickerbocker Press, 1911.

Strasser, Susan. *Waste and Want: A Social History of Trash.* New York: Metropolitan Books, Henry Holt and Company, 1999.

Tanner, Gordon. *Reports of Cases Argued and Determined in the Supreme Court of Judicature of the State of Indiana Vol. 13, Containing the Cases Decided at the November Term, 1859, from the First to the Twenty-Second Day, Inclusive.* Indianapolis, IN: Merrill and Company, 1860.

"The National Home for Disabled Volunteer Soldiers." *Prologue Magazine,* 36. No.1: Published by the National Archives (Spring 2004).

Thomson, Rebecca W. "A History of Wyoming Territorial Supreme Court Justices." *Annals of Wyoming* 53, No. 2 (Fall 1981).

Trenholm, Virginia Cole. *The Shoshonis Sentinels of the Rockies.* Norman, OK: University of Oklahoma Press, 1964.

Ulrich, Laurel Thatcher. *A Midwife's Tale.* New York: Random House, 1990.

United States Department of the Interior. Bureau of Land Management. General Land Office Records: glorecords.blm.gov.

Utley, Robert M. *The Story of the West: A History of the American West and Its People.* Washington D.C.: Smithsonian Institution, 2003.

Waitley, Douglas. *William Henry Jackson, Framing the Frontier.* Missoula, MT: Mountain Publishing Company, 1999.

Wellman, Judith. *The Road to Seneca Falls.* Urbana and Chicago, IL: University of Illinois Press, 2004.

Wheeler, Denice. *The Feminine Frontier: Wyoming Women 1850-1900.* Privately Published, 1987.

Willard, Frances E. and Mary A. Livermore. *American Women, 1500 Biographies with over 1400 Portraits, Volume I.* New York, Chicago, Springfield, OH: Mast Crowell and Kirkpatrick, 1897.

Wilson David H. M.D. *Chicago Medical Times, A Monthly Journal* 13, (April 1881 to March 1882). Chicago, IL: Culver, Page, Hoyne and Co. Printers, 1882.

Wind River Agency. Bureau of Indian Affairs. https://www.bia.gov/regional-offices/rocky-mountain/wind-river-agency.

Wood, Edwin O. *History of Genesee County Michigan Volume I.* Indianapolis, IN: Federal Publishing Company, 1916.

___. *History of Genesee County Michigan Volume II.* Indianapolis, IN: Federal Publishing Company, 1916.

Wollstonecraft, Mary. *Political Writings of Mary Wollstonecraft: A Vindication of the Rights of Women.* New York: Routledge, 1993.

Yates, William. "Reminiscences." Unpublished manuscript. Sweetwater County Historical Museum, Green River, Wyoming.

Contributing Museums, Collections, Historic Sites

American Heritage Center, University of Wyoming, Laramie, WY.
Cliff Hall Collection.
Historian, Baptist Church, Owego, NY
Brigham Young University Library, Provo, UT.
Family History Center, Salt Lake City, UT.
Fremont County Pioneer Museum, Lander, WY.
Illinois State Historical Society, Springfield, IL.
La Salle County IL Historical Society, Utica, IL.
Marriott Library, University of Utah, Salt Lake City, UT.
Massachusetts Historical Society, Boston, MA.
Rock Springs Historical Society Museum, Rock Springs, WY.
Salt Lake City and County Libraries, Salt Lake City, UT.
South Pass City State Historic Site, South Pass City, WY.
Sweetwater County Historical Society and Museum, Green River, WY.
Tioga County Historical Society, Owego, NY.
Utah State Historical Society, Salt Lake City, UT.
Wyoming State Archives, Cheyenne, WY.
Wyoming State Historical Society, Wheatland, WY.

INDEX

ACKNOWLEDGMENTS

THIS BOOK WOULD not exist without three people: My sister Marlene Swim Nielsen provided a place for me to write these past three years. My niece Genevieve Muriel Swim Navratil who has the magical ability to decipher Esther's extremely challenging handwriting. And my friend Elsa Glen Perkins (Glennie) who read every word of the book many times over and provided support and encouragement throughout. Thanks to my other readers, Marilyn Davies, Nielsine Archibald, and Constance McCormick and to Janene E. Nielsen (Jani) for her editing.

My 1994 trip to South Pass City Historic Site to meet with the enthusiastic curator, Todd Guenther, carried me into another era. I was hooked and decided on the spot to write a biography of Esther. Thank you, Todd.

This was quickly followed by a trip to Laramie, visiting Michael A. Massie, former curator of the site and author of "Reform is Where You Find it," whose generosity of time and sharing has continued to the present day. Marion McMillon Huseas invited me into her home in Cheyenne for a marvelous chat about her research for *Sweetwater Gold*. Spending time with Bill Dubois led to his unbridled support and a twenty-five-year friendship. A lengthy interview with historian T.A. Larson was a delight. My thanks to Jon Lane, current curator at South Pass City Historic Site; Rick Ewig, American Heritage Center in Laramie; Carl Hallberg, Suzi Taylor, and Robin Everett, Wyoming State Archives.

In Sweetwater County, Wyoming, Cyndi McCullers, Ruth Lauritzen, Brigida Blasi, and Bob Nelson provided ongoing assistance.

In Tioga County, New York, thanks to Jean Alve, Rodger Fritz, and Pamela Goddard.

Cliff Hall graciously allowed me to use his large collections of photographs and documents. I appreciate contributions by Tom Harmon and Rev. Fr. Gregorios (Bruce Forman Pawlak.) Thanks to Jonita Sommers and Joan Petrie Carroll.

Will Bagley read the first rough draft, made pithy comments and suggestions, leading me to a rewrite, which made publishing possible. I appreciate his tutoring and support.

Sincere thanks to Lori Van Pelt, Laura McCormick, Judy Mac, and Patsy Parkin.

Finally, my appreciation and respect for Nancy Curtis at High Plains Press knows no bounds. Not only have I learned a great deal from her but working with her has been delightful.

ABOUT THE AUTHOR

SEVENTY-EIGHT-YEAR-OLD Kathryn Swim Cummings was well prepared to bring to life the story of Esther Morris. Her own story, plus her exhaustive research and interpretive abilities, combined to make her the perfect narrator of Esther's story.

With a life-long passion for history, Cummings has spent over forty-five years doing genealogical and historical research. In 1992 after many years as a single parent and with her children grown, Cummings left the corporate world in San Diego and moved to the Rocky Mountains of Utah.

Her strong interest in western history focused on Esther Morris, leading to twenty-five years of research into the unembellished lifestory of the first woman judge in the nation. At her seventy-fifth birthday party, Cummings realized it was time to buckle down and write the book.

Cummings has three children, eight grandchildren, and nine great grandchildren and lives in Holladay, Utah.

NOTES ON THE PRODUCTION OF THE BOOK

This book was first published as a *softcover trade original.*
It is covered with ten-point stock,
printed in four colors,
and coated with nylon matte film lamination.

The text is from the Adobe Garamond Family.
Display type is Oldbook from ITC.
Supplemental ornaments are
LFF Engravers' Ornaments and
Tesseroni by the Coyote Foundry.

The book is printed on sixty-pound white Kateroo,
an acid-free paper,
by Versa Press, Inc.

The cover design is by Laura McCormick
and incorporates artwork by Mark Schuler
licensed from Wind River Studios Holdings Incorporated
and photography by William Henry Jackson.
from the U. S. Geological Survey Photographic Library.